Educational Potential of Computer Games

Also available from Continuum

Analysing Underachievement in Schools, Emma Smith
Philosophy of Education, Richard Pring
Education and Community, Dianne Gereluk
Theory of Education, David Turner
Homo Zappiens, Wim Veen and Ben Vrakking

Educational Potential of Computer Games

Simon Egenfeldt-Nielsen

continuum

Continuum International Publishing Group

The Tower Building
11 York Road
SE1 7NX

80 Maiden Lane, Suite 704
New York, NY 10038

www.continuumbooks.com

British Library Cataloguing-in-Publication Data
A catalogue record for this book is available from the British Library.

ISBN: 0826497470 (paperback/hardcover)

Library of Congress Cataloging-in-Publication Data

Typeset by Fakenham Photosetting Ltd

Printed and bound in Great Britain by Biddles Ltd, King's Lynn, Norfolk

Contents

Preface

The wicked sirens still sing their song luring me to venture dangerous places

This book is about educational use of computer games. The book has been a journey through a landscape not seen in full by many people. My background as a psychologist slowly but steadily determined this book, supplemented with clear directions from game research. Over the years, game research has become as much my starting point as my psychology training. It feels strange looking back at the road travelled, seeing the twisted passages one chooses, when one could have stayed on the main road. I have, however, more than once been amazed by the rich experience base just under my nose, which seems to have gone unnoticed by me and by other researchers for many years. I hope that the work you are about to read will bring the field forward and show new paths for educational practice with computer games. The book may seem overly critical of educational use of computer games in places, but I strongly believe that this is needed to push the area forward. My optimism in terms of using and developing computer games for other purposes than entertainment has never been greater than now.

The book grew out of my work on a PhD at IT-University of Copenhagen. The more academic discussions and method considerations can been found in the PhD. In this book, I have dissected the field of educational use of computer games, which with a bit of luck will pave the way for new insights. I have taken pride in not wishing to settle with just the necessary findings and discussions, but have kept pushing on. The venture could have gone wrong in so many ways, and in fact did, but still it produced valuable insights for me, and hopefully for other people as well. What you are now about to read can, to the best of my knowledge, be described as 'unfinished business'. For me, the book has left more questions unanswered than answered, though it may not seem so from the outside. I cannot wait to continue the journey and hope to gain more companions.

I would like to thank the following people who have played a significant role in the process: my three supervisors, Anker Helms Jørgensen, Carsten Jessen and Andrew Burn, who have given valuable insights, discussions and academic shelter over the years.

In connection with the course used as an example, I wish to thank Gitte Nielsen, Henrik Wegener, Anders Kloppenborg and Anne Marie Asmussen for making this possible. I also want to thank the 72 students who participated in the two-month-long course.

For academic discussions in general, thanks to everybody mentioned above but also to: Jonas H. Smith, Fin Egenfeldt-Nielsen, Susana Tosca, T.L. Taylor, Jesper Juul, Jesper Tække, Miguel Sicart, Troels Folmann, Debra Lieberman, Caroline Pelletier, Siobhan Thomas, Diane Carr, Gareth Schott, David Buckingham, Espen Aarseth, Jørgen Bang, Sara de Freitas, Drew Davidson, Marie Laure-Ryan, Martin Sønderlev, Lars Konzack, John Kirriemuir, Rikke Magnussen, Patrick Bergman, Thorkild Hanghøj, Thomas Duus and all the anonymous reviewers of papers along the way. Thanks to Pernille Heegaard Deichmann, Ann Heegaard, Tasha Buch and Sande Chen for proofreading and editorial work.

In addition, warm thanks to the listeners at conferences, public talks and seminars who raised their hands with comments, criticism and questions. Moreover, thanks to the people that went before me and to those that come after me.

Simon Egenfeldt-Nielsen, October, 2006.

Dedicated to Sidsel Egenfeldt-Nielsen
who paints life in bright colours.

Introduction

Many people still reject the educational potential of computer games. However, times are changing and this book is about these changing times. There have been few serious attempts to harness the potential of computer games and even fewer critical accounts of such endeavours. The new millennium has seen an increasing interest in what is often referred to as serious games, or computer games used for other purposes than entertainment. Educational use of computer games is the largest subcategory within serious games with a life of its own. Marc Prensky and James Paul Gee, in their books, argue convincingly that computer games are replete with learning potential, but so far less has been said about actually using games in educational settings. This book provides some answers by building a framework for the educational use of computer games based on concrete examples while not limiting the frame of reference to classical edutainment.

WHO IS THIS BOOK FOR?

This is hardly a how-to book, but researchers, educators, policy-makers and developers should all find something of value. The knowledge and thoughts in this book come from a variety of perspectives that I have gained over the last ten years – from the very hands-on experiences in game development to the more theoretical angles in game research that will be more pronounced in this book. These days I have gone beyond theorizing and thinking about educational use of computer games. Today, my company Serious Games Interactive develops next-generation educational computer games by relying on many of the ideas you will read about in this book. However, I still have strong roots in research and educational circles and truly believe that a mixed approach can enrich the educational use of computer games. My diverse profile points to the usefulness of the contents of this book in terms of studying, designing, developing, implementing and evaluating educational computer games. Hopefully, you will agree.

WHAT IS AN EDUCATIONAL VIDEO GAME?

To explain what makes a video game become educational is not a simple task. It relies on our perception of several key concepts such as games, education and learning, which this book will explore in later chapters. Indeed, presuming what an educational video game is before reading this book may severely limit your understanding of the educational potential of computer games. Below, I outline the most important kinds of educational computer games.

The first, most obvious and recognizable category is commercial educational computer games, often known as edutainment. Edutainment focuses on teaching the player certain specific skills: mostly algebra, spelling, problem-solving and other similar basic skills. Edutainment titles include *Math Blaster*, *Pajama Sam* and *Castle of Dr Brain*. Edutainment titles have a strong educational component but often lack the intrinsic motivational drive found in commercial game titles and many do not consider them to be similar in quality to entertainment games. Some even question whether they qualify as games.

The second category is commercial game titles used for education, more or less haphazardly. These rarely focus on an exclusive topic or on basic skills. Titles in this category include *SimCity* and *Civilization*, which have been used by several schools for many years. The educational goals of commercial computer games are indirect rather than direct, which can lead to a skewed focus in the learning process. However, their strength is that the motivational part is well documented from the success on the commercial entertainment market – they feel and play like a 'real' computer game.

The third category is research-based educational computer games that often try to challenge the existing formula of edutainment. Educational computer games coming from research often present new approaches and have strong documentation for learning outcomes. However, they often lack the budgets and technical quality to compete with the more commercial titles. The titles often make a greater impact if published on the commercial market with some modifications. Exemplary titles are *Oregon Trail*, *Logical Journey of the Zoombinis*, *Global Conflicts: Palestine* and *Phoenix Quest*.

WHAT IS IN THIS BOOK?

I start out by looking at previous research and then look at a concrete course using the commercial computer game *Europa Universalis II*. This concrete example is then used in connection with existing theory to develop a general theory on the educational use of computer games.

Chapter 1: The State of Research on Educational Use of Computer Games
This chapter outlines the current trends within the area and the theoretical foundation that this book is built on. It straightens out some potential confusion surrounding terminology, research traditions and game types.

Chapter 2: The History of Educational Computer Games

This chapter provides the background for educational media use with a focus on the emergence of educational use of computer games. The chapter presents the influential forerunners, characteristics of the titles and current market conditions and describes recent trends in the approach to educational use of computer games.

Chapter 3: Research into Educational Use of Games and Simulations

This chapter examines the research conducted on simulation and games, and how it leads to important research questions and knowledge that is also relevant for the educational use of computer games.

Chapter 4: Research on Educational Use of Computer Games

The area of educational use of computer games is vast, and therefore it is necessary to address different paradigms and sub-areas before venturing further in the book. This chapter presents the most important contributions up to the current day.

Chapter 5: Getting to Third Generation: New Trends in Educational Use of Computer Games

This chapter discusses the most recent research contributions to the area and outlines different approaches to the educational use of computer games. These approaches make up three generations.

Chapter 6: An Initial Educational Framework

This chapter discusses the educational theories that steer the empirical studies. These include educational theory, computer games theory and media theory. The chapter establishes the necessary terminology for examining educational use of computer games in the chapters that follow and prepares the way for the final theory in Chapter 11.

Chapter 7: Initial Preparation for the History Course with the Strategy Game *Europa Universalis II*

This chapter presents an initial analysis of the title used in the concrete course as an example to understand the implications of using computer games in an educational setting and the reflections one should consider before using computer games. The analysis is kept to a common sense approach to clear the way for more in-depth discussions later.

Chapter 8: Practical Barriers and Perception of History

This chapter focuses on the trajectories of different student groups through the experimental course with *Europa Universalis II* and how barriers persisted for the course. In addition, the chapter discusses the struggle between different understandings of history among the students and its impact on the learning experience with computer games.

Chapter 9: The Balance Between Play and Learning
The chapter outlines, analyses and discusses the problems related to play and learning in an educational setting. Often this relationship is taken for granted or outright dismissed. However, as the chapter argues, a balance needs to be found between play taking over learning, and learning subduing play.

Chapter 10: A Theory on Educational Use of Computer Games
This chapter delivers a general theory for understanding the educational use of computer games. The focus is on how the use of computer games in an educational setting can provide concrete experiences that teaching can extend, thus providing stronger and richer educational experiences.

Chapter 11: Final Thoughts
The last chapter summarizes the results and presents some final thoughts on the scope and implications of this book.

1

The State of Research on Educational Use of Computer Games

Tell me and I will forget. Show me and I may remember. Involve me and I will understand.

Confucius, circa 450 BC

More and more active researchers worldwide are looking at computer games as a topic of serious research. As a mainstream entertainment activity, computer games are increasing in popularity, with a broader player base and a rising number of sold titles (ESA, 2003). One area of early and continuing interest is the educational use of computer games. Not surprisingly, the increased general interest in computer games research has helped educational computer games research. However, many questions remain unanswered, largely due to the fragmented nature of the research into the educational use of computer games and the lack of thorough case studies. There exist only incomplete attempts at integrating research within this area. This does not imply a lack of recent research in the field of computer games, education and learning. Primarily, researchers have mostly written from one perspective with a limited wish to present overall empirical results or to engage in the entire research field. Recent research examples include, but are not limited to, Prensky (2001b), Konzack (2003), Gee (2003) and Squire (2004).

This book's primary goal is to build a framework that can bring some of the many pieces together, challenging the dominance of edutainment. Edutainment plays the role of the villain in this book and is defined, with a few exceptions, as the current dominating titles on the market for educational computer games. Edutainment titles are characterized by their use of quite conventional learning theories that rely on training more than learning, thereby providing a dubious game experience. They rely on simple gameplay and are mostly produced with strict reference to a curriculum. Thus, the framework I intend to build is in opposition to conventional learning theory. It avoids a narrow-minded understanding of education as curriculum and shuns simple gameplay to facilitate strong learning experiences through computer games. The most important focal point of this framework is the ability of computer games to offer concrete experiences that provide relevance and engagement, which in turn leads to students' investment in the learning activity. Instruction extends from the concrete experiences undergone in the game, and the students' investment in these experiences leads to the comprehension of abstract concepts. Instruction provides the necessary direction, order, exploration and linking to other areas. This approach sees computer games from the start as an integrated part of existing teaching forms, rather than an entirely new beast by itself. This implies that using computer games in education should be thought of not as a substitution but rather as a supplement.

AN EXAMPLE OF EDUCATIONAL USE OF GAMES

Computer games provide strong experiences that can be expanded to deeper knowledge through instruction. An example from my own company's title *Global Conflicts: Palestine* illustrates the idea. In *Global Conflicts: Palestine*, the player is a journalist who must solve different missions by finding the best sources and build up trust to get the best information for the next scoop on an article.

The player is confronted with everyday Palestinian and Israeli experiences. For example, the Palestinians will resent the collective punishment and the dire repercussions that cut them off from relatives, work in Israel and studying. On the other hand, Israelis will give you their side of the story focusing on security and the perils of suicide bombing. This example points to the power of computer games in providing concrete experience from different perspectives and personal stories which is often difficult in teaching. Furthermore, instruction is crucial to expand on such game experiences. The teacher should follow up afterwards, ensuring that all students appreciate the implications, and explore them beyond the immediate game actions and even link them to other clashes between overall policy and everyday repercussions in the conflict or society in general. With this overall steering point established, we start the building of a new framework for educational use of computer games.

THE IDEA BEHIND EDUCATIONAL USE OF COMPUTER GAMES

We start by asking where the infatuation with computer games for education originates? Is it just a passing phenomenon similar to other emerging new media or does it have more holding power? Simply put, is it worth our time? Educational researchers have embraced radio, television, computers and computer games for their ability to engage and motivate students, but the fascination often dries up relatively fast. The current focus of many researchers on computer games' ability to increase motivation and interest among students is somewhat superficial as it only addresses the manifestation of other underlying factors. It doesn't get us very far to conclude that computer games in general lead to increased interest and motivation when the underlying variables continue to influence the learning process haphazardly. We need to describe these underlying variables as well (Buckingham and Scanlon, 2002; Calvert, 1999; Loftus and Loftus, 1983; Prensky, 2001a).

The idea of using computer games for education is not just a concept forged by hopeful educators and ambitious researchers; it is also found in leading game designers' descriptions of the most basic incentives for playing computer games. In the words of game designer Chris Crawford, 'The fundamental motivation for all game-playing is to learn' (1982: Chapter 2, unpaginated). Crawford points out that learning is not necessarily a manifest motivation when playing computer games, but that it lies latent. He is especially referring to the games with a universe that can be explored. I will add that, for a computer game to work, one is required to learn on a very basic level, that is, playing computer games is not just explained by an abstract idea of a basic human desire to learn new things. Learning is incorporated into the structure of computer games; learning is a prerequisite for playing. In order to advance within the game, one needs to learn different things depending on the genre and game. The elements that support learning in computer games may take very different forms. In the action game *Space Invaders* the player improves the ability to react swiftly with utmost precision and shoot down those damn aliens. In adventure games, like the *Leisure Suit Larry* series, the player is constantly forced to acquire new knowledge and solve puzzles in order to advance. Failure to get hold of a clue or figure out something leads to a quagmire; the game will come to a halt. Computer games may have different tolerance levels for 'bad' learners since they rely more critically on constant learning and changing demands on the player's capacity for learning, but in the majority of games, the player needs to learn to advance further. This learning mostly involves improving a skill or acquiring certain knowledge, and this takes a very concrete form when the player uses that skill or knowledge in the right place at the right time to get further in the game. Of course, the skills and knowledge are not always interesting from an educational point of view, but the basic structure and process is in place.

A very basic premise of playing the majority of computer games is to engage with an unknown universe, slowly learning more about this universe. Because the structure of computer games demands learning, this makes them different from other media in which the pupil can move forward without necessarily learning more to gain access to more of the representation. Computer games have a prerequisite for learning as introduced above, purporting to more than most representations. They have a number of engaging game features, providing a richer experience with different modalities, and have different potentials for interaction compared to other media. When computer games work, they draw the user into the experience, make him lose sense of time and place and they demand the user's full concentration, focus and energy, forcing the user to invest in the learning experience. Computer games challenge the user to his limit and the user loves it. For every action the game demands a counteraction – a constant and often a high-paced ping-pong in the most popular genres. The actions are performed within a simplified game universe where the player experiences the consequences of different actions and observes the relations between actions. It is these characteristics above that make researchers, developers and educators believe in the learning potential of games and their superiority in some areas compared to other media. They believe that the computer game is potentially a very valuable supplement to traditional teaching methods by virtue of its engagement. This despite the fact that evidence of computer games providing better learning experiences compared to other learning forms remains somewhat ambiguous, mostly due to difficult conditions for testing the learning effect of games exactly, but also out of flawed methods in many studies conducted so far.

Against the above background, it doesn't make much sense to treat learning in computer games from a narrow perspective in which learning is perceived as occurring only in computer games specifically constructed for educational purposes (that is, with a curriculum in mind). Obviously, we must see all computer games as relying on the player's learning to ensure the progress of the computer game, and the educational part is to a high degree a matter of framing. A beat'em-up computer game with female avatars fighting bad guys may be considered educational in connection with a self-help class for battered women but from a parental perspective it may be considered deeply antisocial. The context of a computer game obviously has an impact on its perceived educational value. In addition, without instruction both of these examples will probably have limited effect beyond the game universe.

Gee (2003) points out that computer games today are mostly coined as entertainment and that the educational framing may be alien to many. Players do learn the relevant actions in a given computer game in order to acquire the desired game outcome. However, it is highly unlikely that we can automatically expect the computer game to also facilitate a desired educational outcome, since this is seldom part of the game universe or the game culture. For this, we need to consider different educational interventions that form the computer-game experience through the surrounding context, instructional interventions or the design of computer games with an educational framing. This is the role educators need to take upon themselves to facilitate educational quality in game experience. They need to incorporate the following process: transform the concrete experiences in computer games by building an appreciation of relevant elements, all the while exploring these elements and linking them to other areas external to the game experience.

The significance of the surrounding context for facilitating educational experiences could indicate that the specific computer game used is of minor importance. However, this is not the case. Some computer games are more useful for educational purposes than others, as exemplified by the popularity of *SimCity, Civilization* and *Oregon Trail* in educational circles. One computer game may lend itself better to educational use as a consequence of the contents in the game, the skills required in the game, the challenge of established attitudes, its ability to support the learning experience or the closeness of the genre to the students' expectations. The hard part is to identify the strong learning features of computer games in connection with educational practice and to determine how specific computer games facilitate learning in alternative ways compared to traditional teaching methods. This doesn't indicate that the computer game as a medium has one unique educational characteristic separating it from all other educational media. If anything, the opposite is the case. It has consistently been found that focusing on a medium in itself for providing better learning experiences is not that fruitful (Mayer, 2001). We should rather examine how the new medium connects, expands and stresses important parts of education in new ways, such as how it will affect teaching style and student role. Therefore, this book will also quite naturally include quite a lot of discussions of more traditional educational theory. One returning question in educational theory is the transfer of knowledge across contexts, which will also play a role in this book.

For some knowledge forms in computer games, like behaviours and low-level skills, there seem to be better indications of a direct transfer. This is especially clear in research on health-related use of computer games (Brown, 1997; Lieberman, 2001). Still, even these studies indicate that a great deal of the transfer may be dependent on peer discussions and a generally improved home climate for health-related considerations. This indicates that the transfer doesn't just happen but has to be facilitated by the context surrounding the computer game experience. The facilitation and qualification of this transfer remains a key topic in studying educational use of computer games. Transfer is in this book not conceived as automatic or unproblematic, but as depending on a variety of factors, most prominently the richness of the learning experience combined with the construction of supporting structures in and around the computer game. Based on the introduction above, some key areas for our further enquiry in the field of educational use of computer games emerge.

First of all, the inherent learning features of computer games should be maintained when designing and thinking about educational game titles. Commercial computer games should not be seen as alien to educational practice. The learning features in commercial computer games, especially the strong engagement, should be explicitly nurtured in the educational context where the computer game is used. An educational computer game should, in theory, be able to exhibit the same holding power on players as any other commercial computer game, although such a game will probably be considerably harder to design, due to the extra constraints imposed by the educational framing.

The second area concerns the facilitation of learning in computer games and how we perceive this process. It is important to resist seeing the current practice for educational use of computer games as the way forward or to be limited by current teaching practices in the educational system. Computer games should challenge educational practices while seeking the realization of realistic educational scenarios (see also Squire, 2005). This balance is delicate but also critical if computer games are to have a real impact and justification in educational efforts. Without the challenge of current practice, computer games risk becoming of little interest to anyone, trapped in the caricature of edutainment, pointing educators backward in time instead of forward. This happened in the past as will become evident in Chapter 2.

The third area we need to address is how we can be certain that knowledge obtained in relation to the educational use of computer games is accessible in other contexts and establish ways to support these links. This is seen as one of the main areas where computer games, through their more rich experiences, can really bring something to the table. Computer games offer concrete experiences that can be elaborated on by the teacher, thus resulting in knowledge that is not merely abstractly tied to the teaching process but is more accessible in different contexts and provides a strong experience-base for student development of concepts.

These guidelines should be kept in mind when trying to fulfil the ultimate goal of this book, which is to provide a counterweight against the tidal wave of unsubstantiated and dissipated claims that computer games are a serious contender in the educational system. Instead, this book should build a serious and solid starting point for educational use of computer games. This ultimately entails developing an understanding of how to use computer games in education that goes beyond the current limited focus on edutainment.

RECENT INTEREST IN EDUCATIONAL USE OF COMPUTER GAMES

Building a framework for educational use of computer games requires a thorough discussion of the current contributions to the field. In recent years, the research area of educational computer games use has received increased attention from researchers, educators and government bodies, but only partly from the game industry, most likely due to the tricky market conditions. Government interests have especially been on a content level trying to pinpoint existing computer games' educational potential. British Educational Communications and Technology Agency (BECTA) has been one of the main forces in the UK, saying:

> Titles such as Caesar III and Age of Empires operate within the context of ancient history and so include factual information about that period. With the increase in processing power and memory capabilities of new computers, there is an increasing demand for technically accurate simulations involving situations that would normally be impossible for the user to experience in real life. Genres such as real time strategy (RTS) can lead to the development of game play, which demands that the user is able to test and develop strategies and reassess decisions.
>
> (BECTA, 2001)

In the US, the Games-to-Teach project has helped kick-start the field with collaborative efforts between the Massachusetts Institute of Technology and Microsoft to build a number of game prototypes to explore computer games from a learning perspective. Recently, work at the University of Wisconsin at Madison has taken over the lead in the US with a strong research group on the educational use of computer games championed by James Paul Gee and Kurt Squire. Current US research is less interested in examining whether or not existing computer games push some content that may be of relevance to educational purposes and it opposes a narrow focus on content, skills and attitudes (Squire, 2004). Instead, it looks to the structural characteristics in computer games that could be used for educational computer games and the social processes surrounding the educational experience. Lately, educational computer games in the US also seem to be finding their way to policymakers.

The research area of educational use of computer games is by no means unexplored, but it remains haunted by fragmentation and unclear boundaries. From the onset, the research has been distributed over a number of disciplines with little in common except perhaps the interest in computer games. Some of these are literature, psychology, media studies, anthropology, ethnography, sociology, history, business studies, military tactics, literary theory, educational theory, instructional technology and computer games studies. This variety gives the area vitality and nerve. However, it has also somewhat hindered the field from moving forward. This may seem counter-intuitive to some and it is in opposition to the increasing recognition of the potential of cross-disciplinary work both on an overall research agenda and within computer games research.[1] There are, however, a number of problems within the field related to its interdisciplinary nature. The two most important are scattered information and the lack of a common theoretical frame.

These two factors make scientific progress hard since we cannot locate relevant work, and if we do, we have trouble discussing it, and certainly building on it. Although this is to a certain degree unavoidable, we can benefit from a closer adherence to educational use of computer games as a specific research area. A closer adherence to a specific field implies that a shared foundation is constructed that addresses what is seen as relevant and important theory, practice and discussions. There is a 'canon' that a researcher is expected to know, although not necessarily in-depth. However, currently it is often haphazard what earlier research is acknowledged. Relevant work goes unnoticed and broader discussions in education are embarked on without reference to basic educational research. For example, several research projects on computer games for teaching maths have been started up without acknowledging each other's existence (see Chapter 4). A first step in such an overview is the awareness of the two parallel communities researching educational use of computer games, simulations and non-electronic games described in the following. The acknowledgement of these two communities is especially important for examining the educational use of computer games as the two communities each have made significant advances in the area that we ignore at our own peril. Unfortunately, too often ignorance prevails.

THE CURRENT STATE OF GAME RESEARCH

Although the last five years have seen strong progress, the research field of computer games is not yet well established. This is true on several levels. On the individual level, researchers still struggle for acceptance and academic credibility. On an institutional level, the field is characterized by the lack of common terminology, basic theoretical discussions and, despite progress, scarce funding of research. Within game research, there exist two parallel research communities and one is often ignored in favour of the other. The split between the two communities is supported by the fact that game researchers in general have quite diverse backgrounds and the majority of references within the field are still from neighbouring disciplines. The result is that a lot of the research is not published in specific journals for game research, but rather in well-established traditional peer-reviewed journals within a researcher's own field. (Although, compared to a couple of years ago, journals are less of a problem today, now that there are several specializing in game research.) Furthermore, researchers already need to follow up on their background discipline and the game research discipline. This makes it very hard for them to keep up with any developments and build on top of earlier research. This results in pockets of research in different hubs. The Ivory Tower column has discussed this issue of a cross-disciplinary approach as both a strength and a weakness for game research (Kirkpatrick, 2003; Pearce, 2003).

Seldom are both communities consulted when approaching computer games, and it is, therefore, initially worthwhile to stress the strength of each community. A historical awareness will benefit us so that we don't constantly reinvent the wheel.

The simulation research community

The simulation community is older than the computer game research community. It is today centred on the journal *Simulation and Gaming* and the supporting academic organizations in different countries like ABSEL, ISAGA, JASAG and NASAGA. This research tradition started in the mid-1950s, especially promoted by business gaming and the perceived potential of learning through games (Butler, Markulis, and Strang, 1988). The focus is on games in general, not necessarily computer games, but a majority of the research is relevant for computer games research.

The field broadens from the early 1970s and up through the 1980s with books like *Simulation Games in Learning* by Sarane Boocock and E.O. Schild (1968), *Learning with Simulations and Games* by Richard Duke and Constance Seidner (1975) and *Gaming-Simulation: Rationale Applications* by Cathy Greenblat and Richard Duke (1981). Conferences have been regularly held over the years and have maintained a good foothold up to present times, especially in the business area. The business area has increasingly come to dominate, with a strong emphasis on simulations and less focus on games. This development is clear when looking at the older issues of the *Journal of Simulation and Gaming*, where fundamental discussions on games and simulations occur especially in connection to educational use. The simulation and games research community has seen a decline over the years and needs to reconsider its organization and goals, which was also an explicit goal of the anniversary conference in 1994 (Dorn, 1989; Duke, 1995).

The computer games research community

The other community focuses on computer games and took its first steps in the early 1980s with classic books like Chris Crawford's *The Art of Computer Game Design* (Crawford, 1982), Geoffrey Loftus and Elizabeth Loftus' *Mind at Play* (Loftus and Loftus, 1983) and Patricia Greenfield's *Mind and Media* (Greenfield, 1984). These books were quite broad in their treatment of computer games, although Crawford's book was an important exception.

Within the 1980s and the 1990s the closest we came to seeing active academic achievements aimed primarily at computer games were *The Journal of Computer Game Design*, a few research projects mainly within maths and science and some quite extensive studies of the potential negative effects of computer games. The focus on small specific areas lasted until the late 1990s. From the late 1990s, the research into games slowly accelerated with the appearance of resource sites like Game-culture, Ludology, Game-research and Joystick101. At the same time, quite a few research-oriented conferences exclusively on computer games saw the light. The IT-University of Copenhagen held Computer Games and Digital Textualities in March 2001, and the University of Chicago hosted Playing by the Rules in October 2001. There was a conference as early as 1983 but the research area never really caught on back then. From the conferences in 2001, several initiatives emerged: several other conferences exclusively on game research, the peer-reviewed journal *Game Studies* dedicated to humanistic game research, and the forming of the *Digital Game Research Association* (DiGRA).

The two research areas above still live in their own domains, but games and simulations (on a computer or not) are too similar to be separated into parallel research tracks.

DEFINING COMPUTER GAMES AND SIMULATIONS

The discussion on how to define computer games and simulations has a long history and it has been the primary interest of a number of theorists (Aarseth, 1997; Coleman, 1970; Crawford, 1982; Salen and Zimmerman, 2003; Seidner, 1975). In particular, the differences between computer games and simulations are a returning problem, which will be discussed at some length below. The computer game versus simulation discussion is important when we later look at the problems related to the learning experience when considering the representational nature of computer games.

I will start with the game definition by Jesper Juul (2003), which is one of the most recent, grounded in an extensive examination of previous attempts at defining games.

> A game is a rule-based system with a variable and quantifiable outcome, where different outcomes are assigned different values, the player exerts effort in order to influence the outcome, the player feels attached to the outcome and the consequences of the activity are optional and negotiable.
>
> (Juul, 2003: 30)

It is obvious from the definition above that computer games are quite far-reaching and maybe the definition does not really exclude educational software or simulations. The major difference seems to be the attachment of the player, which can also be instilled in educational software and simulations. Juul (2003) is aware of the problem since he discusses a number of borderline examples that share a lot of characteristics with games. The addition of conflict to the game definition solves some of the problems, especially in relation to differentiating games from simulations and most educational software.[2] One example of an early definition of a simulation is by Seidner (1975):

In the broadest sense, simulation refers to the dynamic execution or manipulation of a model of some object system. In education, simulation entails abstracting certain elements of social or physical reality in such a way that the student can interact with and become a part of that simulated reality.

(Seidner, 1975: 15)

The definition by Seidner may seem to cover computer games, but if we look to other game definitions, important properties are missing, namely artificial conflict and the player's investment (Salen and Zimmerman, 2003). These elements are far from trivial, as they point to the focal point of most computer games. The construction of an artificial conflict and the balancing of this conflict to best challenge the player is one of the trademarks of a good computer game. When this element is missing, we have a simulation. Seidner (1975) also describes this when she points to the lack of goals in simulations as the difference from games. The close relationship is best captured by Coleman's (1970) definition of 'simulation games', which are simulations that become games when goals are applied to the possible activities in the simulation. Goals are tied to the conflict and necessary for the player to really invest strong feelings in the game. Even when computer games do not set up specific conflicts and goals, many players will invent their own and use the simulation to achieve these goals, making up their own game experience.

The difference between implicit and explicit goals has important consequences in how the game universe is constructed. The explicit goals are those set by the game, whereas implicit goals are those the players are capable of setting and very often do (Salen and Zimmerman, 2003). Relying on implicit rules will provide a more open-ended game universe akin to a simulation, whereas explicit goals will make the game universe more game-like.

Also, in simulations, the realism of the model has high priority, whereas a computer game will often sacrifice realism if it benefits the overall game experience. The computer game is not primarily about simulating, but rather about providing an interesting experience when the player fulfils certain explicit goals. Thiagarajan (1998) suggests a useful division between low-fidelity and high-fidelity simulations to address the difference between game and simulation. High-fidelity simulations attempt to resemble the real world as closely as possible, whereas low-fidelity simulations 'focus on only a few critical elements and use a simplified model of the interactions among them' (Thiagarajan, 1998: 37). Most computer games will be low-fidelity simulations.

The closeness between computer games and low-fidelity simulations is due to computer games' priority of entertainment over realism. This is captured in relation to the design of conflicts in computer games, which favours an interesting and balanced conflict at the expense of realism. Few would say that the *Civilization* series embraces realism, but it certainly includes simulation properties with a dynamic model representing civilizations that can be manipulated. Most computer games have degrees of simulation, but it is not necessarily a property of computer games. In an adventure game, a branching structure can exist that does not have the characteristics of a dynamic structure. It has a finite number of options contrary to a simulation, which has a basic set of rules that the player can manipulate in almost endless ways. Simple action games are basically low-fidelity simulations where one can engage in a simulated universe with explicit rules for the potential activities. On the other hand, some action games, specifically those designed in collaboration with the military, like *First to Fight*, have a high-fidelity level. The truth is that setting up borders for just what makes something a game or a simulation is hard. Indeed, just agreeing on a definition for either is hard.

EDUCATIONAL THEORETICAL BACKGROUND

Along with a basic understanding of computer games, it seems obvious to gain a better understanding of the educational dimension. Within educational theory, there is a very wide range of theories and one has to be selective. Research into the educational potential of computer games spans the entire spectrum of theories of education, teaching and learning. For some, learning is conceived as achieving skills like system-thinking, analysis and problem-solving. Others refer to concrete facts, while some will focus primarily on the social setting around the learning experience. This book intends to show an inclusive understanding of learning, education and teaching.

Learning, education and teaching

The concepts learning, education and teaching are certainly broad and potentially very inclusive. We need to get a firm idea of what we really refer to when we use these different terms. Some overall criteria for the definition of these central concepts is helpful for guiding the unravelling of educational use of computer games, since a number of different paths can be taken. Our understanding of learning should not be limited to, for example, the education of children or education in a school context or deal exclusively with edutainment titles. Our definition should be able to describe both the interaction with the computer game and the interaction around the computer game. The definition should also be able to provide a perspective for understanding and exploring different practices that lend themselves better to using computer games for educational purposes. These criteria are critical if we are to uncover the existing spectrum of research done on the educational use of computer games and build a viable framework. The first important property is that learning, education and teaching is not conceived as limited to any one context or person. In some distant past, it may have been easy to say what education was: education took place at school. This is hardly the case any more, when there are broader, newer concepts that have expanded the scope of education beyond childhood, school and teachers, like home-schooling, lifelong learning and supplementary training. Education and learning often take place within an educational system, but cannot exclusively be limited to a certain context. On an overall level, education is still an attempted controlled socialization and qualification of a given individual for the benefit of society (Ljungstrøm, 1984). However, this happens through still more subtle practices, handing over responsibility to the individual. Education is continually becoming a task for everybody other than teachers. The increased practice of home-schooling, which has strong ties with edutainment, hands over responsibility to the parents and, to some degree, to the students and is partly accelerated by information technology (Egenfeldt-Nielsen, 2001). Also, lifelong learning and supplementary learning tend to transfer responsibility to the student. Finally, schools are increasingly relying on the students to be masters of their own educational fate, with individual teaching plans and 'career' goals formulated by the student at a still earlier stage (Buckingham and Scanlon, 2002; Egenfeldt-Nielsen, 2001). Similarly, teaching is not restricted to a teacher or school and learning can take place in all situations. Inspired by anthropologist Gregory Bateson, I use learning as an overarching term that refers to activities and contexts we engage in to change or support our patterns of action. We can see learning as the ability to appreciate the difference that makes a difference (Bateson, 1972).

In terms of the learning process, this book introduces the experiential approach to learning as formulated by David Kolb, expanded with John Dewey. These theorists cover the development of experiential theory from the early twentieth century and are situated within the constructivist learning approach founded by Jean Piaget. The experiential approach stresses the connection between concrete experience, reflection, concepts and application. This is seen as a learning cycle and, as will become clear later, fits well with the playing of computer games. The important characteristic of the experiential learning approach is the focus on the concrete experience as the starting point for students' learning. Computer games offer such concrete experiences that can be reflected, conceptualized and applied continuously.

An additional argument for drawing on the experiential learning tradition is the foothold it has within the research area of educational games (e.g. Gentry, 1990; Ruben, 1999). It lends itself well to understanding the active processes involved in using games for facilitating learning. Therefore, this theory is a good foundation for understanding computer games that share some basic properties with traditional games.

Overall, education refers to a purposeful learning process and hence is a sub-category of learning. I define education as a mostly planned activity that we engage in with the purpose of changing specific contents, skills or attitudes. These can be contents, skills or attitudes in different forms:

- Defined by curriculum (for example arithmetic, reading or writing)
- Parental interest (for example information on local history or family history)
- Supplementary projects such as youth centre projects (for example build a house, learn basic DIY skills or learn how to cook)
- Self-study (for example learn programming through online tutorials or a Spanish evening course for a holiday trip) (Good and Brophy, 1990).

When I defined education, I stated that we learn contents, skills and attitudes. These are imprecise concepts, but are inspired by the work of Bloom et al. (1956) and Kratwohl et al. (1964). The delimitation serves as a starting point and is throughout this book a useful analytic tool. The work on the taxonomy was initiated in 1948 with the explicit goal of including the different educational theories to construct an overarching description of what outcomes were relevant in education. The aim was to describe three main areas: cognitive domain, affective domain and psychomotor domain. However, the taxonomy was never fully developed for the last area and I will not concentrate on this last area as it seems to have limited bearing on the current educational research related to computer games.[3] In the affective domain, there are five categories: receiving, responding, valuing, organization and characterization. The first two categories describe the necessary basic attitude of the students towards the learning process, whereas the next levels refer to how values will be internalized in the students. This taxonomy has not experienced the same success among educators and researchers as the cognitive domain, but is still useful for pointing to the importance of the affective objectives in the educational process. It basically describes what I will refer to as relevance and investment, namely the student's willingness to approach a given area and continually invest in it, thereby making it part of the student's perception of the world.

The taxonomy of the cognitive domain (often referred to as Bloom's taxonomy) includes the following hierarchy: knowledge, comprehension, application, analysis, synthesis and evaluation. The last levels presuppose to some degree mastery of the basic level and comprehension. It is worth noting that the first levels are what we would call facts or information, whereas the next levels are actually skills used in constructing knowledge. We will later see that the higher levels are relevant especially in computer games, but they require the basic levels, which are often not in place in today's students.

Above, I have outlined the important bricks for building an understanding of the educational use of computer games. To limit the scope of this book, I will concentrate on the particular challenges of the school setting, which despite everything is still the prominent site for education. This delimits the more informal and incidental learning processes around computer games that have earlier been a topic of research, for example by VanDeventer (1997), Jessen (2001) and Gee (2003).

A WORD ON TERMINOLOGY

I have throughout this introduction used some terminology that typically causes great confusion. In the following, the most important terminology is listed going from general to more specific. There is also an expanded list in the Glossary that the reader can refer to:

- *Educational software*: The concept refers to all computer programs with an educational aim. Educational software is, therefore, a broader group than educational computer games, and the applications are quite different in that they do not necessarily have game elements. When they have game elements, it is seldom an integrated part of the experience, but rather small separate activities. Educational computer games are often included under the heading educational software.
- *Educational computer games*: Computer games developed for educational use or titles often finding their way to educational settings, including the fake, bad, ambitious and superb. This includes edutainment, but is not limited to it. In this book, educational computer games often implicitly exclude edutainment when used.
- *Edutainment*: Edutainment is a sub-group of educational computer games that are heavily criticized. Typically, edutainment titles are characterized by their use of quite conventional learning theories, which provide a questionable game experience and simple gameplay. They are often produced with reference to a curriculum.
- *Educational games*: Refers to traditional non-electronic game-like activities developed for educational use spanning board games, simulations, role-playing games, etc.

THE FOCUS ON COMMERCIAL COMPUTER GAMES

This book will have a stronger focus on commercial computer games than one might initially expect. This is a logical consequence of the perception of computer games presented earlier, when I discussed computer games as having a stronger inherent claim to learning than other media forms. It makes sense to treat most computer game genres as potentially educational, depending on the framing, although the educational quality has different degrees. Thus, the basic premise for using commercial games is met, but a number of other factors for choosing commercial games should be mentioned.

First of all, the majority of educational computer game titles on the market are lacking in quality and, therefore, are questionable examples for researching educational potential. The titles are mostly produced on a low budget, sold at low retail price and are constantly on sale (Buckingham and

Scanlon, 2002; Leyland, 1996; Taylor, 2003). As senior designer Margo Nanny of the company Interactive Learning states:

> Both the gaming industry and the educational software industry are acting in a short-sighted fashion by driving their product design entirely from the latest software fad and short-term bottom line.
>
> (Stern, 1998:1)

The rationale for using a commercial computer game was that I had a proven commercial title. I knew it worked gameplay-wise and could concentrate on its educational potentials. With most educational computer games, I would have been concerned with whether the results were contaminated by a flawed gameplay that would have made the computer game of little interest to students. It remains a constant problem whether studies on educational use of computer games are addressing the lack of a specific title or the educational use of computer games in general.

On the other hand, the commercial game title might fail because it lacks support for the learning experiences and is not specifically developed for educational purposes, which was indeed the case in the course that I will extensively refer to within this book. The choice of a commercial computer game for the course leads to speculations concerning the external validity of studying the use of computer games for educational purposes in general. However, I decided to use a commercial computer game because the existing educational computer games seemed to disqualify themselves on both accounts, working as neither education nor computer games. This was especially evident for the target group I wished to address; educational titles were practically non-existent for high-school classes. Studying an older group of students in the educational system provided some clear advantages as they were better able to give feedback. Computer games can be complex and older students have more background information for playing them. Commercial computer games, therefore, remain central to this book, both reflected in the theoretical approach and the empirical studies carried out to support the development of the field.

NOTES

1   The Ivory Tower column has attested to this several times as a special trademark of computer games research (www.igda.org/columns/ivorytower/).

2   In early research on educational use of games, we find that researchers prefer 'simulation' to the term 'game'. The reason for this may be more cosmetic than a reflection of real use. Simulations invoke fewer associations with fun, making it easier to transfer simulations to a serious educational context.

3   Although researchers have connected computer games with learning psychomotor skills, especially eye-hand co-ordination, it has a fundamentally different theoretical basis from this book (Egenfeldt-Nielsen, 2003d).

2

The History of Educational Computer Games

Unlike the scripted, paper-driven exercises of the past, computer simulation has become a must. In fact, it may be the only way to represent the complexities of future warfare.
        Lieutenant General Eugene D. Santarelli (quoted in Aldrich, 2003: 22)

This chapter provides the historical background for understanding the framework for the educational use of computer games. Often, when considering the educational potential of computer games, we lack an understanding of the realities of life. There seems to be this notion that with the right knowledge of how to produce educational titles, better titles should appear almost by magic. However, one should be careful in assuming that the low availability of high-quality educational titles is merely a result of limited knowledge of producing educational titles. Market realities have clearly influenced the face of educational titles.

The goal of this chapter is to situate educational computer games in a historical context by presenting the related influential areas, describing the historically significant events and outlining the market conditions. The starting point is the strong traditions within the business sector and the military for using games for educating people, which dates all the way back to the eighteenth century for the military. The military perspective is interesting to look at in order to document that educational use of computer games is not merely a new, hyped phenomenon. After an overview of military and business titles, the similarities between the educational use of computer games and other educational media will be examined. These similarities have heavily influenced the current face of educational computer games. The final step is to examine how the area of educational computer games became dominated by edutainment titles.

Educational media increasingly came to shape the form taken by educational use of computer games, although historically there have been other, more ambitious attempts at developing educational computer games. Edutainment became the dominating form despite, or perhaps because of, its conservative approach to education and questionable game titles.

THE MILITARY'S EDUCATIONAL USE OF COMPUTER GAMES

The earliest roots of war games are in *Chaturanga*, the Indian forefather of chess, but the formal introduction of games into the military didn't start until Helwig in 1780 and was refined later by Lieutenant Von Reisswitz. During the nineteenth century, the Prussian military seriously began to use *Kriegsspiel* as a way to simulate strategy on the battlefield. This became the first organized effort to use games for a direct educational purpose in Western culture. In 1824, the game *Kriegsspiel* was recommended for training Prussian officers and a copy of the game was distributed to every regiment in the Prussian army. The Prussian military put the games to good use and, slowly, the idea spread to the rest of the world (Avendon and Sutton-Smith, 1971; Leeson, Unknown).

The US military started to use commercial computer games for training with a modification of *Doom* called *Marine Doom* back in 1998. The impact of the military is considered by some to be a paramount influence on the computer game industry's current focus on warfare and violence (Kline, Dyer-Witheford and Greig, 2003). In the early 1980s, the military tried to use the computer game *Battlezone* for eye-hand coordination, but failed. However, the military has had a long tradition for using games and it was not about to give up (Macedonia, 2003).

Instead, the military took a new starting point, extending more from the approach in *Kriegsspiel*, and developed other types of computer games. Instead of concrete simulations, computer games were conceived in a broader way. The real rationale for using computer games became team tactics, decision-making, conflict resolution and strategy. This is the idea behind using *Doom, Delta Force 2, Guard Force* and *Joint Force Employment* in the military today (Plotz, 2003; Prensky, 2001a; Social Impact Games, 2004). There are still computer games used for more low-level skills, such as torpedo firing through periscope readings in *Bottom Gun*, but they are fewer in number and are more precisely described as simulations rather than computer games.

The military's use of computer games has increased over recent years, most noticeably with *America's Army, Operation French Point, Foreign Grounds, Full Spectrum Warrior, Close Combat Marines* and *Full Spectrum Command*. It has become more affordable to tweak existing commercial computer games for use in a military setting and it has increasingly been possible to hire game developers for a specific game title, often in the form of so-called modifications (mods). Mods refer to computer games built on existing commercial computer game engines, but with some features tweaked. The modifications vary from superficial to extensive.

The military are often hailed as the true champions of educational use of computer games (Prensky, 2001a), but access to their findings and results are for good reasons often limited. Military use also has a number of characteristics that makes it less interesting to look at regarding its experiences with computer games. The military area deals with very different target groups, quite alternative settings for playing and reliance on training more than learning and has serious consequences for not learning well from the game. It may be hard to maintain the importance of play when considering military training games. Some of these characteristics are also shared by another influential area, namely business games and simulations.

EDUCATIONAL BUSINESS SIMULATIONS AND COMPUTER GAMES

Previously, I have hinted that business simulations and games were used early on for teaching a variety of business-related topics, including the general operations of a company, the management of a specialized business or specialized parts of the business area. The area is too large to ignore altogether and a few words proving its existence are important in order to construct an overall inclusive framework for the educational use of computer games.

Business simulations and games have long been a natural part of business schools, especially American ones, whereas computer games with business content are still mostly found at more introductory levels (Faria, 1990). Until recently, the area of business simulations and games has not seriously influenced the research into educational use of computer games, even though sparks have flown between them over the years. The business area is probably the place where simulations are most well established, but games have not really kicked in that much yet.

In 1956, the US Air Force simulation *Monopologs* let players become inventory managers, managing the Air Force supply system. One year later, *Top Management Decision Simulation* made its way into a business college class at the University of Washington. Thus, the way was paved for thousands of business games and simulations.[1] Although games and simulations also spread to other areas, they remained strongest within business studies and the military where games and simulations had originated (Woods, 2004). The area of business games and simulations never really joined forces with the educational use of computer games, probably because business understanding didn't seem the first priority to teach younger children who quickly became the major target group for educational computer games.

From early on, computer games with a business theme were labelled like any other commercial computer game, but the high complexity often points to older players. Almost every business area has been the subject of computer games. One can run a railroad company in *Railroad Tycoon*, become an oil tycoon in *Oil Imperium*, run an airline in *Airline Tycoon*, build up a car company in *Car Tycoon*, form a pizza empire in *Pizza Tycoon* or even control a worldwide company and learn the basics of the market in *Capitalism II*.

The actual use of these for formal learning is more uncertain, but many of these titles are quite successful. Perhaps there is a viable alternative to edutainment that has integrated and engaging gameplay, even if it's not always state-of-the-art computer games.

EDUCATIONAL MEDIA: THE FORERUNNER FOR EDUCATIONAL COMPUTER GAMES

Computer games follow other media surges almost perfectly. Every new media invention is bound to go through a stage when it's considered to be of potentially high value for educational purposes. In the honeymoon stage, the magic of the new medium combines with the traditional need for conveying knowledge to new generations. Unfortunately, the optimism is mostly followed by pessimism, which surfaces when new media forms are brought into educational settings without delivering the promised salvation. Often the first attempts are based on existing teaching practice and well-known media forms, which has indeed been the case with computer games. The theoretical winds from educational media have shaped, inspired and influenced educational use and research into computer games (Calvert, 1999; Cuban, 2001; Saettler, 1968). Educational media maintains its strong grip and continues to influence the form taken by educational computer games, especially in the manifestation of edutainment. Ultimately, the strong ties with other educational media are part of the explanation for the emergence of edutainment that only realizes a quite limited part of the potential for using computer games in education. It is, therefore, also worthwhile to look at educational media to track some of the characteristics brought into educational use of computer games.

Educational media research approaches educational media from at least two perspectives. On the one hand, educational media may contain direct academic content like spelling, maths, history, geography and science. This is the traditional perspective on educational media, but often it has been broadened with a pro-social perspective. In a pro-social perspective, educational media is expanded to also encompass social and emotional development of children. This second perspective is opposed by Calvert (1999), stressing that educational media should address specific curriculum goals. Calvert's approach is continued in the dominating approach to educational computer games, namely edutainment. The narrow focus on curriculum is problematic because it implies a narrow perception of education, which I opposed in Chapter 1. Interestingly, the curriculum focus has triumphed over the years, right from the first instructional films to current edutainment. The curriculum focus often also ties in with existing teaching practice in the form of classroom teaching, where the teacher takes the lead rather than the student. The result is that edutainment often lacks any real innovation in terms of teaching approach and practice.

Instructional films make their mark

The first attempts at using educational media were carried out at New York City school museums as early as 1890. They were instructional films without sound. The use expanded during the 1910s, when some suggested the integration of instructional films into schools. However, Cohen cautioned against this development in 1918. 'This impression that we are ready to supply just what the schools need in the way of educational picture [...] is quite general and absolutely erroneous' (Cohen, quoted in Saettler, 1968: 97). Still, they were introduced to many schools and subsequently caused a lot of problems. Finally, in the 1930s, the instructional films market crashed, not only due to the general depression, but also as a consequence of deep structural problems. In 1937, McClusky evaluated a lot of the problems in an effort to turn things around. He echoed some of the same concerns that are with us today regarding educational computer games.

Among the problems identified by McClusky (Saettler, 1968) was the widespread scepticism against combining entertainment, commercial interest and education. Instructional films were considered low culture and below the dignity of both educators and educational institutions, though educators on the surface might seem positive toward the enterprise of educational media. Another well-known problem was a lack of seriousness in the instructional films produced and a tendency to aim for fast profit. The sales methods and propaganda used by proponents of instructional films alienated educators and eroded the confidence in instructional films. Educational media was oversold. Regular technical problems, copyright issues and confusion regarding restrictions of use also discouraged educators. The commercial operators were hit hard by competition when subsidized production resulted in a saturated market. A lot of universities, school museums and companies engaged in both distribution and production of subsidized instructional films directly or indirectly with government funding. In addition, in some early attempts, there was a clash between commercial interest, instructional film directors and the subject experts who were consultants on the production. What worked in a film wasn't necessarily in accordance with curriculum. McClusky suggested a market of independent developers would solve the problem, along with a strong committee to advise and validate products. Nothing came of it (Saettler, 1968).

The concerns discussed above related to instructional film were increasingly being raised after the consolidation in the edutainment business during the 1990s, when the big companies began dominating the market. These structural problems remain a part of educational computer games even today. Indeed, all of the problems from the instructional films in the 1930s are found when considering the dominance of edutainment in the current market. Before looking closer at edutainment's road to power, it is beneficial to look at how educational television is rejuvenating instructional films.

Educational television experiences similar problems to edutainment and influences the educational approach favoured in edutainment.

Educational television dawns on us

Educational television was broadcast for the first time by the University of Iowa in 1933. During the early years, educational television was aimed at college students and proceeded at a slow pace with one-way communication. The result was often boring and somewhat ineffective educational programmes with the exception of more concrete programmes in science subjects. In science, one could visualize the processes of driving, show pictures of space and depict dynamic presentations of systems. The first slow years were succeeded by more active years from 1967, when legislation enforced broadcasters to air educational television (Calvert, 1999; Federal Communications Commission, 2003). This legislation also led to more attempts at reaching younger age groups. However, there was little success until *Sesame Street* was launched on 10 November 1969.

Early on, problems were caused by the inability to know the viewers' baseline knowledge, the age variety in viewers, and the desire to run the programmes live without needing to build on earlier programmes (Calvert, 1999). One couldn't assume that all viewers had seen the last episode. Some of these problems are clearly present with regards to educational use of computer games, which also aim at a broad target group. Computer games also give very different experiences through dispersed patterns of play and more choices for the player. *Sesame Street* solved some of these problems and, despite some criticism, became the model for future educational programmes as it won the hearts of the viewers.

Interestingly, educational media almost disappeared from broadcast television in the US during the 1980s as a consequence of new legislation. It would take several new legislation attempts before educational television would re-emerge in the mid-1990s. Educational programmes have now become popular and some stations, like Nickelodeon, Discovery Channel, the History Channel, the National Geographic Channel and Animal Planet, specialize in educational content, although interestingly often more for adults than children (Calvert, 1999; Miller, 2002).

According to Calvert (1999), the evaluations of the effectiveness of educational programmes are controversial, but in general lend support to the notion that educational media prepares children for school. Some of this effect is due to a general appreciation of learning in the home, where educational programmes are viewed. Children from middle-class families are especially inclined to view educational programmes. This suggests that educational programmes may actually widen the gap in preparedness for school between social classes rather than bridge the gap. The middle-class families secure and extend their head start by using the educational programmes that are relatively more expensive for lower classes. The educational programmes are also more easily embraced by middle-class culture because education is closer to those parents' hearts (Calvert, 1999).

THE APPEAL OF COMPUTERS FOR EDUCATORS

From the birth of television, interaction with the audience, as implemented through live shows, has been seen as an important characteristic. The potential of computers was, however, soon to dawn on educators. Although live television came one step closer to interacting with the user when compared to books, the computer was believed to take it at least several steps closer. As Loftus and Loftus state,

> Educators began to realize that the computer, with its powerful interactive abilities, might be used to aid in instruction. Thus the concept of computer-assisted instruction (or 'CAI') was born.
>
> (Loftus and Loftus, 1983: 116)

The 1960s saw massive investments in computer-assisted instruction, or CAI. For example, 4000 students during 1967–8 completed 300,000 arithmetic lessons. The lessons mostly covered simple maths like addition and fractions, but most importantly, CAI appeared to work (Cotton, 1991; Loftus and Loftus, 1983; Willis, Hovey, and Hovey, 1987). The expansion continued up through the 1980s and 1990s with the appearance of a range of terms covering the use of computers in school for educational purposes, e.g. computer-based education (CBE), computer-supported collaborative learning (CSCL) and computer-based instruction (CBI). Computer-based education refers in the broadest sense to the use of computers in education, but the sub-area that historically most clearly affected the use of educational computer games was CAI.

The term computer-assisted instruction is actually quite a narrow term and refers to drill-and-practice, simulation or tutorial activities offered as stand-alone activities or with limited guidance from teachers. The area has been heavily researched and while early studies showed that CAI worked (Cotton, 1991; Loftus and Loftus, 1983; Willis et al., 1987), it has more recently been noted by Soloway and Bielaczyc (1995: 1) that, 'By and large the impact of computers on education has been minimal.' Educational computer programmes continue to be caught in restrictions imposed by learning theories, hardware limits, structural problems and market conditions, a point also vigorously pursued by Cuban (2001). This is perhaps especially true for CAI, where drill and practice remains one of the most significant trademarks.

Although CAI has been shown to improve learning, it is unclear whether CAI is more or less effective than conventional teaching. The common conclusion is that a combination is preferable (Cotton, 1991). Still, CAI is often caught in the drill-and-practice approach to learning. Developers have apparently consistently found it hard and cumbersome to construct real alternatives to drill-and-practice programmes that can work in school settings. This is interesting as the drill-and-practice model used in early CAI is apparent in the early educational computer games and continues to be present in a lot of the popular educational computer game titles (Brody, 1993; Miller, 2000). The easy way out, one might say.

However, most of the current titles use an adventure-game format to contextualize the drill and practice. This has led to the critique of educational computer games as sugar-coated learning (Egenfeldt-Nielsen, 2003e; Healy, 1999). The major difference between educational computer games and CAI is primarily the role of motivation for engaging the students. Computer games are primarily seen as being able to offer both stronger intrinsic and extrinsic motivation. From the start, this is the major ambition of educators and researchers for turning to computer games – to alter educational computer programmes so that students become more motivated. This is where Thomas Malone's research in the early 1980s starts and this is the real birth of educational computer games. Over the years, motivation becomes the sole excuse for producing educational computer games instead of other educational software.

Parallel to the maturation of educational computer games, educational software increasingly turns towards multimedia learning to study the advantages of integrating different media forms. The term multimedia learning is coined in the 1990s to describe the advantages of computer-mediated learning from a primarily cognitive perspective influenced by modern thinking in cognitivism like Howard Gardner (1983). The overall conclusion in multimedia learning is that the different modalities give a better learning experience when the content is encoded in different modalities: text, pictures and sound. Furthermore, theorists within multimedia learning stress the opportunity for different cognitive learning styles to be nurtured in multimedia learning (Mayer, 2001).

EDUCATIONAL COMPUTER GAMES SINCE THE 1970S

Naturally, the success of educational software and educational media was touted when educational computer games appeared. It influenced the form and content of the titles produced, but also the market approach. Over the years, this resulted in educational computer games turning into edutainment.

Despite the early discussions and a search for the educational potential of computer games, the area's history has for years been conspicuously missing in the mainstream computer game research community. The long line of articles and books on computer games history largely ignores educational computer games (e.g. Hunter, 2000). One exception is Broderbund's highly acclaimed series *Where in the World is Carmen Sandiego* (see DeMaria and Wilson, 2002). The industry lacks a coherent perception of what signifies important game titles in the history of educational use of computer games. We need good examples for reference and a shared terminology to address recurring elements in failed educational titles. The first step is to identify some of the more successful and influential titles over the years and how specific companies influenced the development. There is an abundance of interesting titles that have been more or less designed for educational purposes, as the market previously was not structured into tight little boxes like now. For example, the game designer Chris Crawford could go from producing *Patton Versus Rommel*, a war game with little educational appeal, to *Balance of the Planet*, an ambitious attempt to educate people about the environmental problems facing our time. The title *Balance of Power*, about the Cold War, is also a very interesting example of a game living on the border between being entertainment and having educational content (Crawford, 2003).

As mentioned previously, the current market for educational computer games suffers from a good deal of the problems also present in the 1930s when the instructional film market crashed. This is not to say that a crash is imminent, but it explains the falling and stagnating market that Buckingham and Scanlon (2002) also mention. According to senior designer Margo Nanny from Interactive Learning, in regards to pitching a concept, the market is quite conservative. She quotes a publisher as saying, 'All we're interested in now is "meat and potatoes", which is essentially reading and math with a licensed character' (Stern, 1998: 1). However, it was not always only meat and potatoes.

THE EARLY YEARS

The first years were influenced by research projects that later led to some of the most successful educational titles. In 1971, the Minnesota based research center MECC produced *Oregon Trail*, a bestseller even today. MECC also produced the famous *Lemonade Stand*. It took the journey all the way up to the hyped 1990s. In the late 1980s, the research centre was sold to a North American venture capitalist for merely $5 million. When the Learning Company bought MECC a year later, the price was $250 million (Educational Software Classics, 1999; Lauppert, 2004).

In 1973, a project named PLATO emerged with a focus on maths and educational software. Computer games played a central role in this project, which avoided the typical drill-and-practice educational software. The inspiration for this project was not behaviourism but rather Jean Piaget, the founder of cognitivism, and educational philosopher John Dewey. The inspiration manifested itself in an attempt to teach maths through more everyday maths examples. Instead of relying on abstract arithmetic, like two plus two, questions were as such: if you have two bananas and get two bananas, how many will you then have? The measures of effectiveness in evaluation studies indicated a significant positive effect on maths achievement and attitudes towards maths (Olive and Lobato, 2001).

The approach favouring maths and science was later continued with the Learning Company's two popular titles, *Rocky Boots* from 1982 and *The Robot Odyssey* in 1984, where children had the chance to acquaint themselves with some of the basic concepts of maths and programming. *Rocky Boots* won several awards and is fondly remembered by many educators and children, thus paving the way for later interesting potentially educational titles such as *The Incredible Machine* (1993). *Rocky Boots* was described as, 'a visual simulation that made it possible for upper-grade-school students to design simple digital logic circuits, using a joystick to move around circuit symbols on the screen and plug them together' (Robinett, 2004: 1). Thus, *Rocky Boots* was among the first educational software titles with simulation as key to the learning environment. Although *Rocky Boots* wasn't the first educational game, it was certainly one of those with the greatest impact in the early years. The integration between the educational content and game mechanism was quite successful. According to the author, it ended up selling more than 100,000 copies – a staggering number in the 1980s (Robinett, 2004).

Among the initial commercial educational computer games, *Basic Math* from 1977 was one of the first titles to exhibit the characteristics of edutainment. It was followed by a similar title in 1979's *Electric Company Math Fun*, which is closer to an actual computer game that is trying to hide the underlying basic edutainment instructional structure. In *Electric Company Math Fun*, two players each control gorillas competing against each other. The more right answers, the faster the player progresses through the jungle. If the player fails an answer, the corresponding gorilla is thrown in the river and cannot get up until the player answers a new question correctly.

From the beginning of the 1980s, the educational computer games wave came rolling, indicated both by the large number of released titles (Willis et al., 1987) and research targetting the area. As indicated by titles listed in two leading game documentation websites, The Underdogs and Moby Games, the trend is clear. Educational computer games were seriously contesting traditional computer games for a place in the shopping bag of ambitious and worried parents. And it was a trend strengthened by the continuous debate on the risks associated with mainstream computer games (Egenfeldt-Nielsen and Smith, 2004).

EDUCATIONAL ADVENTURE GAMES TAKE THE LEAD

Snooper Troops was one of the first examples of a successful educational adventure game that became one of the preferred and dominating genres for the educational computer games market. Here, children would play detectives, solving different assignments. The game primarily based its educational value on the ability to facilitate better problem-solving skills like many later titles would. It was followed by several other educational adventure games, which is hardly surprising as this was the decade of the adventure game. A not-so-classic educational adventure but influential title was *In Search of the Most Amazing Thing* from 1983, where the player explores a science-fiction universe with long-lost uncle Smoke Bailey.

It is clear that *Snooper Troops* (1982), along with 1985's commercially successful *Where in the World is Carmen Sandiego* and *Oregon Trail*, offered alternative educational computer games. Edutainment had not taken over just yet in its purest form. This probably accounts for the success of the latter titles, now, even 20 years afterwards. Although these titles are focused narrowly on transferring information from the computer to the player, it is less mechanistic. They also have a closer integration between motivation and gameplay in line with Malone's theory, which is discussed later. The player must work for the knowledge, solve meaningful puzzles and travel through a meaningful game world. The connection between the play experience and the learning experience is also stronger. The tool used by instructional designers in those years for a closer integration of learning and gameplay was mostly the adventure genre, which had its best days through the 1980s and early 1990s. The success of the adventure game was promoted by new technology and the introduction of the graphical user interface. The market leaders LucasArts and Sierra both produced educational game titles with some success. Among these were *Winnie the Pooh in the Hundred Acre Wood* (1984), *Mickey's Space Adventure* (1986) and *Troll's Tale* (1984). Al Lowe, who later went on to make the classic *Leisure Suit Larry* series, produced several of these games. The success of educational computer games peaked in the mid-1980s with the two most famous titles, *Oregon Trail* and *Where in the World is Carmen Sandiego*. The *Carmen Sandiego* series continued for years and has spanned several sequels. The integration of geography in the gameplay won it an educational reputation.

Oregon Trail was an early hit for the company Broderbund, and has been republished several times in refurbished versions; the latest is version 5 (2000). The basic gameplay doesn't change significantly. The player follows in the footsteps of the early American settlers and has to make decisions concerning his journey. Through the game, schoolchildren learn about the American pioneer spirit, as the advert does everything to convince us of:

You can almost smell the dust from the wagon train! Kids will build real-life decision-making and problem-solving skills as they choose their wagon party and supplies, read maps, plan their route and guide their team through the wilderness.

(Broderbund, 2003: 1)

Despite the promising description, there is not really any evidence to support the claims for educational value. While some of the highlights in educational computer games see the daylight, the term edutainment is coined.

EDUTAINMENT BEGINS TO MAKE ITS MARK

The well-received and popular game *Seven Cities of Gold* (1984) was the first game title to be marketed as edutainment, despite not really having the characteristics of edutainment. The legend goes that it was Electronic Arts founder Trip Hawkins who coined the term for computer games. *The Seven Cities of Gold* sold 150,000 copies across several platforms and won several design awards. The game had an educational feel with its exploration, strategy and actions taking place in a historical setting (Mamer, 2002).

In 1987 *Mavis Beacon Teaches Typing* followed; it was something of an oddity, not really a game, but it still had extreme success in adhering to the edutainment formula. Not only does the title *Mavis Beacon* make you wonder but so does the gameplay. In the game, you can set up different races against time as you type to the best of your abilities. Although some might hint that most children could have learned this just as well on a traditional typing machine, it was a success and continues to sell. This concept has been reproduced several times over the years; perhaps most famously in the more recent morbid cult title *The Typing of the Dead* (Sega, 2000).

The edutainment title *Reader Rabbit* (1989) also enjoyed success. It attempted to teach spelling and reading, paving the way for toddlers' future schooling. This brand continues to serve the Learning Company well in the market today, with a number of different instalments over the same brand. The graphics have improved, but the gameplay is pretty much the same. As will become evident, educational computer games over the years have gone from innovative titles to re-hacks of old classics. In comparison, the remaining games industry's talk of sequels, licences and betting on the same game seem like wild exaggerations. When we look at some of the most popular titles over the years, more than 75 per cent are sequels (see Table 2.1), and this number increased as the edutainment industry consolidated throughout the 1990s.

The current historical presentation runs the risk of underestimating the impact of edutainment titles as they often are not fondly remembered, contribute no real innovation and, therefore, are not mentioned in historical accounts. It is worth stressing that the edutainment market grew and slowly became a dominating force, pushing other types of educational computer games out of the market. It is noticeable that the use of edutainment has from the beginning been driven by business and market interests rather than by the needs of educators. Arguably, the edutainment genre has become home for a lot of questionable titles, developed by hopeful amateurs or greedy business people seeing a chance to capitalize on parents' desire for educational computer games. The criticism of edutainment has, of course, weakened the appeal of using the edutainment label. Currently, edutainment titles are sold at discount price in a stagnating market with more critical consumers (Buckingham and Scanlon, 2002; Facer et al., 2003; Leyland, 1996; Mamer, 2002).

This development happened despite Lucas Learning's emergence as a separate company in 1998 with *Star Wars DroidWorks*. *Star Wars DroidWorks* uses a first-person-shooter game engine from LucasArts' other commercial computer games. The idea is to make 'solid educational content to create something different: a thoughtful game that's actually fun and helps kids to learn within the game medium' (Blossom and Michaud, 1999: 1). However, in general, the games industry has given up on educational computer games. Initiatives like Lucas Learning are rare and the general change is best indicated by the way leading educational computer game developer the Learning Company has ended up under the educational publisher Riverdeep with little room for manoeuvring and innovation. The tendency for less innovation in a harsh market is increasingly bemoaned by people in the edutainment industry, who see little change over the years despite an outspoken desire for better titles (Children's Software, 1998).

The transfer of the production of educational computer games from the games industry to educational publishing is bound to influence the approach taken to designing educational computer games. As a consequence, edutainment has strengthened its grip on the market. Educational publishers look to other educational media and adopt similar business models and educational thinking for all of their educational products (Buckingham and Scanlon, 2002). The decline is accelerated by the unpopularity of adventure games among players. This influences the development of educational adventure games. As a result, quality suffers, leading to less innovation and smaller budgets in educational adventure games (Sluganski, 2001–4).

THE TWITCH-SPEED GENERATION

In the mid-1990s, the idea that computer games might fit well with the demands of a new generation's special characteristics gathered momentum. It has slowly gained a stronger foothold with the general enthusiasm about children's knack for digital learning. Thus, computer games challenge edutainment's narrow focus on curriculum content, but end up promising even more about the potential of educational computer games than proponents of edutainment. Supporters of the new twitch-speed approach talk about a Nintendo generation, and twitch-speed learning reflects this development (Gros, 2003; Hostetter, 2003; Papert, 1996; Prensky, 2001b; Provenzo, 1992).

The basic proposition is that new media is changing a generation's way of learning. The twitch-speed generation is not comfortable concentrating on one task at a time, but is engaged in a variety of tasks at the same time. The traditional educational system is not challenging enough and is in opposition to this new way of learning. The following ten points are listed as characteristic of the new generation: twitch speed, parallel processing, graphics first, random access, connected, active, play, payoff, fantasy and technology-as-friend.

> This game generation is used to a twitch speed, parallel processing, active, fantasy world. Games have changed the learners' cognitive skills so that the game generation can process a lot of information at the same time. Video games are an excellent learning tool because the computer can adjust its difficulty according to the player's preference or need.
>
> (Hostetter, 2003: 1)

It has been suggested, but with little research backing, that computer games are well equipped to become learning devices for this new generation. Tackling a game's difficulty levels could be similar to learning. Prensky (2001a) has especially been an influential proponent of this view in his book, *Digital Game-based Learning*. The most important characteristics of computer games are their knack for engagement and interactive learning. The way these are put together is the real trick and Prensky sees a true potential in computer games for revolutionizing the educational system (Prensky, 2001a, 2004). This approach is currently the most optimistic and reflects a general increased interest in computer games for educational use. The main idea is that players can use computer games to learn important skills that are necessary to navigate modern society, to cope with the increasing information bombardment, and to acquire an alternative learning style. However, just like many claims about edutainment, the arguments lack substantiation. In particular, this idea about computer games glosses over the problems, focusing only on the potentials.

EDUCATIONAL COMPUTER GAMES GO OUT OF FASHION

Despite twitch-speed learning's great promises, educational computer games throughout the 1990s began to acquire a bad name with commercial game developers. As a consequence of the dominating edutainment's quality problems, developers outside the narrow circle of edutainment producers increasingly avoided explicitly labelling their computer games as educational. Educational computer games were increasingly seen as low-budget titles aimed at pre-school or early-school children and having little shared heritage with the still fiercer market for commercial computer games. Nevertheless, some of the educationally most interesting titles were produced in these years, interestingly never marketed as educational.

Around 1990, a couple of quite interesting titles were released but most were not explicitly labelled as educational computer games. These developers avoided being placed in the same category as the increasingly criticized edutainment titles, presenting the titles as commercial entertainment titles. The most noticeable are *SimCity* (1989), *Lemmings* (1990), *SimEarth* (1990) and *Civilization* (1991). Most of these computer games are well known. *SimCity* is about starting a city and maintaining its growth as mayor. In *Lemmings*, one helps some misguided lemmings to the end of the level by arranging lemmings in just the right way. *SimEarth* is concerned with the development of Earth from prehistorical times until today, whereas *Civilization* starts with the emergence of the first civilizations. In *Civilization*, one wins by managing different key areas of a civilization, including warfare, technology, trade, city management, diplomatic relations and economic planning.

The credibility of educational computer games was still somewhat intact and *The Incredible Machine* in 1993 didn't change that. However, early critical voices were growing still stronger as the edutainment formula increased its domination (Brody, 1993). At Sierra, the aspiring game designer, Jane Jensen, later known for the *Gabriel Knight* series, throws the player into the role of ecologist Adam in 1992. In *Eco Quest 1: The Search for Cetus*, the player, as the dolphin Cetus, must save the ocean from man's destruction. The game is characterized by a very fine mix of gameplay elements and educational information that is acquired within the game.

EDUTAINMENT DEFINES THE MARKET

In the mid-1990s, some of the big edutainment brands that are still with us today were established and came to dominate the market: *Freddi Fish* (1994), *Putt Putt Saves the Zoo* (1995), *MS Magic School Bus Explores* (1995) and *Pajama Sam* (1996). The edutainment games were now mostly centred upon pre-school children and early school age. They covered basic areas like arithmetic, reading, typing and spelling. Most titles had close adherence to school curricula in major countries suggested by titles from the US, the UK and Sweden (Buckingham and Scanlon, 2002; Softbase, 2004; Veta, 2004). The most noticeable series and games were *Dr Seuss Preschool* (1999), *Oregon Trail* (2000), *Reader Rabbits* (2000), *Bioscopia* (2002), *Math Missions* (2003),

Table 2.1: Important titles over the years

Title	Year	Edu-game	Series	Genre	Subject
Basic Math	1977	Yes	No	Puzzle	Math
Electric Company Math Fun	1979	Yes	No	Puzzle	Math
Word Fun	1980	Yes	No	Puzzle	English
Rocky Boots	1982	Yes	Yes	Puzzle	Programming
Snooper Troops	1982	No	Yes	Adventure	Cognitive
In Search of the Most Amazing Thing	1983	Yes	No	Adventure	Cognitive
Mule	1983	No	No	Strategy	Cognitive
Winnie the Pooh	1984	Yes	Yes	Adventure	English
Seven Cities of Gold	1984	Yes	No	Strategy	Social studies
The Robot Odyssey	1984	Yes	Yes	Puzzle	Programming
Balance of Power	1985	No	No	Simulation	Society
Lemonade Stand	1985	Yes	No	Strategy	Math
Oregon Trail	1985	Yes	Yes	Adventure	Social studies
Where in the World is Carmen Sandiego	1985	Yes	Yes	Adventure	Geography
Math Blaster	1986	Yes	Yes	Puzzle	Math
Mavis Beacon	1987	Yes	No	Action	Typing
Hidden Agenda	1988	No	No	Strategy	Social studies
Life and Death	1988	Yes	Yes	Simulation	Health
Reader Rabbits	1989	Yes	Yes	Puzzle	English
SimCity	1989	No	Yes	Strategy	Social studies
Balance of the Planet	1990	Yes	No	Simulation	Environment
Designasaurus I+II	1990	Yes	Yes	Adventure	Geology
Lemmings	1990	No	Yes	Puzzle	Cognitive
SimEarth	1990	No	Yes	Simulation	Geography
Super Munchers	1991	Yes	Yes	Action	Trivia
Civilization	1991	No	Yes	Strategy	History
Castle of Dr Brain	1991	Yes	Yes	Puzzle	Science
Crystal Rain Forest	1992	Yes	No	Puzzle	Programming
The Incredible Machine	1993	No	Yes	Puzzle	Science

Caesar	1993	No	Yes	Strategy	History
Dinopark Tycoon	1993	No	No	Strategy	Geology
SimHealth	1994	Yes	Yes	Simulation	Society
Freddi Fish	1994	Yes	Yes	Adventure	Cognitive
Millie's Math House	1995	Yes	Yes	Puzzles	Math
Backpacker	1995	No	Yes	Adventure	Geography
Putt Putt Saves the Zoo	1995	Yes	Yes	Adventure	Cognitive
MS Magic School Bus Explores	1995	Yes	Yes	Adventure	Science
Logical Journey of the Zoombinis	1996	Yes	Yes	Puzzle	Cognitive
Pajama Sam	1996	Yes	Yes	Adventure	Science
My Make Believe Castle	1998	Yes	Yes	Strategy	General
Dr Seuss Preschool	1999	Yes	Yes	Puzzle	English/Math
Roller Coaster Tycoon	1999	No	Yes	Strategy	Society
Virtual U	2000	Yes	No	Simulation	Administration
Lightspan	2000	Yes	Yes	Adventure	English
The Sims	2000	No	Yes	Simulation	Society
Globetrotter 2	2001	No	Yes	Adventure	Geography
Freddi Fish 5: Creature of Coral	2001	Yes	Yes	Adventure	Math
Math Missions	2003	Yes	Yes	Adventure	Maths
Jumpstart Study Helpers	2003	Yes	Yes	Adventure	Maths/English
Disney Learning 1st and 2nd grade	2003	Yes	Yes	Adventure	English

Jumpstart Study Helpers (2003) and *Disney Learning* (2003). The brands formed in the mid-1990s also continue to be marketed today. The majority of these titles fall under the edutainment label although some older republications are an exception.

The infatuation with fitting educational computer games to existing curricula has hardly helped the creative development in the market. The market is definitely suffering from a bad image and conservatism.

THE CURRENT MARKET FOR EDUCATIONAL COMPUTER GAMES

Despite the promise of edutainment, the market only makes up a fraction of the total computer games market. According to Entertainment Software Association, edutainment had 7.6 per cent[2] of the total US console sales in 2002, estimated at a total sale of 25.1 million units of edutainment for the US market with a revenue of $322.6 million (The ESA, 2002, 2003). Other sources put the PC edutainment market at $235 million in 2002. Indeed, the situation for edutainment has deteriorated in recent years. The NPD group suggests that revenues from educational computer games have plunged from $495.8 million in 2000 to $152 million in 2004 (*BusinessWeek*, 2005). One would think that a drop in revenues of that size would make educational publishers desperate for innovations. Still, the existing market is not insignificant, although the revenue may be small since the retail price of educational computer games is often low and sold with reductions (Buckingham and Scanlon, 2002; Taylor, 2003). On the other hand, the budgets for the development are often smaller. The market is currently split between the large players after a number of mergers in the educational publishing business.

Early on, the market saw entry from some of the largest companies within entertainment and publishing like Disney, IBM, Simon and Schuster, Scholastic, McGraw-Hill Interactive and Europress. The educational games market during the 1990s experienced large growth and consolidation with a few dramatic twists along the way. The development was driven partly by bundling with new hardware, but also by the overall change in learning environments mentioned earlier (Facer et al., 2003). When the 1990s began, the market was still made up of a lot of small players. Through the mid-1990s, a bubble was built up with a lot of takeovers and mergers. The bubble burst due to different reasons and, to make matters worse, the market leader CUC International's takeovers proved to be too expensive. In 1998, CUC International was finally sent down due to accounting irregularities.[3]

In 1992, educational software grew 47 per cent – more than three times the average growth of other software categories. That year's sales from the maths, reading, writing, science and history titles of market leader Davidson and Associates added up to $40 million. The company's flagship was the award-winning *Blaster* series, which had at that time sold more than 5 million copies throughout the series' lifespan. The two other market leaders were the Learning Company and Broderbund Software (Guglielmo, 1994).

Forced by retailers, the consolidation really took off in 1996. There were 2000 titles in the edutainment category, but major retail outlets only had room for 250 titles at the most. CUC International tried to snatch the market by buying up others, securing control of Sierra and Davidson, but ended up paying too much compared to takeovers just one year later. Humongous Entertainment was bought by GT Interactive and later by Atari. Disney and

Mattel also entered the market in these years with a strong presence. In 1996, Microsoft Learning and Entertainment Division launched with a significant push in the edutainment area. In 1996, Microsoft ranked as number seven in edutainment sales. They were building the brands that are still with us today: *Magic School Bus* and the *Goosebumps* series (Browder et al., 1996).

In 1996, the ten largest suppliers of edutainment controlled 90 per cent of the market. The leading players were SoftKey International and CUC International. Learning Company and CUC each sold about 16 per cent of all education CD-ROMs. From 1996 to 1997, CUC International bought up Davidson and Associates, Blizzard Entertainment, Gryphon Software and Knowledge Adventure. This made the CUC International software division the leading publisher of consumer software in North America until their rapid decline in 1998 due to accounting problems. At that time, the company was split up and sold to different publishers (Armstrong and Hamm, 1997; Packaged Facts, 1997).

The Learning Company is one of the most successful and strongest players on the market. It has been developing educational computer games from the beginning with *The Robot Odyssey, Reader Rabbit* games and *Super Solver*. It has had a bumpy journey over the years, with all the mergers and buyouts. In 1998, the Learning Company merged with Broderbund, and thereby became a part of the major toy manufacturer Mattel. The Learning Company for its part had a couple of years before it acquired MECC, the father of *Oregon Trail*.

Mattel was also getting in trouble and had to sell Broderbund in March 2001. This didn't include the Learning Company, which was sold separately to Riverdeep, which later in 2002 also acquired Broderbund. This leaves the e-commerce site Broderbund owned by Riverdeep with a strong product set-up for the coming years. It has a strong mix of educational products, covering a wide group of subjects and age groups.

Sierra released a significant number of educational titles from the early 1980s onwards and continues to have some impact. Sierra consolidated in the mid-1990s and became one of the biggest developers, but in 1999 they were bought up by Havas Interactive. Havas Interactive was eventually acquired by Vivendi Universal some years later, strengthening Vivendi Universal significantly on the edutainment side. In combination with the takeover of Davidson and Associates, the ambitious Vivendi Universal got a foothold in the market and this was further bolstered by the acquisition of Knowledge Adventure. Knowledge Adventure early on became the leading company and continues to develop some of the best-selling educational titles.

The innovative game company Maxis also rode the wave of educational computer games without diverting into edutainment. In 1987 the company was formed, and in 1989 *SimCity* was released. Though *SimCity* is not specifically educational, it has been used in a variety of teaching settings.

Later *Sim* series, consisting of *SimFarm*, *SimHealth* and *SimEarth*, were clearer in their educational appeal, but less commercially attractive. All of the computer games from Maxis are described by Will Wright as software toys (Brown, 2002). They are among the most open-ended educational computer game experiences out there. Maxis proved once again its importance to the innovation of the game industry by launching *The Sims* in 2000, which is also used in educational settings. Although Maxis is still a separate brand, it was purchased in 1995 by the world's leading game company, Electronic Arts (EA). Electronic Arts had some edutainment titles over the years, such as *Pong and Kooky's Cuckoo Zoo* and *Scooter's Magic Castle* (both 1993), but it is not a primary area for them any more. The early educational titles were produced under the label EA Kids, but were stopped in 1993 when EA decided to concentrate on sports games (Brody, 1993). It is perhaps fitting that the downfall of edutainment is signalled in 1993 by the largest game company, EA, pulling the plug on its educational titles. Perhaps it is also fitting that EA have just signalled a new interest in the area with the Teaching with Games project (Sandford et al., 2006) and they are backed by the game trade association ELSPA (Ellis et al., 2006).

Overall, the market for educational software (including edutainment and educational games) experienced fast growth during the late 1990s, but has slowed down more recently. This occurred because the internet has begun to offer an increased amount of educational content and parents are becoming more critical consumers. With that perspective, the future looks somewhat gloomy, but it remains to be seen what precise long-term impact the internet will have (Buckingham and Scanlon, 2002). Now that the dotcoms of the edutainment industry are gone, it seems that websites are no longer so eager to offer an abundance of free educational content. The new incentive, however, might prove to be a mix of advertising and edutainment from large companies such as *Cadbury's Chocolate Factory* game. The availability of free edutainment online may be what pushes educational publishers to raise the bar for their titles. In addition, with more museums, schools and libraries offering educational products, we may be travelling back in time to the 1930s, when subsidized products made the market difficult for independent commercial developers of instructional films. This notion was supported by the Serious Games Summit at GDC in 2004 where alternative funding for developing educational titles was put forward by the main organizer, Ben Sawyer, as an important leg in the development of the area.

The main explanation for the hard times in the edutainment market may arise from a year-long narrow focus on the needs of parents and educators rather than on the children's preferences as players, the trademark of good computer games (Buckingham and Scanlon, 2002). Back in 1993–4 the alarm bells should have sounded, when Funk (1993) and Cesarone (1994) found that only 2–3 per cent of the children in a survey named educational computer games as their favourite pastime. Instead mergers ensued, raising share prices. It doesn't really seem to be the adults who are hindering the development; in a study by Booth and VanDeventer (1997), 100 adults were asked: 'Do you think that it is possible for children to learn anything from video games or cartoons?' Of these, 75 per cent answered positively and 25 per cent rejected the idea. The main objection by the small group of rejecters was that children would only engage with violent content in computer games. Hence, this showed that the rejecters did think it was possible to learn from video games and cartoons, it's just that they didn't see violent content in computer games as relevant learning. So, adults do not need convincing that, in principle, one can learn from computer games. However, they lack the skills to actively identify titles that live up to children's expectations and also have sound learning principles. Some parents may be trapped in rhetoric from marketing people, researchers and educators with a preference for twitch-speed learning.

EDUTAINMENT IS DEAD – LONG LIVE EDUCATIONAL COMPUTER GAMES

In research circles, an understanding is emerging that in order to produce educational computer games beyond edutainment, one must combine the talents of commercial game developers, educators and subject matter experts. This is best reflected with the initiatives of Education Arcade and Serious Games that aim to bring developers, educators and subject experts together through seminars, websites, conferences and joint development projects. Arguably, in the long run, children are probably too smart to be cheated by the discount games that edutainment often are. If we look at the computer game titles that generally dominate the commercial hit charts, it is clear that these are not discount games, but are the result of state-of-the-art expertise in all the areas necessary to make a game.

Overall, it seems that educational computer games, including edutainment, are dying out as a separate breed. Edutainment lives on through old brands and gameplay forms and is increasingly being seen as educational software. The links to the computer games industry have become weaker with the mergers over the years. This process probably explains the current lack of explicit focus on the game part of edutainment. The structures that operate within are educational software and this is an entirely different breed from computer games. To name a few important differences: educational software lacks the coolness of the games industry, the state-of-the art technology, the constant innovation in gameplay but perhaps, most importantly, the basic desire to produce entertaining products beyond anything else.

SERIOUS GAMES: A NEW MOVEMENT IN EDUCATIONAL COMPUTER GAMES

The starting point for modern educational games researchers is often a critique of edutainment as it manifested itself up through the 1980s and its continuing domination of the market. Such a critique is important for building a better educational foundation for computer games.

Edutainment started as a serious attempt to create computer games that taught children different subjects. Arguably, it ended up as a caricature of computer games and a reactionary use of learning theory. The conservatism in educational computer games seems to be maintained by a vicious cycle leading to a still smaller target group: limited investment results in little innovation and low quality erodes the market, which subsequently results in less investment (Egenfeldt-Nielsen, 2004).

However, in the new millennium, a broader approach to education and computer games is becoming stronger, and educational computer games are re-emerging on the agenda as a serious topic. This is perhaps best illustrated by the increasing number of initiatives in the US, the UK and the Nordic countries.[4] These initiatives may provide the impetus for more innovation and higher quality products that can drive the market forward and get investors to take a new interest.

In the US, the Serious Games Initiative is regularly hosting conferences between developers and researchers to discuss new roads for educational computer games, and this is supported by another separate initiative, Education Arcade, with a similar agenda. Also, the Games-to-Teach project at MIT has put educational computer games on the agenda. Furthermore, the group of researchers, including James Paul Gee and Kurt Squire, at the University of Wisconsin at Madison is forming the field.

In the UK, initiatives have been pushed more by government funding through Becta and Future Lab, resulting in interesting new research and collaboration between industry and research. At the University of London, several projects aimed at the educational use of computer games are in their last phases, like the Making Games project. This is a three-year project that is trying to develop authorware for schoolchildren so they can design their own computer games. The research project collaboration between Future Lab and EA Europe is also interesting, with its attempt to find ways to harness the educational potential of commercial computer games (Facer, 2003; Oliver and Pelletier, 2004).

In the Nordic countries, Learning Lab Denmark is establishing a centre for educational games as an extension of several ambitious educational game products produced in collaboration between researchers and industry. At Malmö University in Sweden, a project has also just finished between a medical company and researchers to produce an educational computer game dealing with ethical dilemmas in the medical industry. At the IT-University of Copenhagen, there is an ongoing research project to develop a new form of serious game. Most researchers in these projects share the belief that it is possible to go beyond earlier educational computer games that had dubious learning experiences and limited technical platforms. The hope is to avoid common pitfalls like separating learning content and computer game by focusing on a close integration of gameplay and learning experience. There is also a broader concept of the educational experience around the computer game. Rather than seeing educational computer games as operating in a social vacuum, a socio-cultural understanding of the surrounding educational environment's importance is emerging. The learning experience is not limited to the interaction between player and game. This is most distinct in research conducted by Gee (2003) and Squire (2004). There are several reasons why educational computer games are back on the agenda. A variety of sources serve to push this new order on both a societal and an individual level.

First of all, there is a general increase in awareness and knowledge of computer games in the public. People are more open toward computer games and their influence on several levels. This is a consequence of the general higher percentage of the population playing computer games (ESA, 2002). It means teachers are less sceptical, inexperienced and stigmatized when approaching computer games for educational use. It is becoming increasingly common for parents to be more open towards educational computer games and hold the necessary competences to critically choose between good educational titles and poorer ones. This forces the publishers to reconsider using an edutainment formula that is more than 30 years old.

A second major influence is the general level of research in computer games, which is booming. Since 2001, the Digital Game Research Association has been established and the number of conferences dedicated to research in computer games has increased. This helps to move the field forward through collaborations between industry and research institutions.

Third, and this is perhaps the most controversial claim, given the games industry's obsession with better audio-visuals, game technology has reached a level at which decent educational computer games can be made within a reasonable budget. This discussion is wider but is supported by the establishment of the Games-to-Teach project's collaboration with Microsoft. To some degree, this runs contrary to the general development in the games industry, where computer games are becoming increasingly expensive to produce. However, the rising development budgets are to a large extent tied to the new console platforms. Traditionally, educational computer games have lived on the PC platform and should therefore not be hit so hard by skyrocketing development budgets (Newman, 2004; Vogel, 2001).

The fourth factor is the changing learning environment, where learning is expanded to the home and to the entire lifespan. The coining of terms like home learning, lifelong learning and supplementary training indicates a more flexible approach to learning (Aldrich, 2003; Buckingham and Scanlon, 2002; Egenfeldt-Nielsen, 2001). This calls for learning products that are capable of engaging people in more entertaining ways, as learners can choose to abstain from dedicating time to learning. Now in competition with other leisure activities, learning must live up to its best.

CONCLUSION: EDUTAINMENT IS PREVAILING FOR NOW

This chapter has staged the scene for educational computer games by outlining its roots, the significant changes, important titles and the current market conditions. The market is defined by the dominance of edutainment extending from a long tradition in educational media for reinforcing existing teaching practice. Since the 1980s, edutainment has slowly and increasingly overtaken the market, allowing less room for innovation and resulting in declining revenues. Educational computer games are fighting many of the same problems faced by earlier educational media and they still have not found their form. In these last few years, we have seen new initiatives on the horizons that may change the nature of the market and its products, a development especially carried forward by a new research interest in the area.

NOTES

1　In particular, business education has taken games to its heart. The website www.marietta.edu/~delemeeg/games lists more than 130 non-computerized classroom games for college use.
2　It is very unclear what type of titles this number covers.
3　The following sources are used throughout this section: The Underdogs (2004); Buckingham and Scanlon (2002); *Wired* (1994); Browder et al. (1996); Armstrong and Hamm (1997).
4　For links to the different initiatives, see Resources.

3
Research into Educational Use of Games and Simulations

Some educators feel that the content of these games has educational value. Others are sceptical about the content of 'pure' electronic games but acknowledge that the motivational game format could perhaps be the perfect packaging for otherwise mundane educational content. The idea of using games to package content predates electronic games altogether.

(McGrenere, 1996: 82)

The previous chapter looked at the influential ancestors to educational computer games and outlined the history of educational computer games. However, one area deserves more attention, namely the research into educational use of non-electronic games. As indicated in Chapter 1, this research tradition is quite strong and can help build a foundation for educational computer games usage. The goal of this chapter is to identify the significant theoretical findings and discussions on research of educational use of games, which is partly recyclable for building a framework for the educational use of computer games.

This chapter evolves around three key areas that are identified as the most important in previous research. The first key area is the *learning environment* for games, which is often found to have a number of unfortunate characteristics complicating the educational use of games. The second is the role of *personal learning factors*, which is an overlooked area. Lastly, the *learning outcome* is examined, which sheds light on the problems with measuring learning outcome from games.

It is concluded that, especially in relation to the more practical problems of teaching, one should be careful not to underestimate the difficulties. Problems like lesson plans, physical space, learning theory, the importance of debriefing and teacher qualifications are well described in the literature. In relation to learning outcome, it is found that games may have something to offer, but we should not settle for just asking whether students can learn from a game. Rather, we should ask the harder questions: who, what, why and where do games work? This is equally important for computer games.

Several relevant insights are carried forward to the later examinations and discussions of computer games. We do not need to start from scratch when researching the educational use of computer games.

TRADITIONAL GAMES MAKE THEIR WAY INTO SCHOOL

One of the first social studies games is the *Inter-Nation Simulation* from 1958 about international relations, in which the players role play one of between five and seven hypothetical nations. Another is *The Sumerian Game* from 1961, targeted at 11 years olds, in which the player learns about some of the economic elements in Mesopotamia around 3500 BC. These are commonly referred to as simulations to differentiate them from games and stress their educational nature. In reality, however, they are very close to our definition of games and share a lot of the same dynamics and problems (Gredler, 1992; Lee, 1994; Seidner, 1975; Wolfe and Crookall, 1998).

When simulations first started to appear, they were not really in keeping with the trends within learning and education in the 1950s. Simulations and games extended from learning theories prioritizing appreciation of the underlying dynamics and processes of events rather than rote memorization of facts and principles. Games became a strong supplement to teaching by virtue of their concrete experiences leading to learning. Instead of being taught about topics, students engaged with these topics and played them out. Therefore, students made their own experiences and got feedback on their specific actions in a safe environment. This is believed to give a stronger experience drawing on the theories of David Kolb and John Dewey especially, which I will return to in Chapter 6. Overall, games were believed to increase motivation, focus attention and change the teacher's role. The teacher is no longer the authority but facilitates the learning experience (Abt, 1968; Coleman, 1967; Coleman, 1973).

Another premise of the educational use of games is their complex nature that potentially prepares students for the challenges in modern society. Traditional teaching methods are not conceived as capable of preparing students for the increased complexity in society and the learning skills necessary in real life. This overall approach to games' potential for facilitating alternative learning experiences is also clear in the previously mentioned twitch-speed approach to learning. The rationales for using computer games are often quite similar to the arguments brought forward above, when games were initially introduced in schools (Coleman, 1967).

EARLIER RESEARCH ON NON-ELECTRONIC GAMES: SIMILARITIES AND DIFFERENCES

The implications of using games for educational purposes have been examined in numerous studies over the years. The overview below attempts to identify some of the important trends that we should also look for when considering educational use of computer games. One of the main problems with the findings below is related to actually evaluating the games. It has been questioned if it is at all possible to use traditional methods for measuring the learning outcome, which will be addressed towards the end of the chapter (Druckman, 1995; Saegesser, 1981). Below is an overview of the factors (see Table 3.1) that I examine in the rest of this chapter and find relevant to carry forward to educational use of computer games.

A frame for reviewing learning through games

The following examination of different important aspects of games promoting learning is based on the categories in earlier reviewed studies. It is not

Table 3.1: Overview of important findings from simulation and gaming research.

Domain	Factors to consider
Learning environment	Awareness of the impact of time schedule, physical space, debriefing, learning theory and existing role scripts.
	Teacher's attitude, general skill, specific knowledge.
	Variations in gameplay and introduction of the game.
Personal learning factors	Individual in relation to gender, age, academic ability, race and game experience.
	Group matters in relation to size, organization and relations between students.
	May promote underachievers more than traditional teaching methods.
Learning outcome	Methods for measuring should be game-specific, problems with basic principles for quantitative designs.
	Assesses basic influencing factors on learning outcome: motivation and student–teacher relation.
	Different domain of learning, such as cognitive and affective.
	Learning theories favour overt signs of learning.

possible to go into detail with separate studies, so instead I aim to present the results from the most important overview articles over the years (Bredemeier and Greenblat, 1981; Clegg, 1991; Dempsey et al. 1996; Dorn, 1989; Druckman, 1995; Randel et al., 1992; Van Sickle, 1986; Wentworth and Lewis, 1973). It should be noted that the reviews are quite dated, which is perhaps a sign of the decline of research into educational games in favour of research on the educational potential of computer games as argued in Chapter 1. I will supplement some areas with more recent research studies to expand on areas not covered sufficiently in existing overview articles. The review is split into three areas. Each of these areas will be presented and discussed to give a status for the research field. They are also reflected on and used in the course presented later in the book.

- **Learning environment**: What properties of a learning environment have a bearing on the learning outcome and what variables are important?
- **Personal learning factors**: What personal factors can play a role for the learning outcome of a specific game experience and how significant is the impact?
- **Learning outcome**: What are the effects of using games for learning within different areas and in relation to different domains of learning?

Before entering into the specifics of these areas, it is worth considering more overall factors of the research such as the type of games used in educational settings and the prevalence within different subjects. It seems obvious that games could lend themselves better to some subjects and that not all game genres have been equally used. Early on, there were few studies comparing different game genres (Roberts, 1976) and this remains a problem. In a search for what game genres were encountered in research articles on simulation and gaming, Dempsey et al. (1996), reviewing both computer games and traditional games, found 43 simulation games, 26 others, ten adventures, four puzzles and one experimental. They attribute the large number of simulations to the history of the research area, which grew out of business and military training. The problem with their distinction is that the simulation category is quite broad, since simulation is in a majority of games almost an intrinsic property. When we look at computer games, the simulation category becomes especially vague.

The scourge of the setting

Often, the setting for educational games use is the school and this holds certain problems related to the quite rigid structure of the educational system. Saegesser (1981; 1984) and Coleman (1973) point out that the time schedule, physical space, learning theory and existing role scripts hinder the use of games and this potentially influences the learning outcome. The time schedule in schools is not structured to accommodate games that stretch for hours and may be hard to contain within a specific time limit. Also, the actual physical classroom causes problems, where there could be more than 25 students playing actively. The existing theories of learning and teaching are not very adaptable for games since they favour classroom teaching. The precise impact of these factors is hard to access; however, we should be alert to implications derived from the overall structure in current educational systems.

Furthermore, Bredemeier and Greenblat (1981) and Dorn (1989) state that the attitude of the instructor toward games influences the outcome and that the instructor's knowledge and skill in using the game is also a factor. In addition, the concrete use of the game can change the outcome if the instructor uses a variation of the gameplay or introduces the game differently. For example, it is far from trivial whether a game is introduced as a competition or a joint exploration. The game experience can also suffer if it is regularly jeopardized by the teacher's lack of knowledge about the applicable rules in different game situations. It seems that the importance of the learning setting has been somewhat neglected in the research in the later years, perhaps as a consequence of the richer hunting fields in adult learning, especially business and military training. In those cases, the constraints and traditions of learning are less tainted by the factors put forward above.

In his interesting article, Dorn (1989) draws on earlier research to outline some factors for instructors to ensure that they achieve the best setting for facilitating learning when using games. Dorn stresses that games should not be the only teaching style in a course, but should be supported by other teaching methods with a clear educational aim. Depending on the use and timing of games in a course, they can serve different purposes. For example, games at the beginning of a course can serve to introduce theory and core concepts or provide some shared concrete experience while giving the students a way to know each other. More specifically, the instructor should have some experience with the games used and the following competencies: skill at administering the game, a desire to use the game, mindfulness of the role scripts in the class, the ability to perform a debriefing, the ability to evaluate different games and an awareness of the physical limits with regard to time and space in school. These seem like basic and reasonable demands, however, they may prove much harder to implement in school life (Dorn, 1989; Elder, 1973).

The complexity that opens up with the many variables in the learning environment is staggering and quite overwhelming for anyone with a practical focus. Even though they might not all be cleared up, they are certainly worth considering when planning on teaching a course with computer games.

Personal learning factors

The role of personal characteristics has been examined to some degree, but Dempsey et al. (1996: 12) found that in reality, studies are 'very unclear in reporting these characteristics'. In their review, the most frequently reported variables were gender, age, academic ability and to some degree race. The limited reporting of such characteristics is quite interesting as the early work in the field stresses the importance of individual differences (Greenblat and Duke, 1981). These individual characteristics are interesting by themselves but also important in examining a sample to minimize methodology problems related to matched samples research design (Remus, 1981). The matched samples design is often a given experimental set-up, as one must conduct the study within the existing class structure in schools, where the randomization of the sample is difficult. The fact that the basic factors like age, race, gender and academic ability are only cited in approximately 25 per cent of the studies indicates that the problem is not very high on the research agenda.

It is argued that games might be a way to reach students with weaker academic abilities. According to Coleman et al. (1973), games are indeed more effective for students with high academic ability. However, Bredemeier and Greenblat (1981) find more mixed results and point out that games *may* be able to reach less advantaged student groups but this depends on a variety of factors. They especially point out that the prior attitude of the student toward games plays a role. In consequence, it seems the less advantaged students may benefit from games, but primarily if they are initially favourable toward educational games. Perhaps this is not that surprising.

Other indications of the role of personal factors are the structure of the group in relation to size, organization and relations between students. The argument is that the composition of the group facilitates different learning experiences while adding to the dynamics in both the environment and for the specific student. For instance, winners and losers of the game have very different experiences. It seems that the initial group cohesion is quite important for the performance in a game environment and remains relatively stable as the game progresses. Some studies indicate that the initial attitude of the students is of limited consequence for the performance, whereas group cohesion is central (Bredemeier and Greenblat, 1981; Clegg, 1991; Wellington and Faria, 1996).

One area that has received little attention is the importance of earlier experiences with games, which could be expected to play a role for the learning outcome. Knowledge and experience with playing games makes it possible for students to concentrate on playing the game and, consequently, they can spend more time mastering a new game form. This is an area that becomes even more relevant in relation to computer games with more complex interfaces and the larger variations in student experiences with computer games.

A Procrustean bed: assessing learning outcome

The question of the precise learning outcome from educational use of games is one of the areas that has received the most attention over the years within the research area of educational use of games: how can we measure the learning effect of games on students? As I have implied in Chapter 1, this question is far too broad and needs to be qualified with: 'For what purpose, under what conditions, and how can we be sure?' (Bredemeier and Greenblat, 1981: 307). This also implies that the interesting question is not whether we learn from games, but rather if this learning experience is better under some conditions, for some users, for some purposes, and if the nature of what we learn is different. I have tried to clear the way for these questions in the sections above and will try to give a general verdict on the learning outcome associated with games.

The list of claims for what games can do is very long, even as early as 1981 when Greenblat summed it up. Greenblat's (1981) list is too long to reproduce here, and in short form it spans two pages with 30 different claims. The 30 claims and other claims over the years[1] have been hard to document due to problems in measuring learning in a school context and constructing methods for measuring learning from games in accordance with existing dominating theories on learning. It has also been pointed out that several studies in general are flawed, challenging the findings on learning outcome so far (Dorn, 1989; Wolfe and Crookall, 1998). Evaluation problems have been clear from early on, but continue to influence the research.

Bredemeier and Greenblat (1981) and Dorn (1989) point out the necessity of awareness toward the basic learning theory we ascribe to and what assessment is feasible to confirm learning outcome within the chosen theoretical frame for understanding learning. One choice relates to what signs of learning we accept and, as Saegesser (1981) points out, many learning theories with strong backing in schools favour external signs of learning over more subtle forms. Although these notions of warning are more than 20 years old, they still hold true even though the theoretical landscape of learning has changed. We still run the risk of not realizing the full potential of games if we try to put them into the Procrustean bed of specific learning theories. On the other hand, we need to be specific about the learning outcome we expect and identify alternative ways for measuring learning. Otherwise, the learning may become repetitive, undocumented and confusing and point in different directions, which is a very real risk when using games for teaching (Elder, 1973). A risk found to still exist in some of the most recent research at Future Lab (Sandford et al. 2006).

The assessment of learning has given rise to numerous problems over the years. One of the most persistent is the lack of taking the most basic factors into consideration when conducting a study. Wolfe and Crookall (1998) have argued for more qualitative methods and a more critical stance towards an automatic acceptance of traditional research designs for educational research, which is also stressed by Bergman (2003). Others also encourage the establishment of a basic foundation for pursuing research, like a clear definition of games and a shared taxonomy of games. Some within the research field also find that researchers with educational research backgrounds are in short supply even though this is quite necessary in order to conduct the necessary rigorous research on educational use of games (Wolfe and Crookall, 1998).

Wolfe and Crookall (1998) list nine goals that draw on traditional research methods in educational theory, but are less suitable for studying games. Some of the principles they challenge when studying games are: control groups receiving placebos, all course sections being identical and that tests should be administered under controlled circumstances. They conclude that applying these principles is almost impossible in relation to games due to their open-ended and flexible structures. However, problems may also arise from giving up on these principles. The principles are important because the validity and reliability of the study is otherwise compromised. Or, in other words, one might as well not perform the study because one wouldn't know what one was studying and whether the results were just a fluke. Solving these problems requires that we look at assessment from a variety of perspectives which can make us aware of the weaknesses and imprecision of each assessment type. This is true whether using qualitative or quantitative methods. We need to triangulate methods because games are in flux.

There is some consensus that three areas need to be measured to gauge the learning outcome in a given game. The overall variable is substantive learning, which can be both learning about a subject or about oneself (cognitive and affective). When assessment of learning outcome is divided into cognitive and affective, we can distinguish between different domains of knowledge and learning methods extending from the outline in Chapter 1. The split between cognitive and affective is also sometimes seen as the division between specific skills and more general principles, concepts and orientations. The problem with distinguishing between these two areas has influenced game research from the start and is shared with other educational research (Bredemeier and Greenblat, 1981; Elder, 1973). The two other areas that as a minimum should be assessed are those having a bearing on the overall variable learning outcome. These are motivation to learn and the relationship between students and teacher. Most of these variables are taken into consideration in serious new studies (e.g. Kashibuchi, 2001).

The outcome of cognitive and affective learning

The reviews are not consistent in their conclusions on learning outcome, but in general it can be concluded from reviews as follows: in some instances, games seem to be more appropriate for affective learning, while for cognitive learning, they are found to be generally as good as other teaching methods (excluding retention over time which is better for games) (Bredemeier and Greenblat, 1981; Butler et al., 1988; Butler, 1988; Dorn, 1989; Druckman, 1995; Lee, 1994; Randel et al., 1992; Van Sickle, 1986).

The review by Dempsey et al. (1996) following Gagne's taxonomy[2] shows that the cognitive ability problem-solving is the most researched learning outcome followed by the more general affective ability attitudes. This implies that, in general, much of the research has been aimed at identifying learning outcome in more overall competences and not necessarily the learning outcome of facts and concepts. This also ties in well with the overemphasis of research in the social sciences, where problem-solving and attitudes have traditionally been an important area (Abt, 1968: 70–71).

The success of maths games reported by Randel et al. (1992) to some degree runs counter to the general consensus, as maths is a subject that also teaches very specific skills. The review concludes that the most successful learning outcome is achieved in games with very specific required skills. This implies that it may be relevant to revisit games for learning more specific skills, such as those found in algebra, physics, chemistry and grammar rules. However, positive findings on specific skills may also be due to the methods used for measuring learning outcome. As discussed above, measurement of learning outcome tends to favour specific facts and skills over more complex knowledge acquired in more general games.

The increased retention over time of learning appears to be one of the most consistent findings within the research areas (Bredemeier and Greenblat, 1981; Randel et al., 1992; Van Sickle, 1986); however, Dorn (1989) challenges this claim, citing older studies that show no difference in retention over time. The newer and more thorough study by Randel et al. (1992) supports the claim for better retention over time. Although not all the studies in the meta-analysis by Randel et al. (1992) examined retention over time, the ones that did generally found a better retention over time compared to traditional teaching methods. This leads to different speculations as to the origin of this increased retention. When considering retention, most of the above researchers relate better retention to the higher motivation, interest and relevance experienced when using games for educational purposes.

CONCLUSION: IMPLICATIONS FOR RESEARCHING EDUCATIONAL USE OF COMPUTER GAMES

We have seen that games are used in very different subjects with varying degrees of success. One may conclude that games have been used in almost every imaginable setting, subject and age group and one would not be entirely wrong. I have painted a somewhat positive picture of the area, and it is worth remembering that the reviews of the area are somewhat contradictory especially in relation to learning outcome. One explanation for the conflicting results is that we are talking about an object of study that is too broad. The difference between role-play games and simulations is not trivial. When we approach computer games, we should be alert to this problem. It does matter what genre of games we are studying and furthermore we can have a large number of badly designed games. We should be careful not to equate a specifically bad or extraordinary game with a general claim for using games for learning. A lot of the early studies on educational use of games were based on titles developed by passionate souls and with little training in designing games. The designers of these first educational games were learning as they went along and the results are still with us today for better or worse. These results may not show problems with games for education per se, but rather with badly designed games.

There are still a lot of problems left when we look at the research on learning and games, but it would be a shame if we didn't build on the rich results from the early days to achieve a strong foundation for studying educational use of computer games. The above review does indicate that educational computer games may be a worthwhile area to study, as the research into educational simulations and games in general is quite positive.

NOTES

1   For example, see the claims at the Educational Simulations website, www.creativeteachingsite.com/edusims.html.

2   The taxonomy includes attitude, motor skills, cognitive strategy, problem-solving, rules, defined concepts, verbal information and other skills.

4

Research on Educational Use of Computer Games

Research into the use of mainstream games in education is relatively novel, but growing rapidly. Research is mainly concerned with the development of related competences and literacies during game play or the role of games in the formation of learning communities either while gaming or related to game play.
(Kirriemuir and McFarlane, 2003: 3)

The previous chapters gave the background for building a framework for the educational use of computer games, but without really getting much into the specific research. The findings presented in the next chapters are important pieces in establishing the field of educational use of computer games, while informing on the empirical studies and theoretical work later in the book. The area is split into several themes that have been influencial and they represent very different approaches to the object of study. More than anything, it illustrates the breadth and potential of educational computer games. This chapter's goal is to present an elaborate overview of early research and, in doing so, contribute to an appreciation for previous research results and identify the key areas for understanding the use of computer games in educational settings.

The chapter looks at the early research in the area, which extends from instructional technology with a strong focus on motivation. Edutainment extends from this research, but simplifies the results of instructional technology. The conservatism in relation to learning theory and gameplay makes edutainment a winner commercially but increasingly unpopular among researchers, teachers and even parents.

DO WE NEED AN OVERVIEW OF STUDIES ON EDUCATIONAL USE OF COMPUTER GAMES?

There exist few attempts at an overview of the field of educational use of computer games and most are dated, aimed at a specific area or have a profound bias toward educational use of traditional games. The field is scattered without internal consistency, with few successful applications and questionable research. The first attempts at an overview of the research areas have appeared within the last ten years, but have not delivered much (e.g. Cavallari, Hedberg and Harper, 1992; Dempsey et al., 1996; McGrenere, 1996). Some of the obvious problems, even with the more serious attempts, are:

1 A lack of division between the different ways of using computer games.
2 Weak theoretical knowledge of computer games.
3 Underdeveloped theory for facilitating learning.
4 Confusion about the educational area.
5 Incomplete literature due to the variety in terminology, publication places and researcher backgrounds.

Lately, we have seen some more ambitious attempts at surveying the area. However, they suffer from the same problems, only covering parts of the area despite having the foresight of previous reviews (e.g. Bergman, 2003; Kirriemuir and McFarlane, 2003; Mitchell and Savill-Smith, 2004).

There are good reasons for the lack of a viable overview, mainly the cross-disciplinary and young nature of the field encompassing a wide area of disciplines. To make matters worse, the closest established research field, computer game research, is still just beginning and remains fragmented despite converging trends (see Chapter 1). The area of education and learning has a longer, more solid tradition, but is overwhelming to review and hard for researchers to handle. In effect, the area of education and learning supports the fragmentation. One researcher may use a constructivist approach whereas another will draw on behaviourist theories, both without knowing the opposing theoretical background in depth.

The overview could have been structured in different ways, but I chose to maintain the thematic areas that have slowly surfaced during the research to show the different satellites around the research field of educational use of computer games. The different satellites will be covered in the following chapters.

THE EARLY BASIC RESEARCH ON EDUCATIONAL USE OF COMPUTER GAMES

This research overview starts by looking at the early insights into educational use of computer games from instructional technology research and how these insights slowly become more twisted in edutainment.

Instructional technology launches the research interest

When computers were first introduced into classrooms in the US, the learning principles were drawn from behavioural theory and were inspired by previous experiences with television for education. The first computer games for educational purposes were naturally strongly coloured by the learning approach to computers, which instructional theory attempts to change by examining educational use of computer games in its own right. Over the years, instructional technology has strongly influenced educational computer games research, although the somewhat narrow focus on motivation has gone a bit out of fashion in research circles.

American educational psychologist Edward L. Thorndike supplied the theoretical background for instructional theory at the beginning of the twentieth century. His work initially concentrated on animal learning, but was later expanded to human learning. His major achievement was the introduction of the concepts of reward and punishment. Not content with the narrow focus on practice, or repetition, he stressed that feedback was a strong tool for shaping the learning experience. Thorndike argued that instruction of a given individual was necessary to support the connection of what should be linked and to discourage things that shouldn't go together. The stimuli presented to the learner should not be random, but based on the learner's experience and feedback that is adjusted consequently (Saettler, 1968). Thorndike's account of future progress in instruction from 1912 is strikingly similar to educational software today:

> If, by a miracle of mechanical ingenuity, a book could be so arranged that only to him who had done what was directed on page one would page two become visible and so on, much that now requires personal instruction could be managed by print.
>
> Thorndike in 1912 (quoted in Saettler, 1968: 52)

Thorndike believed books and teachers each had their place in education. Teachers should not be used for conveying information that a book might as well supply. Instead, a teacher should guide the student through insight and sympathy (Saettler, 1968). Although somewhat appreciated, the importance of social context was not well integrated in his theory. Reflection was not very explicit in Thorndike's thinking, but was forcefully introduced by his contemporary John Dewey who attempted to set a new course for education. Dewey influenced the early movement in instructional technology, but his contributions were watered down over the years before re-emerging again after the cognitive revolution had slowed down. I will not go deeper into Dewey's thinking here, but the book later presents him as part of the attempt to reframe our understanding of the educational use of computer games.

The design of computer games in accordance with instructional theory somewhat accounts for the rigid and conservative educational use of computer games that is still with us today. The theoretical heritage is apparently hard to throw away, especially since it is an easy starting point for designing educational computer games. Thorndike's prophecy in the quote above attests to the link between instructional theory and educational computer games. It is possible to actually change the feedback to the student playing a computer game by using educational software based on previous input. The educational software, especially computer games with strong rewards, is the dream of Thorndike come true.

Another trend in early instructional theory is the focus on overt behaviour that Skinner proposed, a theory that caught on in educational circles during the 1950s. According to his theory, only overt actions are interesting in a learning perspective, but not any thoughts, understanding or reflection that may or may not happen. In 1958, Skinner actually did build a drill-and-practice machine resembling later edutainment titles. Behaviourism implies a narrow focus on the ping-pong between player and computer games; the computer game will ask a question and the player will answer. When the question and answer are linked enough times through rewards, learning will occur. The player who answers the question $2+3$ correctly with 5 gets points as a reward. Thus, learning arithmetic. There are, of course, a number of problems with the behaviourist approach, which is the reason why the theoretical learning landscape has changed since those days. A behaviourist approach is most useful when we are studying less complex learning phenomena. The complexity involved in figuring out a riddle cannot be boiled down to a number of random attempts during which one slowly will be conditioned just like a pigeon learns that pressing the lever at the right time leads to food (Gleitman, 1995). Some kind of reasoning or understanding is necessary, which becomes increasingly important when considering the educational use of computer games beyond a first-generation perspective.

Instructional technology discovers computer games

The behaviourist approach never really manifests in the research area of educational use of computer games, but is quite evident in edutainment titles. Before turning to edutainment, it is worth presenting some of the early instructional technology research that extends from a cognitivist approach. The research area of instructional technology into computer games primarily became active in the 1980s in relation to computer games. Over the years, it has been represented by researchers like Thomas Malone, Mark Lepper, Richard Bowman and Marshall Jones. Contributions focused especially on the value of computer games for motivating students and how educational computer games can be built to harness these qualities. The basic idea is that drill-and-practice software is not satisfactory by itself but needs strengthening by enhancing the learner's motivation through different mechanisms.

By taking into account player attention, focus, curiosity and fantasy, a second-generation perspective begins to emerge in which the player becomes a more important part in the learning equation.

Thomas Malone (1980) was not as such interested in the educational features of computer games but was interested in providing more efficient educational software in general. He focused on intrinsic motivation, or what makes an activity fun or rewarding in its own right rather than through external rewards. In his early work, he suggested that the essential characteristics of good computer games can be captured in three categories: challenge, fantasy and curiosity (Malone, 1980). He later expanded these in collaboration with Mark Lepper (Malone and Lepper, 1987b) to five categories. Through this collaboration, he expanded his work to encompass computer-based instruction in general with strong ties to computer games (Malone and Lepper, 1987a). Malone and Lepper (1987a; 1987b) identified the following categories that should be considered in designing drill-and-practice computer games to enhance learning:

- **Challenge**: The activity should be of an appropriate difficulty level for the player. This is done through clear short-term and long-term goals, an uncertain outcome, and by facilitating investment of self-esteem through meaningful goals. Furthermore, clear, constructive, encouraging feedback is essential.
- **Curiosity**: The information in the game should be complex and unknown to encourage exploration and organization of the information in relation to both the sensory area and the cognitive area.
- **Control**: The player should gain the overall feeling of being the controlling party. This is done through a responsive environment, a high degree of choice in the environment, and by equipping the player with the ability to perform great effects.
- **Fantasy**: The activity can increase intrinsic motivation by using fantasies as a part of the game universe. These fantasies should appeal to the target group emotionally, serve as metaphors for the learning content and be an endogenous part of the learning material.
- **Interpersonal motivations**: This refers to the increased motivation resulting from the social context of the computer game. Often, this is achieved through direct competition and collaboration with peers. Gaining the recognition of peers also serves as motivation.

Malone and Lepper (1987b) distinguished between extrinsic and intrinsic motivation to sort different forms of drill-and-practice computer games. Intrinsic motivation refers to a motivation that arises directly from doing the activity, whereas extrinsic motivation is a motivation that is supported by factors external to the activity. An example of intrinsic motivation would be students who spend hours learning how to play *Counter-strike* in order to get better, whereas extrinsic motivation would be parents' approval of their offspring playing an edutainment title to learn spelling. In edutainment, the activity in itself is rarely motivated. Malone and Lepper (1987b) pointed out that a long list of educational computer games has extrinsic game elements which can get in the way of the learning experience. These correspond to the heavily criticized edutainment titles, where there is no connection between the computer game and the learning part. The game part is mainly used as a reward for doing some learning activity. However, Malone and Lepper (1987b) argued that intrinsic use of game elements in drill-and-practice computer games can facilitate enhanced learning and sustained interest for a given topic over time. However, the importance of integrating learning elements into the gameplay doesn't make it into most educational computer game designs, which is evident from Konzack's (2003) analysis of a number of titles and several more common sense observations by researchers (Leddo, 1996; Leyland, 1996).

According to Malone and Lepper (1987a), a drill-and-practice perspective assumes that anything else other than the learning material in a learning experience is noise and potentially a hindrance for learning. The graphics, narrative, sound or ad-hoc activities in a computer game get in the way of learning. From this perspective, it hardly makes sense to call edutainment drill-and-practice, as edutainment is ripe with qualities opposing a clean drill-and-practice perspective. However, edutainment is usually described as drill-and-practice due to its adherence to behaviourism in its basic learning mechanisms, which will be pinpointed later in this chapter.

Lepper and Malone (1987a) also brought up classic problems in using computer games for educational purposes. They pointed to the problems between time-on-task, motivation and computer games. Depending on the learning context, the question of motivation may be more or less important. Assuming we have a number of fixed school hours to spend on an educational computer game, the additional features for increased motivation may turn out to divert the students from learning the relevant material, decreasing time-on-task. In a home setting, these additional features will, however, sustain the interest of the player and result in time spent on educational content that is supplementary. Here, any time-on-task is an extra benefit. Related to this is the question of whether it makes a difference if the learner feels in control when learning through a motivating educational computer game when compared to traditional teaching methods. Malone and Lepper (1987a) pointed out that this may be a choice between superficial learning and in-depth learning. When learning is driven by the student's own discovery in computer games, the quality of learning improves, but not necessarily the number of topics or contents covered.

Malone and Lepper (1987a) acknowledged that the real challenge is how to balance the wish for learning specific content, attitudes or skills with the discovery-based approach in computer games. They also envisioned great problems in matching the open environment with learners with different abilities. They referred to the academic level of students, but with the increasingly complex computer games (compared to that time), it also becomes a question of catering to different levels of game literacy among learners.

The research on computer games from an instructional technology perspective has also shown a sustained interest in the theory of Csikszentmihalyi's concept of flow. It has received a lot of attention within computer-game research. According to Csikszentmihalyi, a person's full attention must be centred on an activity in order to achieve a flow experience and the person must feel as one with the activity. An important point is that the flow experience is so strong and intense that people will engage in it without any other rewards, incentives or reasons. It is these characteristics that lure game researchers too, as flow theory might explain the infatuation with computer games. Csikszentmihalyi (1992: 49–66) identified eight characteristics of the flow experience:

- Feeling that one can complete the given activity
- Concentration on the activity
- The activity has clear goals
- The activity provides fast feedback
- Deep involvement in the activity
- A sense of control over the actions necessary to perform the activity
- Self-awareness disappearing during flow
- Sense of time is altered.

Marshall Jones' (1998) work is often cited as the theory of flow in relation to educational use of computer games. Jones found that the flow theory to a large degree explains the motivational aspects of computer games and that they should be catered to when designing educational computer games. Jones' research somewhat echoes Bowman (1982), describing how computer games are constructed in a way that facilitates flow.

Bowman (1982) took a more direct look at how computer games perceived through the flow theory would have a direct bearing on school practice. Through interviews with players, he identified some of those mechanisms that create a more engaging and intrinsically motivating learning experience in games arcades compared to classrooms. The most interesting were clarity of task, choice in problem-solving strategy, possibility for self-improvement, balance between skills and challenges, clear feedback, enjoyment while learning and lack of fear of failure. He concluded that some of these characteristics couldn't be extended to a teacher's practice while others would be transferable. The characteristics reflect the flow theory and it is stressed how altering the teacher behaviour may facilitate a more engaging and motivating learning experience for the benefit of all parties.

When looking at instructional theory, Malone's work has especially served as a guide to many researchers and designers over the years. However, the theory seems too narrowly focused on the relationship between computer-game structure and player. The latest revisions of the theory try to integrate the collaboration around computer games as an additional increaser of motivation identifying co-operation, competition and recognition as important motivators. However, the social context for educational computer games is primarily considered in relation to interpersonal encounters that increase motivation, not as a potential mediator and tool for learning as suggested by Squire (2004).

The legacy of edutainment

> To this point computer games with 'educational' features have not fared well in the marketplace. The 'educational' content tends to come at the expense of the gameplay and control is taken out of the hands of the player ... Game buyers (as opposed to concerned parents) are wary of edutainment.
>
> (Leyland, 1996: 1)

Edutainment is inspired by the instructional approach, behaviourism and later by cognitivism. It tries to focus on simple computer games and the delivery of straightforward information to the player. Many early popular educational computer games have a different understanding of learning and do not fit the label of edutainment. However, there is a plethora of edutainment titles continuously building on the instructional technology approach, supplemented with behaviourist learning theory in particular. Other educational computer games are slowly outmanoeuvred by edutainment, which encompasses a more conservative approach to learning with its promise of simplicity appealing to parents. An exploration of edutainment's nature is important, as it will show the characteristics and problems of current edutainment titles that I wish to avoid when developing a new framework for educational use of computer games.

Edutainment is potentially a broad term that covers the combination of educational and entertainment use on a variety of media platforms including computer games. The term edutainment is quite elastic as a lot of games are put into this category, and game companies are so inclined to strengthen the appeal for parents even though the brand edutainment is not as attractive any more (Konzack, 2003). Parents appreciate the combination of enter-tainment and education, preferring play that teaches children something. This links well with the common rationalizing of children's play pursued by adults as argued by Sutton-Smith and Kelly-Byrne (1984). There is a distinct tendency for both educators and parents to cast play in developmental terms. Children should not just play for the sake of playing, but in the process preferably nurture other skills. This wish for rationalizing play is extended to edutainment and used for creating a new market. Although there are good theoretical arguments for using play for learning, as I will discuss in Chapter 6, it seems these are mostly left behind in edutainment.

Edutainment is a subset of educational computer games that is easily recognizable with a clear reward structure separate from the gameplay. Usually, the game part is a reward for giving the right answer. In *Maths Blaster!* the players must shoot down the right answer and, on completion, one's balloon will move towards a needle. The first player who pops the balloon wins. It is assumed that constant shooting of the balloons will automatically lead to a conditioned response no matter what the learning, context, or previous experience. In the recent *Maths Missions Grades 3–5: The Amazing Arcade Adventure* by Scholastic, the player earns money for every correct answer. This money can be spent on buying arcade games and the player even gets to run the arcade. Here, the rewards are still used as a way to push the learning forward without really being related to understanding the learning experience as such. There is not really any connection between the arcade games and the maths questions. It is not that different from a mother promising her noisy child an ice cream if he will be quiet and do his homework.

We should not think of edutainment as a fixed genre but rather as different titles which share some assumptions about motivation, learning theory, learning principles and game design while being produced, marketed and distributed differently from commercial computer games. The characteristics are outlined below drawing on the above discussions and Chapter 2.

- *Little intrinsic motivation*: Edutainment relies more on extrinsic motivation through rewards, rather than intrinsic motivation. Extrinsic motivation is not really related to the game and consists of arbitrary rewards, e.g. getting points for completing a level. An example of intrinsic motivation would be the feeling of mastery from completing a level.
- *No integrated learning experience*: Usually, edutainment lacks integration of the learning experience with playing experience, which leads to the learning becoming subordinated to the stronger play experience. The player will concentrate on playing the game rather than on learning from the game. One example is the skipping of text about the pyramids and going straight for the mini-games located in the game universe, such as Othello.
- *Drill-and-practice learning principles*: The learning principles in edutainment are inspired by drill-and-practice thinking rather than understanding. This means that the player will constantly get arithmetical problems like $2+2$ and can memorize the answers, while not necessarily understanding the underlying rules that make $2+2 = 4$. You can also describe this as training rather than learning.
- *Simple gameplay*: Most edutainment titles are built on a simple gameplay often from classic arcade titles or a simple adventure game with a world that can be explored.

- *Small budgets*: Edutainment titles are often produced on relatively limited budgets compared to commercial computer games and with less than state-of-the-art technology.
- *No teacher presence*: Edutainment never makes any demands on teachers or parents. Rather, edutainment assumes that students can simply be put in front of the computer with the edutainment title and learn the given content or skills. There is no required teacher or parent guidance, help or involvement.
- *Distribution and marketing*: Edutainment titles are distributed and marketed differently from commercial computer games. They can be found in bookstores, supermarkets, schools and family magazines.

Edutainment games probably do teach children bits of things, but edutainment is mostly simplistic in its facilitation of learning experiences. Rote learning in relation to spelling and reading for pre-school and early school children may see some gains from edutainment. However, edutainment does not really teach the player about a certain area, but rather lets the player perform mechanical operations. This will lead to memorization of the practices aspect, but probably not a deep understanding of the skill or content. Just like a parrot, the student doesn't really grasp the concepts and while this may work for some areas, like spelling and reading, this is a quite limited scope. In general, the parrot-like learning will result in weak transfer and application of the skills, content or attitudes learning, as it is not fundamentally understood but only memorized as a mechanical action in the game environment (Gee et al., 2004; Jonassen, 2001; Schank, 1999). The learning may show up on assessment, which formulates questions that are very close to the aspect learned, not requiring much reworking of knowledge, but not if the assessment strays away from the specific aspect learned.

There is also common agreement that edutainment fails to integrate the learning with the computer game. Hence, there is a change of focus in the learning experience from the educational part to the game part. This results in weak learning experiences especially if the time-on-task issue is considered. The player won't spend a lot of time on educational experiences, but rather will gain a lot of game experience (Brody, 1993; Fabricatore, 2000; Facer et al., 2003; VanDeventer, 1997). In general, the information in edutainment is fed to the player in chunks separated from the games, like in the Swedish game *Chefren's Pyramid*. In this game, one starts with a presentation of Egyptian history and an overwhelming amount of facts that a player scrolls through and *sometimes* reads. Then, one can start the 'game', in which the player walks inside a pyramid finding different puzzles or small games like backgammon. These game dynamics have no connection to Egyptian culture, which the game is supposed to teach the player about. Most players will learn to play backgammon though.

Edutainment is also criticized for supporting a superficial and problematic construction of learning in the new generations. As Okan (2003: 258) asked,

'Should learning be fun?' This is supported by Healy (1999) and Kafai (2001) who asked whether we in our eagerness to revolutionize learning are undermining the very foundation for learning. Students need to be able to endure frustration during learning and stay on track despite problems. This is argued to be rare in edutainment titles, and that may be right, but it is certainly not a feature of computer games in general. Frustration and challenge is central in Gee's (2004b) account of the learning qualities of the commercial computer game *Rise of Nations* and, in general, computer games fit Papert's term 'hard fun'.

Overall, the shortcomings of edutainment have led to an overall negative attitude towards edutainment titles. To put it mildly, there is widespread scepticism toward almost every aspect of edutainment. The gameplay, learning principles and graphics are all criticized heavily by users, both children and parents, especially after all the mergers in the early 1990s. As edutainment has conquered the market place it has increasingly moved away from early research on instructional technology.

HOT SPOTS WHERE EDUCATIONAL USE OF COMPUTER GAMES HAVE BEEN STUDIED EXTENSIVELY

The research on educational use of computer games is not equally distributed across all areas, with basic subjects like maths, science, reading and spelling exhibiting more research. It is worth spending more time on these areas because this is where there is some aggregation of results.

There is little actual research on how much computer games are used in educational settings. However, McFarlane, Sparrowhawk and Heald (2002) asked students whether they played computer games in school. Depending on the age level, a rather large number of students did play computer games in school, but with the smallest number at the highest Key Stage (Table 4.1). This is in line with edutainment's strongest showing in the pre-school and early-school area as discussed in previous chapters. A Canadian, English and Danish study of grades K-12 use reported that almost 60 per cent of the teachers had used games and that most were interested in using games (Becker and Jacobsen, 2005; Egenfeldt-Nielsen, 2005; MORI, 2006).

Table 4.1: Number of students playing computer games in school (the statistics are from McFarlane, Sparrowhawk and Heald [2002: 28])

Key Stage level	Age group	Percentage playing computer games in school
2	7–11 years	63.4%
3	11–14 years	70.8%
4	14–16 years	23.2%

The study is unclear on whether or not the computer games were part of the lesson plan or purely entertainment played at breaks or in after-school activities. However, it seems unlikely that it should exclusively be educational as the difference between boys and girls is quite significant; indirectly pointing out that this is partly a voluntary activity.

The obsession with maths and science

> Most of the early mathematical computer games focused on drill and practice of simple number operations and concepts. Such games are easy to develop. Moreover, playing such games are an effective and motivating method of increasing fluency for many students. However, drill and practice is only one of many components of mathematics learning and can also be achieved via a variety of non computer-based methods.
>
> (Klawe, 1998: 9)

There has been a significant number of research projects dedicated to using or constructing computer games which can rejuvenate the teaching of science subjects and especially maths. This has partly been facilitated by a political concern in increasing the interest in natural science in order to stay competitive in the global educational race. The increased interest and preparedness for using computers and hence computer games among teachers in natural science subjects has also played a role. Finally, the early educational computer games within maths (in reality, mostly edutainment) may have provoked a response, more as a red flag than as state-of-the-art games. Researchers are convinced it could be done better.

Over the years, a surprisingly large number of projects have focused on this area and, compared with other subject areas, it is quite well researched. The studies concerning topics of general interest to the educational use of computer games will be reviewed in chronological order, starting out with the PLATO project.

The PLATO project yielded positive results from 1973 in relation to using computer games for maths and these results supported the initiation of later research into the field. This was clear, for example, in the research by Levin (1981) on using computer games to learn alternative and everyday arithmetic. In Levin's perspective, we need a new way of learning arithmetic, as the current models are not appropriate when we have calculators and microprocessors to do most of our maths in everyday life. Levin (1981) constructed the two educational computer games *Harpoon* and *Sonar* in 1981, based on the *Darts* game from the PLATO project. The two games were intended to facilitate new understandings of arithmetic closer to everyday needs. They proved to be motivating and engaging and were ultimately successful in teaching children the planned maths concepts. Based on the results, it is suggested that computer games may be appropriate for teaching different ways of approaching maths that cater to individual differences. Through the 1980s, the educational programming language Logo was the favourite flavour within mathematics and attempts were also made to combine it with earlier progress on computer games. The approach was especially formed around children designing maths games themselves. Here the results were also encouraging, as the students engaged with designing Logo maths games outperformed the control group (Kafai, 1995; Kafai and Resnick, 1996; Olive and Lobato, 2001; Papert, 1996). We will return to constructionism later in this chapter since this theoretical approach's bearing on educational use of computer games deserves more attention.

The 1990s kicked off with the E-Gems study overviewed by Maria Klawe (1998). It is impressive in its findings and is probably one of the first cross-disciplinary academic research groups dedicated to studying computer games. The study focused on two educational maths computer games designed in connection with the research project: *Super Tangrams* (1996) and *Phoenix Quest* (1997). These were the basis of several empirical studies, where different variables were manipulated to determine the most active elements in facilitating the learning process. The results were particularly strong, as they have been replicated by different research designs and research teams. The total number of students in the empirical studies was also quite impressive. Approximately 200 students participated in the controlled studies of *Super Tangrams* and a similar number in the research on *Phoenix Quest*. On an overall level, the computer games produced in the project proved to be motivating, popular and highly effective in teaching maths to students (Klawe, 1998; Sedighian and Sedighian, 1996, 1997).

Klawe (1998) summed up the results of the E-Gems project and stressed that computer games should be used for maths activities that are otherwise hard to introduce in a classroom. Special attention should be aimed at elements in computer games that are particularly strong, such as the unlimited number of activities, visualization, manipulation, symbolic representations, adaptive sequencing, feedback and meaningful, contextualized activities. These elements are not believed to be limited to educational maths computer games, but should apply to all educational titles. The generalization is not based on research, but connects well with earlier ideas of intrinsic motivation and flow theory.

In the discussion of the challenges during the game design process, Klawe (1998) raised some of the central problems with educational computer games. Most of these are backed up by an earlier study by Sedighian and Sedighian (1996), the researchers responsible for the *Super Tangrams* part of E-Gems. Klawe pointed out that the immersive effect of computer games leads to a lack of awareness of the mathematical structures and concepts integrated in the computer game. This result is a weak transfer of game experience to other contexts. In an earlier study by Klawe and Phillips (1995), the use of paper and pencil during gameplay was found to be valuable for transferring computer game maths experiences to other classroom practice. In the same study, debriefing and shared discussions were also stressed. They did not draw on research from the simulation and gaming community presented earlier, but the findings are in line with the heavy focus on debriefing in educational game research.

Klawe (1998) argued that transfer can especially be improved through careful game design that integrates the maths elements, echoing Malone and Lepper's previously discussed work. Also, it seems that a teacher's explicit and constant probing of the educational relevance of the computer game during play will increase the value. She suggested that both *Super Tangrams* and *Phoenix Quest* solve the problem, but at least one study challenged the ability of *Phoenix Quest* to make explicit the maths concepts and structures (Jillian et al., 1999). This transfer problem appears in most research into educational use of computer games, and we will continuously run into it.[1] It seems to be an unsolvable double bind. On the one hand, it is assumed that the learning must be by stealth and undetectable by children. This is based on the premise that an educational computer game should resemble a traditional computer game. It shouldn't give itself away because then children will shy away from the educational title (Brody, 1993). The learning elements should be integrated into the game experience and not stand out. On the other hand, it seems that if the players are not aware of the learning elements, it will undermine the learning experience and especially the transfer value (Bransford et al., 1999).

The idea of stealth learning and the close overlap with commercial computer games runs contrary to the emphasis placed on debriefing in research on educational games, which was discussed in Chapter 3. Especially in E-Gems, the issues with implicit learning elements become problematic. They are not only concerned with teaching the students the basic arithmetic, so often encountered in drill-and-practice educational titles, but also aspire to use computer games for more advanced maths concepts and structures. These concepts and structures are more complex and can be hard to automatically uncover in a game context. It can also be argued that these concepts require a more reflective process than the rote learning of arithmetic. This may also be generalized in other more complex topics presented through computer games.

Another basic problem addressed by the E-Gems project is the clash between the player's control when playing and the need to scaffold the learning experiences. Again, there seems to be a conflict between the computer game medium and pedagogies for facilitating learning. The solution suggested by Klawe (1998) is to carefully integrate a reward system that will steer the player in the right direction. However, this seems to entail some problems considering the classic time-on-task issue. Even with a proper reward system, the student will sometimes take the wrong path and may experience failure and waste valuable time on an insurmountable problem. Depending on the concrete learning experience and one's theoretical background, it may be a complete waste of time or one of the essential factors of computer games. According to Gee (2003), in the long run, the students faced with such hopeless situations will learn how to steer clear of difficult problems and frame them in a sufficiently precise way to avoid problems in the future. This may sometimes be possible, but it also seems that this may be the reason for the relatively simple simulations and representations in computer games. They mostly require a minimum of skills and knowledge from the outside world in order to be playable. It may be necessary to reconsider this approach if we want more complex educational computer games than just drill-and-practice. Today it is unthinkable for most players to read the accompanying manual to a computer game, but this doesn't mean that it might not in fact be more efficient as computer games increase in complexity. Interestingly, many players will after some playing consult the manual expecting to find more information on different game areas. This can point to good points of departure for introducing an educational perspective.

The research project Through the Glass Wall had a slightly different focus than E-Gems. It took the role of supporting the concrete educational use of computer games for maths more seriously. The researchers reviewed existing educational maths computer games and set up guidelines for educators and parents to choose better educational computer games (Kliman, 1999; Murray, Mokros and Rubin, 1998). The project resulted in fewer research findings and there were not the same kind of iterations as the E-Gems project, but they did have some interesting findings. They focused on an educational title called *Logical Journey of the Zoombinis* (1996), which somewhat resembles the classic computer game *Lemmings*. The *Logical Journey of the Zoombinis* was developed as an offshoot of educational maths research and took children's own experience and fun with maths-related issues as a starting point. Their approach could be described as learning maths in another way through computer games (Hancock and Osterweil, 1996). The developers of the *Logical Journey of the Zoombinis* shared this ambition with other research projects in this area. The Through the Glass Wall project suggested that, compared to traditional educational maths titles, maths is an integrated part of playing *Logical Journey of the Zoombinis* and encourages maths-related reflection, thinking and discussion (Murray et al., 1998; Rubin et al., 1997) The researchers stressed the importance of the narrative frame and the gender-neutral game universe. They also found that the game teaches the children basic maths concepts although they did not compare it directly with other teaching methods. However, the results from the Through the Glass Wall project are hard to generalize as they build on limited qualitative data and what counts as learning is quite vague. They do not really measure the difference between different educational computer games, but purely observe the dialogue around the computer game. The results of playing, reflecting and discussing are never really examined. Furthermore, the critical question of transfer is not tackled. The problem of recognizing and transferring the maths skills is also a real issue here, when maths is never really mentioned in the computer game and a debriefing context is never established.

Despite the large number of research projects within the maths area, it is also tainted by a lack of awareness of prior research. Each project starts from the assumption that little or no earlier research has been done, each reinventing the wheel. They do draw on larger theoretical frameworks but not on specific research into educational maths computer games.

The dominance of educational adventure games

The most consistent claim on the educational potential of computer games is in relation to adventure games, especially promoted by Australian researchers. This link may be due to an integration of computer games in the curriculum goals in the Australian primary schools as early as 1989, which is still maintained (Beavis, 1999a; Cavallari et al., 1992).

The support for adventure games is expressed by researchers, journalists, educators and parents. Additionally, the amount of research into adventure games is larger than that of any other genre. Adventure games are bestowed with the ability to increase problem-solving as a basic part of their puzzle-based structure. The success criteria in adventure games are often identified as logical thinking and puzzle-solving (Cavallari et al., 1992; Egenfeldt-Nielsen and Smith, 2000), which are well respected qualities in the educational system. In addition, the close relation to reading a text when playing adventure games is appreciated by educators (Heaney, 1989). The relationship between text and narratives is considered a strong educational feature, although the increasing graphical representation somewhat diminishes the direct parallel to more classic text forms. However, few studies have used the purely text-based adventure games, with Grabe and Dosmann (1998) the exception. One could easily claim that adventure games are the 'easy' transition from traditional teaching methods in the softer subjects (e.g. English, history and geography) to game-based learning. Adventure games offer a close connection between existing theories within a subject field and computer games.

Cavallari et al. (1992) summed up the claims in educational circles for adventure games as teaching knowledge, skills and attitudes which are transferable to other contexts. It is stressed that most adventure games are not explicitly educational, but that they 'provide opportunities' for interested teachers. The teacher's role is perceived as imperative for the learning experience. Cavallari et al. (1992) encouraged the teacher to consider the following options, although weakly documented:

- Use adventure games across curricula and do not be limited to one subject.

- Encompass the adventure game within an overall topic that the students preferably have previous knowledge of.
- Finally, provide additional resources concerning the topic to extend the scope of the computer game.

The last point on providing additional material is strongly supported by later research on a strategy game by David Leutner (1993).

A majority of the researchers in the early 1990s ended their papers by calling for more research directly comparing use of adventure games with traditional teaching methods. Such studies are still scarce within the adventure games area, but an interesting study by James Wiebe and Nancy Martin (1994) supported the cautious attitude by the majority of researchers. In their study, they used the classic adventure game *Where in the World is Carmen Sandiego* for teaching geography. They compared students playing the adventure game with a group of students learning through non-computer games. They found no significant difference between these two groups and this led them to question heavy investment in educational computer games. The study had some flaws though, especially the short time span of 40 minutes for both groups. In this period, half of the time was dedicated to non-geography-related activities to control for the Hawthorne effect, the potential bias arising from researchers' interest in the study. However, that only left 20 minutes for the computer game to have an impact, which is a short learning experience in traditional teaching, especially with computer games that usually span longer periods of play. The students would need to start up the computer game, learn the interface and link the game to geography. This is a type of empirical design that Wolfe and Crookall (1998) warned against, as the results are jeopardized by not really taking into account the special characteristics of computer games.

Another work answering the call for studying educational use of computer games is by Shirley Grundy (1991) and, interestingly, she studied the same game, namely *Where in the World is Carmen Sandiego*. She examined the game through mainly qualitative methods, focusing on student competences and student decision-making processes. The educational potential of the game is initially described as knowledge about computers, feeling of success, factual knowledge, literacy skills and problem-solving. These potentials are in opposition to Wiebe and Martin (1994), who focus narrowly on one subject. The findings by Grundy are not quantifiable but emerge through systematic data analysis of student interaction around the computer game. Grundy did not find support for students gaining more knowledge about computers. She found that *Where in the World is Carmen Sandiego* could support a wide area of relevant topics, but learning these is not an integrated part of the game. Most students had successful experiences with the game, solving the assignments. Overall, students drew on earlier subject experiences and the computer game fitted well with the current theme in the course that was about different countries all over the world. The background information from earlier work in the class was used heavily. However, the game's almanac was only used to a limited degree, as it proved too cumbersome. It was also clear that knowledge and information provided by the computer game that was not perceived to be directly applicable to the specific computer game situation in question was not considered relevant and interesting enough to invest time in. The learning was therefore only superficial, exposing:

> A real need for the program to utilize information provided in the information frames in the early game, so that students learned the benefits of remembering and assimilating the knowledge.
>
> (Grundy, 1991: 49)

This problem is a recurring one in the research literature (e.g. Jillian et al., 1999; Squire, 2004) and challenges the very notion of using computer games for learning since the relevant educational material may be quite limited.

Furthermore, the students had a blind belief in the computer game's ability to present accurate and valid information. When students experienced a conflict between their own knowledge and information presented in the game, they believed the game. The superficial approach to knowledge was also present in the general reading of the text in the game, which was perfunctory. Most students skipped the text or scanned it. This was also made worse by the problematic game design. The clues in the game were presented in short sentences, but always at the end. Therefore, the unfortunate consequence was that the students skipped to the end. Not surprisingly, they put the game goals higher than the learning goals, which we could put down to bad game design, but it seems to run deeper. One can say that students lived up to the principles for playing the game in that they completed the assignments as fast as possible without thinking about the educational goals (Healy, 1999; Magnussen and Misfeldt, 2004). Another game design might have changed this situation, but the suggestion by Grundy (1991) that the game should have mechanisms that draw on information presented earlier in the game is not easily implemented. A computer game consists of a quite basic gameplay and it is almost impossible to get even a fraction of the background information to have a bearing on the game. In the strategy game *Civilization* there is an encyclopedia describing a range of objects, events and inventions and most of these have at least a one-page description. This is also true for the *Colossus of Rhodes*. However, the game effect of the *Colossus* is to double trade in the city where it is built. This is the real impact it has and this is what most players will learn. Squire's (2004) analysis of the strategy game *Civilization III* has similar examples.

Grundy (1991) concluded that although limited explicit learning potential existed in the computer game, it offered many implicit learning possibilities that the teacher could harness. Alternatively, the computer game should be redesigned to support the learning experiences more closely. Grundy ended up cautioning against investing heavily in an area with so few clear advantages.

A more fine-grained approach to the learning process in adventure games and the potential implications for transfer was presented by Oluf Danielsen, Birgitte Olesen and Birgitte Holm Sørensen (2002). They set up three different potentially active dimensions of learning in the computer game *Miljøstrup* (*Environtown*): informative, attitude and action. Each of these dimensions gave a different optic for understanding how the computer game can facilitate learning. The informative dimension is concerned with the facts presented in the computer game and the comprehension of this information. The action dimension looks at the learning that occurs when the students do something in the computer game and whether this transfers to actual everyday environmental behaviour. The attitude dimension refers to learning that results in reflection or alteration of attitude to environmental themes based on game experiences.

Unfortunately, they did not adjust their methodology to match the different learning dimensions: informative, attitude and action. All of the results are based on qualitative methods, and the conclusion that children do acquire some specific knowledge of environment is left hanging in the air. Further questions remain: what information?, by whom?, and to what extent? The same is true for the attitudinal dimension, where they also found that the engaging experience with environmental content in the computer games made students' attitudes more favourable towards environment. The really interesting part is their observations and interviews with students in their home environment, where they determined whether the knowledge obtained through the computer game is transferred to everyday activities. They found that this is the case for some students. These students are characterized by already having a home environment that can facilitate the experiences with the computer games. The researchers concluded:

> Each pupil may well build up knowledge and attitudes about correct environmental behaviour and healthy food habits supported by computer games. But if there is no space for action, the acquired knowledge remains in the individual as potential physical action competence. For many children the learning will thus remain isolated and tied up with the game if it is not picked up and connected with everyday actions, for example initiated by the teacher at school and/or the parents at home.
> (Danielsen et al., 2002: 78)

Overall, the study pointed to important distinctions in accessing learning outcome and different types of knowledge in computer games, which is further addressed in Chapter 6. There is a close connection between adventure games and computer games as a way to teach media literacy. Often, adventure games are used to discuss what makes computer games different from more traditional media forms.

Computer games as a way to media literacy

Computer games as media literacy has strong roots in the research on adventure games, but broadens the scope more and sees the computer game as an interesting medium in its own right. How do media, including computer games, play a role in relation to literacy, culture, curriculum and society (Buckingham, 2003)? Computer games are seen as tied to children's culture and, as such, potentially relevant to reflect upon to increase literacy in new media.

The closest example of a representative for computer games in media education is Catherine Beavis (1997; 1999a; 1999b) who has extensively examined the relationship between using computer games and new forms of literacy. She stresses that computer games in general are a way to engage with new culture forms prevalent among children and youngsters. The educational system should not be limited to transferring a classic high-culture vision of society.[2] This claim is seldom used as an argument in itself for using educational computer games, but it holds interesting perspectives for general use of computer games. It is reasonable to suggest that new media culture (including movies, TV shows and computer games) could benefit from a general higher critical awareness. This should be supplied by the school and therefore computer games have a place in the curriculum, which is also the case mirrored in the national curriculum of Australia and Denmark where games are explicitly mentioned in recent curriculum descriptions.

Beavis (1999a) argues that there are great advantages in integrating computer games into teaching because they are complex, engaging and well known by many children. However, she warns against perceiving computer games as neutral. Their closer connection with everyday life, current media practice and culture generally leads to anything but neutral objects of study. They are violent, stereotyped, ideologically loaded, and will be very differently approached by different students. Still, this just underlines the relevance of engaging with the media and Beavis (1999a) suggests the following approach based on two studies in Australian schools:

> How might we work with computer games as part of the literacy curriculum? I suggest we approach computer games much as we do other texts, particularly those to which they seem most closely related, novel and film. As part of the spectrum of texts we examine, we can explore elements in the construction of the texts from aesthetics and structural patternings through to the values they imply and the subject position they seem to ask of their readers. We can discuss with students the appeal of the texts, what they take the dominant values or ideologies to be, how they position themselves in relation to the main characters, particular issues raised by the game and so on.
>
> (Beavis, 1999a: unpaginated)

Beavis (1997; 1999a; 1999b) is optimistic about the role of computer games in the educational system, as it seems to be a way to approach new literacy forms that is meaningful and motivating for students. Of course, there will be classic problems, especially in relation to computer game licences and technological barriers. Since her latest work, these problems have somewhat diminished as computers are slowly becoming a more integrated part of school life and playable computer game demos are wide-reaching enough to serve as objects of study. The theoretical work on computer games is also becoming increasingly accessible to teachers, making it easier to bridge the gap between existing subjects and analysis of computer games (Egenfeldt-Nielsen, 2003a; Squire, 2003a, 2003b).

The approach to media education should not be confused with the narrow focus on teaching ICT skills in schools. Research into the ability of computer games to teach these is not widespread, but examined in a pilot project by Becta (2001). Becta also stressed collaboration, motivation and relevant content as apparent in the educational use of computer games, but ICT was the one most strongly supported by teachers' assessment.

The titles studied were the *The Sims, SimCity, Age of Empires* and *Championship Manager*. The skills especially observed to be used were 'multi-tasking, switching between windows, and practice at finding and applying rules from menus' (Becta, 2001: 8). This was done with high motivation and interest from all students. The teachers in the study intuitively used computer games for ICT, but they did also find some indication in relation to learning thinking skills, collaboration and some relevant content depending on the specific computer game. The measurements were, however, quite informal and participating teachers were not entirely representative.

Healthy computer games can change your behaviour

Research on computer games aimed at supporting more healthy behaviour have some interesting results. Researchers within the field have strengthened their claims by comparing educational use of computer games directly with learning in other media forms. It is also noticeable that studies of health games have the advantages of being able to measure more overt changes in behaviours and external signs of learning.

Educational health computer games are mostly inspired by Albert Bandura's social learning theory, and the field spans some successful titles along with interesting research findings. Proponents of Bandura's theory assume that, by watching and enacting specific activities, one will learn the activities, especially when enforced by appropriate role models. Computer games provide a safe frame for these activities and one is able to make children repeat otherwise tedious actions. There are a lot of health games out there. *Bronkie the Bronchiasaurus, Packy and Marlon, Traffic Jam, Hungry Red Planet* and *Aids Prevention – Catch the Sperm* are some examples.

The area is characterized by thorough empirical studies, especially when it comes to examining the learning outcome from computer games. This is due to its roots in medical science and psychology, fields in which the documentation of effect is an inherent part of performing research. Most of the results are quite positive and indicate a significant behavioural change.

One of the most interesting health computer games is *Bronkie the Bronchiasaurus*, which is within the action genre, in the sub-genre called platform games. The player controls the character of Bronkie who must fight the bad Tyrannosaurus Rex to assemble a wind machine to clean the air. The story has minor significance except for setting the scene and is quickly forgotten once the player becomes engrossed in the gameplay. The player jumps over enemies and avoids obstacles that will bring on asthma in order to make it to the next level. However, embedded in the game universe are a lot of necessary asthma management tools and activities that the player must perform. The factual knowledge is limited to a few multiple-choice questions between levels, but students will perform asthma management and change their behaviour.

Debra Lieberman (2001) compared playing the computer game for 30 minutes with watching an educational video for 30 minutes. The children who played the computer game expressed more enjoyment and learned the same as the children watching the television programme. Lieberman stressed that this is interesting, as the video will only be watched once and needs to convey all its information in one chunk. The computer game will deliver a limited amount of factual information in 30 minutes but will be played for longer periods. Still, it measures up on the short-trial period.

This hints at a problem lurking beneath the surface that may arise when using educational computer games, namely the computer game's ability to deliver large amounts of information. Computer games consist of basic rules and do not deliver the same density of information as videos or books. It has basic rules covering the most important information which the game designer or educator wishes to convey about a subject through the game. This information is introduced, re-used and re-applied but seldom with the same details as, for example, in a textbook. The cyclical nature comes at the expense of introducing large amounts of relevant educational material. The above findings by Lieberman suggest that this might be a pseudo-problem, as children are under all circumstances not capable of receiving and digesting all the information in more classic media like video and books. It is not possible to generalize from such a small study, but it is worth noticing as we approach other studies and consider how to evaluate educational use of computer games.

Brown et al. (1997) found the similar game *Packy and Marlon* to be quite effective in improving diabetes self-care among children. The player in the game controls an avatar with diabetes and must monitor the level of blood glucose, take insulin injections and choose foods. This is done within the overall narrative of saving the diabetes summer camp from evil rats and mice who have stolen the diabetes provisions. The course of the game indicates that well-designed educational computer games can be effective. Players improved on self-efficacy, communication with parents about diabetes and self-care behaviours, and the number of urgent doctor visits decreased. The post-test showed a 77 per cent drop in medical visits in the experimental group compared to the control group (Brown, 1997; Lieberman, 2001).

Interestingly, the players did not improve their knowledge of diabetes significantly, which links back to the problems with a narrow focus on seeing computer games only in a knowledge-acquisition perspective. It also conflicts somewhat with the results described by Lieberman, but she didn't measure the actual knowledge acquired. She merely stated that computer games, in terms of knowledge acquisition, are just as effective as an educational video. The effect on factual knowledge may, however, be limited by both teaching styles when considering the general problem of transfer. The classic view on transfer has in general been heavily criticized in educational psychology for its reliance on a simplified understanding of learning (Döpping, 1995). Alternative approaches to understanding transfer are clear in relation to educational use of computer games. Transfer is seen as quite hard and cumbersome and computer games will not change this, even though computer games seem to include features for enabling transfer (e.g. Gee, 2003; Gee et al., 2004).

The results by Brown et al. are somewhat supported by other research findings (Dowey, 1987; Johansson and Küller, 2002; Noble et al., 2000; Thomas et al., 1997; Turnin et al., 2000) but contradicted by another study that failed to find a transfer of knowledge from the computer game *Foodman* to everyday contexts (Sørensen, 1997). This one study on *Foodman*, however, might be more related to limitations in the actual game design and applying the results to educational computer games in general may not be appropriate. *Foodman*'s interface is quite arbitrary, hindering the players from understanding the content about healthy food behaviour and from seeing the connection between their actions and consequences. The general challenge in the building of interfaces for healthcare games is partly related to the students' existing level of knowledge about the subject, which was also recognized in a prototype study by Lockyer et al. (2003).

CONCLUSION: SCATTERED SATELLITES

The research into educational use of computer games has indeed covered some ground. However, the research lives on in its own dedicated pockets where the wheel is constantly reinvented. Approached separately, each area still has a number of blind spots but taken together, we see quite a few trends. Many of the problems remain with more recent research traditions that we will approach in the following chapter.

NOTES

1 Indeed, most educational research struggles with the transfer problem (Bransford, Brown and Cocking, 1999).
2 There have been similar discussions in Denmark (Egenfeldt-Nielsen, 2003b; Walther, 2004).

5

Getting to Third Generation: New Trends in Educational Use of Computer Games

The latest research approach, the third generation, extends from a sociocultural and constructionist starting point, where educational use of computer games relies on the surrounding context rather than the game per se. In a third-generation perspective, the educational use of computer games is seen as an activity that is accomplished in the interplay between game, student, context and teacher. The following six key areas are identified:

1 Learning vs. playing
2 Drill-and-practice games vs. microworlds
3 Transfer vs. construction
4 Teacher intervention vs. no teacher intervention
5 Depth vs. superficiality
6 One subject vs. cross-subjects.

The chapter concludes that the research into educational use of computer games has gone through three generations, although not in strict chronological order as the generations overlap. The first generation maintains a narrow focus on learning with the computer game, filling players up with knowledge. The second generation perspective is more inclusive, trying to understand the more complex processes between player and computer game. We are now beginning to see the third generation become more dominant, where player, computer game, teacher and context all become important elements for understanding educational use of computer games.

Until now, we have primarily talked about research which relates to computer games in a first- and second-generation perspective, focusing on the player and/or the computer game, but this is, as suggested previously, too limited. The research presented in this chapter is less elaborate than the previous themes, but points forward to a third-generation perspective that includes player, computer games and context while stressing learning as understanding. In that sense, it paves the way for the next chapter, where I will present a new educational foundation for understanding educational use of computer games.

CONSTRUCTIONISM'S DREAM: VIRTUAL WORLDS AND CHILDREN AS GAME DESIGNERS

Inspired by Piaget's constructivism, Seymour Papert formulated the theory of constructionism. The mission was initially to teach children hard subjects like maths in alternative ways, but slowly it became a well-established overall theoretical learning approach. The most influential tool for constructionist thinking is the programming language Logo. Logo lets students draw computer-generated drawings by using mathematical concepts. The concepts are not explicit, but are implicitly used when one draws figures. The so-called turtle, which is not too different from an avatar in a computer game, can, for example, draw a square. The student observes the turtle drawing a line and then gives it the command, 'turn 90 degrees'. This is repeated three times and a square is drawn. The active approach to knowledge and use of external artifacts for facilitating the learning experience is essential for constructionism.

Turning to computer games, these principles have been used in several ways. For some constructionist thinkers, computer games are the lost paradise. Here is a universe where the learner can engage with a microworld and construct different objects and connections (Papert, 1980).

The most noticeable contribution within this field is the work by Yasmin Kafai (1995; 2001), which has stood the test of time. Through the 1990s, she expanded the idea of children as game designers, turning children into producers of knowledge and, in a very concrete way, letting them play with objects in different ways. According to Kafai and Resnick (1996), there is no doubt that one can acquire programming experience through designing computer games and learn the maths used in developing computer games. It is believed that designing computer games makes it possible for the learner to approach a subject in an active way, thereby constructing a personal representation of knowledge by using physical artifacts. The student's learning experience draws on different perspectives, giving rise to a variety of actions and, in that way, provides a fuller understanding of a given topic.

The main focus is the construction process and, therefore, research has also focused on open-ended games. This has run the gamut from students designing simple games, engaging in virtual worlds, exploring microworlds and building active worlds online to the playing of open-ended commercial computer games in general. The basic assumptions about learning are different in constructionism compared to the dominating edutainment titles. In a constructionist perspective, learning does not come from the computer game and the challenge is not so much to design an educational computer game with relevant content. Rather, the hard challenge is to facilitate playing that makes the player engage with the material, discuss it, reflect on it and use the computer game as a means for constructing knowledge. A prerequisite for such constructions may very well be relevant content but the content is far from enough.

The interest in microworlds is therefore also obvious, as these are more or less game-like open-ended universes where a certain topic is represented through different artifacts. A microworld can be described as a simulation of a part of the world that is simplified and constructed to facilitate the working between concrete objects. When one interacts with objects in microworlds, one learns about these objects' properties, connections and applications. The player can engage and manipulate these artifacts and thereby construct a perception of the given topic. Kafai (1996) noted that the design of these microworlds proves to be a lot harder than drill-and-practice computer games, because the topic has to be integrated with the microworld. It wouldn't work to just grab a well-tested action formula and use that as the blueprint, as would be the case for the edutainment genre. The interest in microworlds has been especially strong in relation to maths and science (Goldstein and Pratt, 2001; Hoyle et al., 1991; Hoyles et al., 2002; Miller, Lehman et al., 1999; Rieber, 1996; White, 1984) but other attempts have surfaced that draw on constructionism as a different approach to computer games (McCarty, 2001; Woods, 2002).

THE SOCIAL-CULTURAL APPROACH: AROUND THE GAME

Edutainment's narrow focus on computer games offering the full educational experience continues. It is still strongly supported today by some who believe computer games to be optimal learning machines. Squire's continuation of a debate at the 2002 Game Developers Conference illustrates the problem:

> Marc Prensky and others argued for the systematic study of learning environments comprised exclusively of gaming activities; in other words, situations where players sit in front a computer, play a game, learn from the game and then walk away. Jon Goodwin responded that, from such an approach, a game would not only be required to provide a robust, compelling context for learning activities but also would need to be able to adjust to individual players' abilities and preferences, provide just-in-time explanations and background material, present divergent problems, include opportunities for reflection and track user behaviour in order to assess learning and then adjust learning experiences accordingly. The claim that any game can (or should) accomplish all this is dubious at best.
>
> (Squire, 2004: 44)

Since the start of the 1980s, there has been an interest in examining the social context around the computer game experience (e.g. Strein and Kachman, 1984). But it was not until the mid-1990s that the socio-cultural approach really started to influence the area. In the Nordic countries, Carsten Jessen's (1995; 2001) study of the culture around computer games described the informal play and learning experiences around them which are mediated through social relations. This led to interesting findings concerning peer-learning around computer games and appreciation of the rich social interaction that mediates the game experience. The appeal of computer games to children was found to be closely related to the match between children's existing play culture and the computer game culture. This research never really goes beyond the informal learning processes surrounding computer games, but points towards the importance of incorporating these. This is strongly supported by Squire's (2004) PhD dissertation, which discusses several classes that played *Civilization III*. The explicit goal is to facilitate history through *Civilization III*, especially through the surrounding social environment. This approach is supported in observations and interviews. Squire concluded that:

> The most important point in understanding how games engage players in educational environments may be that good games engage players in multiple ways and the interplay between these different forms create dynamic learning opportunities. Different play styles and tastes enriched classroom conversations, often leading to discussions that produce important 'taken-as-shared' meanings. [...] Discussions between different player types drove them to articulate and defend different strategies, even rethinking their orientation to the game as when Marvin, a builder/explorer, implored Joey to rethink waging war.
>
> (Squire, 2004: 241)

It is also stressed that computer games do not lend themselves to learning about history as rote memorization. Instead, the relationships between variables, events and complex patterns should be the goal.

In a socio-cultural perspective, computer games are tools for constructing a viable learning experience. Computer games mediate discussion, reflection, facts and analysis facilitated by the surrounding classroom culture and the student's identity. This approach is argued to be very useful for understanding computer games with their strong social network (Gee, 2003; Jessen, 2001; Linderoth, 2002; Squire, 2004). Since they tend to exaggerate a bit, computer games are not interesting for their content, but for their way of initiating new explorations, negotiations, constructions and journeys into knowledge.

Gee (2003), who spoke from a socio-cultural perspective, has given one of the strongest theoretical accounts for understanding the learning mechanisms in computer games. It may not necessarily be directly useful in an educational setting, however. The overarching idea is that children learn to participate in new domains by playing computer games. They learn to make sense of new areas, especially by engaging with like-minded discussion, reflection and sharing. A key area in the play activity is the role of critical thinking, which is constantly used in the social practice the player engages in around the computer game. Gee presented five main areas of interest concerning computer games, which are also of interest for educational purposes. He saw these as intrinsic qualities of computer games that can be useful in a school setting:

- **Semiotic domains**: Like other activities in life, computer games are a semiotic domain that can be slowly learned. One learns to make sense of and navigate in the domain of computer games, while being pointed to other interesting domains like science. Computer games can also work as a place to reflect on the engagement and processes in domains of practice.
- **Learning and identity**: Computer games give new opportunities for learning experiences when the student is involved with the material. Computer games are quite good for creating agency and identification. This sparks critical thinking and learning that matters. The learning experience in computer games becomes more effective because the student is immersed in the environment. The student can make mistakes without real consequences and is encouraged to keep on trying.
- **Situated meaning and learning**: Computer games are well suited for new forms of learning, in which one can interact with the game world through probing, choose different ways to learn and see things in a context. One can interact and challenge computer games and, over time, build up a more accurate understanding of an area.
- **Telling and doing**: Games can amplify areas and represent a subset of domains that one can practice. According to Gee, games also lend themselves well to transferring between domains. It is possible to transfer what one learns in computer games to other contexts.
- **Cultural models**: The content in games represents ways of perceiving the world and carries a lot of implicit information. This content also has a bearing on other domains of life and can contain both good and bad content, depending on one's values and norms.

Gee's contribution is currently one of the strongest in the field, but is also symptomatic of the area since he fails to really engage with earlier research and findings. This makes his theory weaker and supports the fragmentation of the field. To a large degree, Gee (2003) made up for these shortcomings by providing a strong grounding in educational theories. He made a case for a variety of strong mechanisms in computer games that facilitate learning and we will take a closer look at these, especially in Chapters 8 and 9. In these chapters, we dissect the concrete learning experience in the educational use of computer games.

KEY TOPICS IN THE RESEARCH AREA

The different approaches correspond to different areas of the educational experience in relation to computer games. The instructional technology perspective focuses on the role of motivation and is valuable for examining the narrow relationship between computer games and students. On a socio-cultural level, we appreciate and examine the environment that emerges around computer games for negotiating and constructing knowledge. Here, questions of collaboration, debriefing and discussion will be crucial to understand. For instance, how can we construct, mediate and support the knowledge acquired in relation to computer games?

The different research perspectives clearly have something to offer on different levels and although there may be some internal inconsistencies, we have covered the important areas of educational use of computer games. Most previous research, as we have seen, awarded prominence to one or two characteristics in educational use of computer games.

I have compiled some of the most consistent claims and documented the variation in researchers' assertions for educational use of computer games. These claims are that computer games can provide:

- Increased motivation
- More interest in a subject
- Simulations that present material differently
- A more open-ended approach to information
- Possibilities for interaction with information
- A well-known media form from everyday use
- A safe virtual play environment to experiment in
- More effective learning
- More challenge
- Students with more control
- A fantasy world that interests students
- Facilitation toward a flow experience
- Increased cognitive skills
- A new generation's way of thinking, scaffolding of learning
- Experience that improves learning
- Better transfer to other contexts than school
- Improved learning through construction in games
- More peer collaboration
- More student autonomy.

More importantly, I have also touched upon a number of central problems that reappear across different approaches to educational use of computer games. The most important discussions that have so far been established are the following:

- **Learning vs. playing**: The basic idea of educational computer games is to combine playing and learning and this never ceases to result in conflicts. It is increasingly suggested that it should be made explicit that a computer game is about learning a topic and that one should clarify what is expected to be the result. In line with this, the question of control arises. On one hand, player control is a critical characteristic in computer games stressed by all researchers, but it is also a fact that all findings show the benefit of guiding, supporting, scaffolding, introducing and debriefing the computer game experience. This risks taking control away from the player, especially in a classroom setting. Another question related to this is the fear of the implicit message we are sending by using computer games for learning: Learning is not worth sweating for and must always be fun.
- **Drill-and-practice games vs. microworlds**: All research shies away from a narrow focus on drill-and-practice games like that of edutainment, but when we look closer many researchers still indirectly assume that parts of the game have drill-and-practice elements that can transfer facts and support skills. This may be due to the problems encountered when designing a microworld. Microworld design has proven to be significantly harder than classic drill-and-practice games.
- **Teacher intervention vs. no teacher intervention**: It has consistently been found that teachers play an important role in facilitating educational use of computer games. They can steer the use in the right direction and provide an effective debriefing that can catch misperceptions and interesting differences in students' experiences while playing. This is neglected in edutainment titles, whereas it is central in the socio-cultural approach.
- **Transfer vs. construction**: From a first-generation position, the challenge of educational computer games is seen as simply transferring information from the computer game to the player. This has been somewhat successful but the use of this information in other contexts has been significantly harder to document. From a third-generation position, the simple transfer of information is not enough. One needs to facilitate situations in which players actively engage in the computer game and construct their own knowledge through the artifacts of the game world. When the player integrates knowledge into existing structures, it is also easier to transfer it between contexts.
- **Depth vs. superficiality**: Indirectly, the question of what kind of learning we are looking for is touched upon in several of the discussions. It seems obvious that superficial learning is negatively loaded, but this is what is encouraged by the still dominant drill-and-practice computer games. Bringing depth into use of educational computer games has proven to be a hard task as games are built on simple rules. We should look to the surrounding social context for facilitating a richer learning experience. Computer games may not deliver a lot of information, but they deliver

what the student can grasp and ensure that the information is richly supported. Other media may deliver more detailed information on a given topic, but that is of limited value if the students can only engage in a minor part.

• **One subject vs. cross-subjects**: Another general discussion concerns the cross-curricular nature of computer games. Most especially, commercial computer games can't be categorized into one subject. This makes it difficult to assess the real impact of computer games and to use them in school settings.

These insights are key and are later used to ground the course that serves as an example in this book.

LEARNING THEORIES ACROSS THE DIFFERENT AREAS

Until now, we haven't really talked about the different inherent learning theories that the themes above adhere to. In bits and pieces, I have presented learning theories like behaviourism, constructionism and the socio-cultural approach. But how do they link with broader developments in learning theories? I will make some generalizations below to show that a pattern emerges from the themes presented. Obviously, no area exclusively adheres to one specific learning theory like behaviourism, cognitivism or constructionism, but all of the areas have some kind of core. Figure 5.1 sketches some of the important links. The idea is to identify the views of different generations on the educational use of games, which entails the positioning of different learning theories, the historical progression evident in learning theories and the connection with the use of educational computer games.

The starting point is a focus on learning through changing the behaviour of students. Behaviourism is only interested in directly observable actions split into a stimuli and a response. The theory claims that one can learn by practising skills and contents through reinforcements and conditioning. There is little initial interest in differences between learners, settings and subject material. Through practice, one learns the correct response to a certain stimulus. The first generation perspective corresponds with the description of early edutainment that assumes that learning occurs when one unreflectively practises a skill enough times. Some edutainment titles try to differentiate between learners and take into account different ways of learning, which points towards second-generation educational games.

In the cognitivist approach, the learner becomes the centre of attention. The cognitivist approach criticizes the automatic relationship presented in behaviourism between stimulus and response. Cognitivist theorists see the focus on behaviour as skewed, neglecting other important variables, namely the cognitive structures underlying the responses. People have underlying

Figure 5.1: The different generations' characteristics and how they emphasize different learning theories

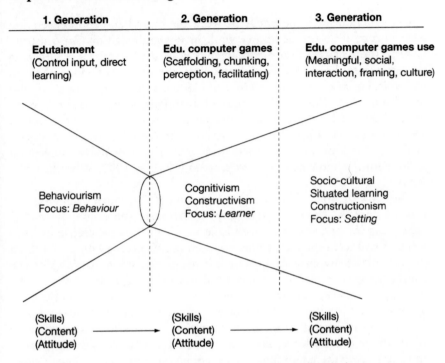

1. Generation	2. Generation	3. Generation
Edutainment (Control input, direct learning)	**Edu. computer games** (Scaffolding, chunking, perception, facilitating)	**Edu. computer games use** (Meaningful, social, interaction, framing, culture)
Behaviourism Focus: *Behaviour*	Cognitivism Constructivism Focus: *Learner*	Socio-cultural Situated learning Constructionism Focus: *Setting*
(Skills) (Content) (Attitude)	(Skills) (Content) (Attitude)	(Skills) (Content) (Attitude)

schemata that represent what has been learned. When students approach a new task, one needs to take into account that they have different schemata. These schemata make up limits and options for each learner that can be addressed by scaffolding information, chunking information, multimedia information and by presenting material in ways that correspond with cognitive abilities. There are limits to the information one can process, better ways to solve problems and different ways of perceiving information. I call this the second-generation approach in using computer games for educational purposes. In this approach, the aim is to build educational computer games that present information in ways that are appropriate to this specific learner and open up different ways of approaching the same topic. The multimedia experience is central for providing these different ways to a topic, and multimedia also supports the player's progression at his or her own speed and ability. Scaffolding information becomes even more central than in the previous generation. The second-generation perspective also differentiates itself from the first generation through its interest in meta-skill: problem-solving, analysing, perceiving, spatial ability, etc. The trend was apparent from the mid-1980s to the mid-1990s, when eye-hand coordination, problem-solving and other cognitive skills were heavily researched. It is still found in many educational computer games and in educators' preference for the problem-solving abilities that can be harvested from playing computer games.

Constructionism is the bridge between the second and third generation with a strong focus on the learner, while involving the setting. For constructionists, the artifacts in the environment can be used to mirror the learning processes from the outside. At the same time, the artifacts provide a platform for exploring new material, mostly from an individual perspective, but also in collaboration. This is further stressed in situated learning and the socio-cultural approach, in which the learning process is seen as mediated in a social context. In a social context, physical artifacts (or tools) are a good facilitator for learning new concepts, as they give a shared starting point and potentially show new ways to proceed (Wenger, 1999; Wertsch, 1991, 1998).

The construction of knowledge, as meaningful through orientation in a social context, becomes paramount in the third generation. Instead of conceiving content, skills and attitudes as residing within the user, knowledge is transferred to culture, tools and communities. Wenger (1999) talked about the interplay between participation and reification, where participants will continuously construct a community through the negotiation of meaning. To support this negotiation, reifications are constructed like school culture, agendas, conception of computer games, hi-score tables, etc. One learns new things by participating in these communities, appreciating and negotiating what counts as knowledge, skills and attitudes. It is worth stressing that in this perspective the educational use of computer games ties in much closer to the surrounding culture. When one uses computer games in schools, the students will draw on a variety of cultural capital to make this experience meaningful. This process is also reciprocal, as the renegotiation of computer games in schools will also lead to new cultural capital being generated, which is useful outside of school. Concretely, this could be introducing computer games as a broader phenomenon than merely action games, or changing attitudes towards computer games. Computer games might actually be something else than just fun.

The third-generation approach doesn't exclusively focus on the specific computer game, but looks at the broader process of educational use of computer games. It stresses the key role of providing a social context that facilitates asking the right questions and going to the right places. Here the teacher becomes central as a facilitator to balance the educational computer game experience as connected to school and other practices, and drawing on other practices to expand the scope of the computer game from 'just playing' to learning.

It should be stressed that each generation is carried forward to the next, but de-emphasized. The learning mechanisms in behaviourism are still partly at play in next-generation titles, and so are the ones from cognitivism, but they are conceived in a broader, overall frame. They will be more or less adequate for explaining different aspects of learning. For example, a socio-cultural approach will have less to say about a student sitting at home playing an educational computer game. In that situation, it would be relevant to look at the interaction between computer game and learner from a more individualistic perspective, like behaviourism or cognitivism.

CONCLUSION: THE NECESSITY OF A BROAD LEARNING APPROACH

The discussion above highlights the need for a broad learning approach to computer games consisting of several layers. We need to appreciate how content, skills and attitudes are not just transferable and a question of interaction between player and computer game. On the other hand, this interaction may very well be severely limited by the concrete implementation of the computer games. An active, interested and strong community that thinks of computer games as its preferred way to learn history will not get very far if the computer game does not scaffold information, has a problematic interface, presumes existing knowledge that is not easily found and bombards the students with overwhelming amounts of information. It will certainly also play a role with the basic reward structure, habituation and connecting experience in time. Students will be steered in directions by being awarded points, getting a high score and beating other players. Students will learn that 'sword' refers to the object sword every time they pick up a sword object with text below it. And they will slowly be less impressed by what this specific educational computer game has to offer them. An inclusive educational understanding is necessary to grasp the full scope of educational use of computer games.

With a preliminary knowledge of how to understand educational use of computer games, we will expand on this perspective in building the third generation. An important element is a discussion of the relevant educational theories, which is the topic of the next chapter.

6

An Initial Educational Framework

What we want is to see the child in pursuit of knowledge, and not knowledge in pursuit of the child.

George Bernard Shaw

So far, we have covered a lot of ground, hopefully gaining a fuller knowledge of the elements necessary to understand educational use of computer games. The framework built in this chapter relates to the third-generation perspective presented in the previous chapter as an alternative to the dominating form of edutainment.

To achieve a more inclusive understanding of educational use of computer games, important theory in respect to knowing, learning, teaching, education, computer medium and computer games is presented. The starting point is experiential learning with a strong focus on concrete experiences, which will serve as the framework of this book's later empirical and theoretical work. Building such a framework entails the introduction of the key concepts: engagement, play, relevance, experience-based, student autonomy, and representation.

It is concluded that experiential learning with its focus on experience is a good starting point to achieve a more inclusive perspective on the learning activity, involving player, computer game and context. Building on Vygotsky, concrete experiences may often be organized haphazardly in spontaneous concepts, but through instruction, scientific concepts can be built. Scientific concepts are what constitute more abstract concepts and thinking, which is central to education. Computer games are potentially a valuable tool for providing the necessary concrete experiences for building strong scientific concepts through their rich universe, engaging nature and dynamic presentation of information, but instruction is needed to facilitate educational relevance in the concepts.

DIFFERENT KINDS OF KNOWING: COMPUTATIONAL VIEW AND CULTURALISM

Experiential learning provides an understanding of the *process of learning* but is less interested in the *outcome of learning* and sees knowing as in flux. However, education has an explicit outcome and, to some degree, works with knowing as a finite size – we have a fixed curriculum that we attempt to hand down to new generations. Before turning to experiential learning, I will therefore discuss two views on knowing based on Jerome Bruner's thoughts: computational view and culturalism. I will argue that it doesn't make much sense to grant exclusivity to one at the expense of the other. But depending on one's purpose, one can of course shift the weight between them, as I will do in this book. Distinguishing between culturalism and the computational view will support an inclusive educational understanding.

The nature of knowing

As was hinted in the previous chapter, the different generations within educational use of computer games speak of different kinds of knowing, but what is understood by knowing? I can know a list of kings by heart (content), be able to use a mouse (skill) or know that I shouldn't drive too fast (attitude). All of these things are ultimately the result of learning and relate to different types of knowing that I have earlier introduced: content, skills and attitudes. However, we can approach the form of this knowing from two sides, facilitated by a split between information and knowledge. This split was recognized by Bruner (1996) when he wrote about different kinds of knowing, distinguishing between the computational view and culturalism.

The computational view operates with information that can be stored, retrieved and transferred between individuals. Information is conceived as a fixed size that does not change as we move between contexts. Bateson (1972) talked about information as the difference that makes a difference. When we draw a map, we choose to promote certain differences and although the map is open to interpretation, it does set some affordances for how we as humans read the map. One map will focus on the national differences, another on religious differences and a third on the terrain differences. The map provides a form of knowing that is finite and in principle transferable across time and space. From the computational view, to put it bluntly, we can actually ask any student where France is and expect the same fixed answer across time and space. In principle, information denotes any of the above types of learning (content, skills and attitudes); I can tell you about the kings, show you how to move the mouse and tell you that speeding is wrong. The information can be transferred between individuals and contexts.

Bruner (1996) was initially somewhat disapproving of this perspective, which has its roots back at the start of the twentieth century with instructional theory, which was discussed earlier and is also apparent in Bloom's taxonomy. He doesn't see the computational view as offering a great many tools for teachers to improve the learning process. To check whether students know facts about France is hardly helpful for improving learning or teaching. We can tell 30 students in a classroom about France, and afterwards some are able to answer correctly that France is a republic whereas others aren't. However, the why seems to escape us. It is also unclear whether they really understand where France is, or if they have merely memorized the explanation the teacher gave. Still, Bruner found that each kind of knowing offers a relevant perspective for approaching knowing and describing different properties. The computational view, to a certain extent, regards knowing as in a vacuum, and this is helpful if we are to generalize across contexts. It may not really be sensible to talk about humans as acquiring information but it is quite helpful when pointing to artifacts, tools, environments and shared spaces that can be used to facilitate learning including computer games. Any of these will in an abstract sense have some differences since we as humans are likely to find relevant differences through our cognitive apparatus, heritage and socialization. However, there is more to knowing than information.

For culturalism, which grew out of constructivism, meaning is central to understanding information. Understanding the differences that make a difference requires human perception, ultimately resulting in understanding a piece of information. The process of seeing the difference is one of linking pieces across different contexts by drawing on previous experiences. From the perspective of culturalism, information is constructed from a given individual's perspective in a specific situation, drawing upon previous experiences. An individual will, in a learning process, approach a given area by drawing on cultural artifacts (including media) and in this process transform information into something meaningful from his or her position. This denotes knowledge. From this perspective, knowing requires that a student actively engages in constructing the knowledge. The student acknowledges the right differences and is able to understand the differences by drawing upon previous experiences, concepts and narratives. Bruner (1996) tried to reconcile the two positions, but I do not find his compromise entirely appropriate for my purpose.

Instead, I will suggest that these two perspectives point to different forms of knowing. The computational view talks about information detached from individuals as an outcome, whereas culturalism addresses knowledge attached to a situated individual involved in a process. We must be careful not to grant exclusivity to one at the expense of the other, which is what I described as one of the problems with edutainment in the previous chapter. Edutainment assumes a computational view, forgetting how the information is put in play. From culturalism's perspective, knowing is personal, meaningful and constructed in connection to more or less generalizable situations, often by using artifacts in a given context. The artifacts, including computer games, set a number of differences, resulting in affordances for the human cognitive apparatus. In some sense, it is actually possible for knowing to travel across contexts and individuals as information. This implies that we are capable of transforming knowledge into information and information into knowledge. We do this constantly and with little thought, unless it causes misunderstandings or problems.

Consider the following example that illustrates the two views concerning students playing a historical computer game: 'Napoleon led the French forces at Waterloo in 1815.' This seems to be a straightforward 'bite' of information that could be part of a curriculum. When one presents this in a school class, it will, however, take on a number of alternative meanings, although as Bruner (1996) stressed, limited by a variety of general constraints in our cognitive apparatus (e.g. language and human evolution). However, students may have very different backgrounds that will make this sentence meaningful. One may not know Napoleon and take him to be a random general. Another might be well versed in the Napoleonic wars and connect this statement with Napoleon's final defeat after re-emerging as emperor from his imprisonment at Elba. Both interpretations result in learning something. For one student, it will support his or her perception of history in the Napoleonic era, while another will gain some factual knowledge of this general called Napoleon. Both of them will know the same piece of information, but the implications and meaning of the information are different – the students' knowledge differs from the information.

The information in the specific sentence leads to different constructions of knowledge based on background, context and skills that will change over time. Thus, students transform information into something meaningful for them at a given time. This something is knowledge. The important implication of this is that we construct knowledge based on earlier presuppositions and our context. However, it also acknowledges that if a finite amount of information concerning a topic is presented in a computer game, the quality and scope of this information is an important variable in the learner's construction of knowledge. It is also worth stressing that the meaning-making of a given piece of information is bound by a number of affordances that support the process of learning (Bruner, 1996; Jonassen, 2001).

Information can also serve as an indicator of learning outcome, although it may be a problematic abstraction to neglect the process the information is layered into. Mostly, when one evaluates a given course, one will focus on the information as a finite size and neglect the knowledge of the student. Evaluation becomes increasingly problematic the further one moves from information to knowledge, implying that the student is generating the knowledge. There is a difference in knowing by reading a textbook on history with the right answers and playing a computer game. In the computer game, the student has to construct the right answers based on actions, consequences and feedback from the computer game, whereas the textbook to a large extent provides a ready-made package. With the reading of a textbook, the student risks memorizing information with few handles for actually using this knowledge at a later time. Computer game experiences, in contrast to the textbook experiences, provide more handles, as one builds concepts through actions, providing a richer contextualization (Schank, 1999). The unfinished state of the potential concepts offered from the game experience also insist on the player's reflection and thought whereas the textbook offers a nice and neatly packed package of the 'right' concepts.

In summary, I will operate with the concepts *information* (computational view) and *knowledge* (culturalism) to describe different forms of knowing. A narrow focus on information lends itself to a first-generation perspective on educational use of computer games, where behaviourism is central. My approach will rather build on the third generation perspective outlined in the previous chapter with an inclusive understanding of learning. In my perspective, the computational view and culturalism are both important to include when approaching educational use of computer games. The computational view points to the potential of a given activity, whereas culturalism points to the actual realization of this potential.

A computer game, textbook or historical city walk will present some differences in the world, but these differences need to be appreciated, explored and linked in a meaningful way, not merely glossed over or memorized. Next, the process of appreciating, exploring and linking the differences in the world is at the centre of the scene.

AN EXPERIENTIAL APPROACH TO LEARNING

Experiential learning offers an alternative to more traditional understandings of how we in school come to appreciate the differences that make a difference by refining concrete experiences. Computer games are well suited to support the focus on the concrete experience as an activity where players are engaged in doing things. Students playing a computer game will point and click, resulting in concrete experiences that are then refined. In the following, we will look more closely at this process of refinement.

The experiential approach to learning is not a close-knit theoretical system, but consists of a number of theorists with a shared focus on the importance of experience in any learning situation. The lack of experience-based learning is evident in the educational system when we consider history, geography, citizenship or religion. We are not actually basing the learning in school on concrete experiences with a given topic, but are primarily relying on students reading or hearing about topics mostly represented by abstract information and concepts with little connection to an actual experience base. This is not a criticism of reading or hearing, as these are strong teaching tools, but rather a challenge of the balance between these and other approaches in education.

The educational system seems to entertain the fantasy that we can skip the concrete experiences altogether. Instead, it favours reading and hearing about abstract concepts, exclusively reasoning based on these abstract concepts. The experiential learning approach challenges this as a viable path by insisting that learning extends from concrete experiences and that the experiences of students themselves are brought to the centre of the scene. We find that in some subjects sole reliance on abstract concepts is challenged, such as in the case when history teachers want to tell what is referred to as the small history. This relates to the history of everyday life from the perspective of those that lived during a certain period.

The strongest proponents of experiential learning are Kolb, Dewey, Piaget, Lewin and Freire, who were all in some ways opposing the educational system of their times. I will start with Kolb's account in the following because he tried to integrate the different approaches. According to Kolb (1984), experiential learning theorists share a range of assumptions about learning:

- Learning is about *constructing* knowledge, not transmitting it.
- Learning should focus on the *process* and *feedback*, not so much the outcome.
- Learning should build on students' *existing knowledge* about a given topic and expand this understanding.
- Learning is fuelled by conflict between *different perspectives* on the world: action, reflection, feeling and thinking.
- Learning is an *interaction* between individual and surroundings.

(Kolb and Kolb, 2003)

We will adopt these assumptions, stressing that they represent culturalism. That remains fruitful for this book's focus, while at the same time remembering that the computational view is also a valid perspective.

The experiential learning approach has, over the years, worked with a learning cycle to stress the hermeneutic nature of learning. Kolb's theory evolves around learning through a four-staged cycle, which historically has roots in similar models by Dewey and Lewin. The model caters for different learning modes, and attempts to present the flow in learning experiences. Different learning modes create a tension that pushes knowledge forward and, in principle, takes the learner through all four modes. The concrete experience is the basis for the observations and reflections. The reflections transform experiences into abstract concepts, inspiring new forms of actions. The experiences from the new actions are then tested and reflected, creating new concrete experiences. The process is then repeated. One would never completely grasp a given area or experience, but continuously explore, closing in on it in a hermeneutic process (Kolb and Kolb, 2003).

I will not use the expanded terminology of Kolb, but merely the basic structure outlined above to explain the dynamics of learning that may

Figure 6.1: The backbone of experiential learning theory that extends from a circular understanding of learning (Kolb, 1984)

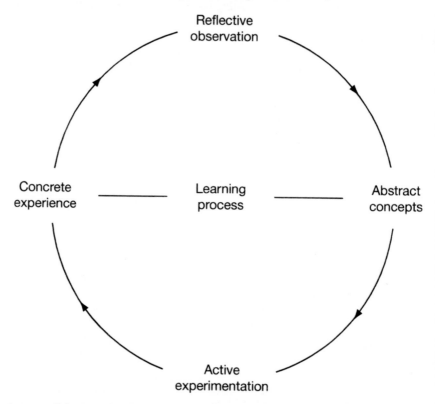

be transferred with relevance to the educational use of computer games. Experiential learning does not convincingly argue for what drives the learning process forward through the cycle (see Figure 6.1). Drawing on Kelly (1963), I find that humans are constantly exploring their surroundings. Kelly (1963) stressed that the individual is constantly testing and exploring the surrounding world to maintain an adequate perception so that he can act appropriately in a given situation. The basic metaphor and starting point for Kelly is man-as-scientist. He stated that:

> Might not the individual man, each in his own personal way, assume more of the stature of a scientist, ever seeking to predict and control the course of events with which he is involved. Would he not have his theories, test his hypotheses and weigh his experimental evidence.
>
> Kelly (1963: 5)

This continuing exploration of the surroundings and testing of concepts is impeded by the threat of damage to our perception of the world that can result from the alteration of subordinate concepts (Kelly, 1963). Thus, we are constantly interested in getting a fuller understanding of the world around us, by exploring our experiences while constructing new knowledge, but are held back by the risks associated with new insights. Education is such a safe place, and as we will see later, likewise is play.

Experience and education

Dewey is one of the first proponents for changing school so that it aligns itself better with students' capacity for drawing on their experiences from all spheres of life and through their natural curiosity for exploring the surroundings. Ultimately, this is based on a wish to increase interest and motivation, leading to improved learning by linking learning to students' existing concepts and experiences while making knowledge from school accessible in other contexts.

The critique of schooling has increased as the educational system fails to make students capable of actually using their education in everyday contexts. We should remember that 'ultimately' education is merely a subset of learning, namely a planned learning experience facilitated by a teacher. In this sense, education must be seen as an attempted socialization of a new generation that can be described in a double perspective: differentiation and qualification (Ljungstrøm, 1984). The basic goal of the educational system remains one of putting students into the right boxes, while providing them with the proper, necessary knowledge to survive in these boxes. This double perspective has often resulted in a detached educational system, in which students are taken out of their everyday context in order to qualify and differentiate them. On graduation, they are inserted back into society in the right places.

The problem of detachment from everyday life was built into the educational system during the formative eighteenth century as a natural consequence of differentiation and qualification. Arguably, students have always experienced the detachment of the school and failed to see the relevance of learning the finer details of algebra, the American Civil War or German grammar, which is certainly far from their everyday life. However, it now makes more of a difference with the changed view on the student role in education. Earlier, the necessary education was handed down to new generations through authorities that have now been weakened. The lack of authorities makes it hard to maintain the automatic acceptance of the curriculum. The perceived relevance among students, therefore, becomes increasingly important (Egenfeldt-Nielsen, 2001).

It has, therefore, been attempted to put these abstract concepts into everyday contexts or links to the student's everyday life. For instance, a mathematics question could be: if you have two bananas and Karen gives you five bananas, how many bananas do you have? This approach builds on Dewey's educational philosophy and Dewey's theorizing will benefit the framework for educational use of computer games. In this framework, concrete experiences are central.

The role of experience

The role of concrete experience in Kolb's cycle is seductively simple, but also quite vague. It is unclear what makes up an experience, but Dewey sheds some light on the concept. According to Dewey (1910), experience is the interaction between humans and their environment, including thinking, feeling, seeing, handling and doing. Experiences are equally present whether we are in a real or artificial universe, on the savannah, in the classroom or in the game universe. In today's computer games, the player is part of a living, breathing, simulated universe with very concrete self-sustaining experiences. It's getting still closer to reality. This is not just in the audiovisual dimensions, but also in the actions in which you engage. In most games the abstraction of chess is gone, and more concrete actions like shooting, driving, picking up and opening doors have replaced it.

What we do, see, feel or think constitutes an experience in any of these places. Dewey also elaborated on education's insistence on starting from the concrete experience and going to the abstract. He stressed that the concrete should not be confused with a detachment from thinking or a prominence on manual work. Rather, he remarked, 'Concrete denoted a meaning definitely marked off from other meanings so that it is readily apprehended by itself' (Dewey, 1910: 136). From the concrete, we make links to other similar experiences, building concepts to group concrete experiences. This suggests that we should start education from experiences that do not assume a number of links are already in place. The concrete experiences can be seen as objects like stones, houses or trees that through internalization become natural to us. The player may not get the full scope of a game situation, but will be able to explore it further within the universe and understand it without reference to abstract concepts outside the game universe. The concreteness of computer games doesn't imply that they lack referentiality, but the referentiality is less of a prerequisite for understanding computer games compared to the abstract concepts delivered through textbooks.

Experiences should not really be thought of in an atomistic sense but rather as a continuum, that is, experiences do not exist in a vacuum in respect to either surroundings or previous experience.[1] However, they can be understood without reference to other concepts. A history teacher explaining the concept of mercantilism will inevitably make a number of assumptions on behalf of the students in terms of existing experiences and concepts. This poses few problems if these assumptions are actually part of students' experience base. However, the assumptions often match the teacher's background and not the students' experience base. Furthermore, the experience bases that are referred to are not easily accessible to the students.

The continuity of experience is the key to Dewey's (1938) thinking. Current experiences will take something from earlier experiences and channel later experiences. In this perspective, education becomes a beacon in people's learning environment that can guide them in the right direction by helping them to appreciate, explore and focus on certain aspects in their future experiences. Dewey (1938) stressed that the experiences do not exist in a vacuum and that experiences are formed as an interaction between internal and external conditions.

> Above all they [teachers] should know how to utilize the surroundings, physical and social, that exist so as to extract from them all that they have to contribute to building up experiences that are worthwhile.
>
> (Dewey, 1938: 40)

From Dewey's point of view, education should rest on experience, but all experiences are not necessarily educational. Dewey (1938) stressed that education tries to facilitate certain approaches to different areas in correspondence with the educator's goals (often set up by a curriculum). The educational value ultimately rests on the 'quality of the experience'. First of all, the quality is decided by whether it is immediately agreeable to the student, which decides whether the student will engage with the experience. This will depend on the student's ability to connect educational experience with previous or future experience. When a computer game gets started, it incessantly builds on previous experiences and instils anticipation in the student that learning something now is useful later in the game. Second, some experiences may limit a student's further progress by changing the student's view on a topic or the process of learning in general. Experiences of a high educational quality will on the other hand have a benign effect on future learning processes in general and open the student's mind to other educational experiences. Playing a historical strategy game focusing on war might educate the student in some aspects of history, but may also limit the possibility of helping the student appreciate broader concepts of history beyond war.

In summary, Dewey focused on educational experiences as characterized by closeness to student experiences and engaging students while promoting future capacity for learning in general and opening up for additional educational experiences. This provides a strong sense of relevance and willingness to engage with a given topic. The student's initial engagement can be thought of as an investment in the object under investigation that pushes learning beyond the initial exploration. We continuously invest in a topic linking our understanding of the world, our experiences and concepts to a given topic. This will sustain our interest, allowing us to further expand our knowledge of a field, but also make us dependent on our knowing within this topic. We build the relation through exploration of the object over time.[2]

Scientific and spontaneous concepts

So far, I have concentrated on the concrete experience in the learning process, but next I extend the framework by elaborating on the role of concepts. The goal is to understand the difference between concepts learned through education and concepts that emerge more spontaneously in any setting. More specifically, I am aiming at the difference between playing a computer game with or without instruction. The concepts formed by education have some advantages that should be considered when using computer games in an educational setting. Vygotsky's (1986) differentiation between scientific concepts and spontaneous concepts is in that connection useful.

Vygotsky's two concepts (1986) describe different ways of organizing and approaching knowledge. The term spontaneous concepts refers to concepts that emerge from the bottom-up – the spontaneous ordering of experiences. The spontaneous concepts are not systematic and often not conscious, but still used to group experiences. Scientific concepts are in comparison top-down, brought about by teaching and instruction. Scientific concepts make the student capable of higher mental functioning and are characterized by being systematic, general, abstract and organized. The scientific concepts are not possible without an experience base that gives the scientific concepts the concrete experiences to build the organization upon. With no experience base to build the scientific concepts, students will merely learn 'parrot-like repetition'. To a large degree, the strength of a concept lies in drawing on concrete experiences, although over time, the concept (as more experiences support the concept) will lose the connections with concrete experiences and maintain only the general characteristics. However, the concept will still be able to activate the experiences under different circumstances, depending on the structuring of experiences and concepts (Schank, 1999). The important point is that it is not hard to teach a student the word mercantilism or to give some rudimentary understanding of it relating to trade. However, the underlying concept is hard to learn if the student has no experiences from which to build the concept and, in particular, the transfer to other situations becomes hard (Schank, 1999; Vygotsky, 1986). This is an increasing problem as school moves further away from society and as the scientific concepts become more abstract and difficult to relate to the experiences of students (Højholt and Witt, 1996). The top-down approach of scientific concepts doesn't imply a direct transfer of concept from teacher to student. Vygotsky (1986) stressed that although scientific concepts are verbal, abstract and systematic, they are still constructed by the student's link to previous experiences and concepts (both spontaneous and scientific). It should be stressed that one of the concepts does not have supremacy over the other as they both serve important purposes. Vygotsky found scientific concepts usually to be ahead of spontaneous concepts if instruction is appropriately based on an experience base.

These observations are clearly relevant to educational use of computer games, where one may downgrade the teacher's instruction by letting the experience in the game universe take primacy. This will parallel Dewey's (1938) warning against letting the progressive school (experience-based) lose sight of the teacher's responsibility to guide and extrapolate the essence from experiences. Students will, of course, acquire a number of experiences immersed in the game universe, but these will primarily be ordered as spontaneous concepts and not scientific concepts that can help students see the experiences in a broader perspective and link them to other related insights within the topic. Indeed, left with spontaneous concepts, due to their 'unconscious nature' students may feel that they haven't learned anything. They may also believe that they are learning many things, but these will on closer examination be hard to take beyond the game universe. In particular, the linking with other scientific concepts learned through instruction will be hard to connect to the spontaneous concepts. Some random spontaneous concepts risk becoming the only result from using computer games without proper instruction and teaching. This is the case seen in the previous chapter with edutainment, which mostly existed in an instructional vacuum. Edutainment may reinforce some links but not add new links. It's training rather than learning.

Dewey (1938) cautioned us that often school works opposite Vygotsky's implicit intention by 'forcing' the scientific concepts upon the students, who lack the experience base to provide the substance to the concepts. Instead of transforming student experiences into scientific concepts, the 'parrot-like' approach is dominating with scientific concepts being empty vessels. Figure 6.2 is an elaboration of the abstract concepts in the basic experiential learning model. The abstract concepts come closest to being a learning outcome that can have two different forms arising spontaneously through actions (sponta-

Figure 6.2: A summary of the connection between experience, learning, instruction, concepts and knowledge

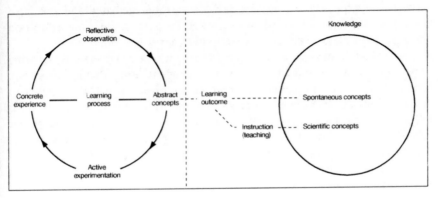

neous concepts) or facilitated through instruction (scientific concepts). The exact theoretical underpinnings of instruction lie beyond this book, but scaffolding is too central in educational use of computer games to be ignored. The potential scaffolding of computer games, as we saw in Chapter 4, has often been stressed by researchers. The zone of proximal development is relevant to understanding the broader potential of scaffolding in educational use of computer games.

In the Introduction, I was initially careful not to conceive teaching and instruction as linked to school and even to education. Teaching is on an overall level best conceived in relation to Vygotsky's (1986) zone of proximal development. This theory is originally aimed at children and parents, but is also relevant for teachers. The theory basically describes the difference between the actual and potential zone of development. The actual zone is the development a child or student can achieve by himself, whereas the potential zone is the development achievable with the help of a parent or some kind of tool. The potential zone of development is achieved by pointing out key elements, reducing complexity or correcting mistakes.

Wertsch (1991) expanded on the nature such instruction can take and found that a number of tools can also serve this role. Tools are quite broadly perceived and include languages, books, hammers and theoretical works, and one can expand this to computer games. In the following, I will expand on how we can conceive of tools in education to understand the potential scaffolding in educational use of computer games. This is central since a computer game can be seen as a tool that mediates the student's approach to a given topic.

The socio-cultural approach: tools, activity and context

The socio-cultural approach focuses on learning as an activity and includes a closer examination of tools as mediating activities. Furthermore, the socio-cultural approach combined with situated learning can include context, culture and history that is not explicitly included in experiential learning theory. The work by theorists like Wertsch, Vygotsky, Lave and Wenger is especially useful. The differentiation between non-mediated and mediated experiences is important when we want to understand how education changes with the introduction of computer games as a tool.

Computer games as a tool extend the action of a given agent by creating both opportunities and limitations for the agent using them. An activity consists of a relation between a subject and an object, which is mediated by a tool. Tools can be a variety of artifacts found in our social and cultural life that endow us with a variety of opportunities. When we use language, we are drawing on a symbolic tool refined through generations. This implies that reading, hearing or writing are experiences that use the symbolic tool language. Language is thick with culture and history, making it useful for a variety of purposes. The same is true when using stories, documentaries, textbooks, blackboards, pencils, calculators, computer games or any other artifact, although few have the extensive range and plasticity of language (Oliver and Pelletier, 2004; Vygotsky, 1986; Wertsch, 1991, 1998). The socio-cultural perspective alerts us to the importance of considering tools and context when thinking about learning and education. Different contexts and tools facilitate a variety of learning experiences, which are also the starting point for situated learning.

Situated learning insists that to learn is ultimately to become part of a community of praxis. A community of praxis is a somewhat fuzzy term. Wenger goes through great lengths to encircle the characteristics of a community of praxis. The central constitutions of a community of praxis are mutual engagement, joint enterprise and a shared repertoire. The mutual engagement refers to a shared commitment latent in relations toward a given activity. It is not enough to merely be physically located together or be interested in the same topic. The engagement has to be connected in a rich and meaningful way (Wenger, 1999). The increasing engagement in a given community of praxis points in the direction of how to speak, act, think, etc. to ultimately what is important and what is not. In that sense, knowledge becomes socially distributed, not existing inside people, but in their connections, shared artifacts and joint activities. People gain what Wenger called a shared repertoire around certain activities. Knowledge is continuously produced and reproduced through everyday praxis. 'This focus in turn promotes a view of knowing as an activity by specific people in specific circumstances' (Lave and Wenger, 1991: 52). Remembering my initial differentiation between computational view and culturalism, here is a clear example of knowing from a culturalism point of view.

Knowing and transfer

Situated learning has levelled a hard criticism against the assumed transfer of information as it finds that information does not really become part of everyday life. Information is not part of the repertoire we use to engage joint enterprises but remains detached and foreign. From a situated learning perspective, we should see real knowing as grounded in a context. The generalization from a given situation and the forming of spontaneous or scientific concepts doesn't ensure that one can use these concepts in all situations. One would have to be able to fit the concepts within a new specific situation (Lave and Wenger, 1991). A radical interpretation of this theory may conclude that we are not capable of transferring knowledge between different communities and contexts. However, this doesn't seem to be the intention behind situated learning. Lave and Wenger (1991), nevertheless, showed that the transfer is very hard and that we should consciously think about creating links between different situations.[3] This is an approach supported by most modern educational thinking (e.g. Bransford et al., 1999; Schank, 1999). To simply learn the facts and knowledge of a given topic is not enough. One would need to apply knowledge to one's own life. In that sense, situated learning is also sceptical toward current schooling practice and sole reliance on language for learning. In school, knowledge is not connected to the existing practice of students and is often limited to being experienced through language providing few handles for using the knowledge in other contexts.

When we talk of transfer, there is constant debate between the situated learning tradition and the cognitive learning tradition. Initially, these two perspectives differ in where they locate knowledge – fixed in the individual (computational) or fluid in the context (culturalism). From a cognitive learning perspective, individuals acquire knowledge that they can bring with them to different contexts. The problem from a cognitive perspective is that the transfer of a learning task and closely related task is often very low. This is usually put down to our limited knowledge about instructional theory and improvements to learning methods are seen as the way forward (Döpping, 1995).

Situated learning is more focused on how knowledge seems to be a part of our everyday praxis and hence bound to the contexts we engage in. The student fails to generalize from one context to a broader application. It is not integrated into the student's existing knowledge structures and is only understood in a quite inflexible way. An analogy to Plato's famous horse example may prove the point. Plato tried to prove the existence of the idea world by pointing to the fact that we can recognize a horse as a horse despite the lack of a large amount of its defining attributes. We still know it is a horse even if one cuts off two legs or takes away its mane. According to Plato, this proves that we have an idea about the horse that enables us to recognize it despite any immediate shortcomings in physical attributes. However, from my perspective, the reason why we can recognize the horse is not because of the invisible idea world, but rather because the horse is integrated in a variety of ways in our minds through numerous experiences. This makes it possible for us to generalize from a given set of characteristics to the horse in full. We have the concept of a horse and a number of concrete experiences we can compare with when we see the horse. By experiencing a number of horses, we increasingly appreciate the differences that make a difference and are able to ignore the missing legs or mane in the example above.

The discussions above show that we should be careful with our assumptions about how students approach a given computer game. They may very well misperceive information in a computer game and construct limited knowledge of a given area. Constructions may depend on context and slowly change as experiences are connected with more experiences. Ultimately, we will have a very hard time actually measuring the educational benefits from game experience because we focus on the outcome while neglecting the continuous process involved. We may especially be trapped if we insist on using traditional ways of measuring learning outcome like factual tests. These factual tests insist on peeling off the layers that according to culturalism make up knowledge. Instead, we should apply methods that are sensitive to both culturalism and the computational view. This is attempted in the later discussed course with a computer game that serves as an explanatory example.

Language and everyday experiences

Often, we will encounter a reliance on language as *the* tool to teach new generations the necessary content, skills and attitudes to become part of society. We certainly have a preference for lectures, group discussions, blackboards and textbooks that lie quite far from the situations in which we are actually expected to make use of many years of schooling. When we observe the development of children, this approach is not used. Instead, different modalities are coupled to guide children: pointing, telling, smiling and showing (Gleitman, 1995; Wertsch, 1998). Preference for language is especially visible in the formulation of curricula and in the forms of assessment chosen to evaluate students as discussed above. We may go on field trips, set up workshops or other experimental set-ups, but mostly, we will not consider it valid assessment. For assessment, we count on multiple-choice tests or essays. The prominence of language is not surprising as it presents one of the most powerful symbolic tools for sharing and transforming experiences. However, language is not *the* experience, but rather a tool for manipulating the narratives that represent our experiences (Bruner, 1991). One must therefore be careful when using language as a tool for assessing learning outcome.

Although language is an intrinsic quality of many experiences, there is a qualitative difference between experiences that promote exclusivity to language and ones where language is used to extend the experience. We should, of course, not remove language from the educational setting, which would be an impossible and absurd endeavour. However, we should consider what the limitations are of the current prominence awarded language. Language tends to promote the general principles, as it is a tool for generalizing and ordering our world. In particular, language is also a tool for manipulating and transforming experiences, but not necessarily for having experiences (Bruner, 1991). Of course, when we read or hear something we are using language as a tool, but the language is never *the* experience. When we return to the difference between spontaneous concepts and scientific concepts, we realize that the latter relies heavily on language. Scientific concepts are possible because we can use language to order, share, structure and generalize from experience. Language is the first choice for describing, presenting, analyzing and discussing scientific concepts. However, one needs to build upon some experience base and this is often lacking in education. In this instance, computer games may be a way to provide concrete experiences in areas that are otherwise hard. Students can immerse themselves into urban planning in *SimCity*, see the evolution of civilization in *Civilization* and experience medieval Europe in *Europa Universalis*.

It is a problem if scientific concepts lack grounding in experiences. We should challenge the notion that most students' experience base in relation to school consists more of scientific concepts than concrete experiences. A teacher will present the scientific concepts that group together history, geography or political systems. However, in many cases there will be little time for more concrete experiences that lack the abstraction, generality and orderliness of scientific concepts. For a teacher, it is natural to present the scientific concepts (often coupled with spontaneous concepts), as this is the teacher's understanding of the field – *la crème de la crème*. However, without grounding in more concrete experiences, whether in school or anywhere else, students' understanding of a given concept will often be limited, superficial and external. This is, of course, ever more problematic if school is alienated from student everyday experiences, which almost seems to be the natural state of educational systems. School is always accused of trailing behind the real society, which is actually quite natural if built on scientific concepts. Scientific concepts need time to be built and formulated and there is a natural sluggishness between generations of teachers, each having their canon with them when graduating from various teachers' colleges. Scientific concepts are a strong tool for facilitating education, but they require an experience base with the students.

The problem of up-to-date scientific concepts is, however, less important than the overwhelming stream of scientific concepts bombarding students. The constant stream of information from lectures, textbooks and talks does not reach students who lack the reason, time and means to invest the necessary energy. The educational experience lacks cracks, roughness, richness, variation, relevance and presence. The redundancy and details found in many concrete experiences may provide just that spark necessary for one particular student to connect with for developing a meaningful scientific concept. The educational system is so pressed to present an ever-increasing curriculum that it disregards the importance of instilling the necessary richness in a student's experience base and ensuring that there actually is a foundation to build upon, which is increasingly considered the significant difference between novices and experts (Bransford et al., 1999).[4]

This is ultimately a question of prioritization in the educational system that is avoided due to its political sensibility. The educational system can't maintain the same breadth in the curriculum if the curriculum actually has to be learned. The breadth requires that some areas are in practice prioritized quite low. The cracks and roughness that language-mediated experiences are deprived of are found in deeper experiences, like computer games that involve students with seeing, doing, perceiving, feeling and thinking. These experiences are fuzzier than a well-defined scientific concept, but provide the important glue and examples for the more abstract concepts. One needs to be able to connect abstract utterances with some more concrete experiences. One needs a rich amount of experiences to generalize from and experiences that can work as metaphors for larger concepts.

The practical problem is that many of the topics in school are quite difficult to get rich experience from, e.g. slavery, civil wars, national depressions or foreign countries. Topics connected to citizenship (social studies) are especially hard to make relevant and experience-based within the current physical limitations and financial realities. Inspecting the trenches in the First World War, feeling the depression of the 1930s or even getting a feel for the current political system in a country are not within the reach of most schools, excluding perhaps the classic field trip to parliament that may give a rudimentary understanding of a political system. Field trips are a popular alternative, but present a lot of practical problems. They are only applicable for a limited number of activities and field trips don't necessarily let the students engage in relevant experiences per se; visiting the White House does not necessarily bring a lot of concrete experiences with the political system. There have been some attempts at making a parallel political system resembling current political systems with quite a bit of success for the few participants (both in real-life and through computer games).

In physics and chemistry, experimental set-ups are another popular way to give students some concrete experience with the quite abstract scientific concepts that make up these fields. However, we do not necessarily have to be physically present to explore a given activity. The insistence on concrete experiences is not necessarily tied to first-hand experience located in a physical environment. First, one can attempt to put the student's everyday experiences at the centre of the learning process, thereby strengthening the links of scientific concepts with the student's existing experience, with the added benefit of strengthening the transfer of knowledge between school and everyday life. Second, one can engage students in activities that are not approaching a topic top-down, but bottom-up. This can be a role play of everyday life in a medieval village or an exploration of the role of horses through history. This is a concrete experience less abstract than traditional teaching. The point I have been aiming at is that a game universe can often provide such concrete experiences. This is later studied in an actual course using a strategy game and unfolded in the theory on educational use of computer games. A crucial factor in the more concrete experiences is the framing of such experiences through scientific concepts insisted on by the instructor. It seems obvious that we can't have concrete experiences with the plague, world wars or depressions. However, the context of play allows for us to explore such experiences in a safe environment.

Playful learning: the relationship between playing and learning

Until now, I have presented a framework for understanding teaching, education and learning, but have yet to discuss the significance of play. Engaging with a computer game is a type of play and this lends it certain advantages compared to other activities (Egenfeldt-Nielsen and Smith, 2000). The focus in the following is on play as a safe environment for exploration and the possibility of paraphrasing actions. This ability makes it possible to gain experiences that would otherwise be hard to obtain. The idea of using play for learning has a long tradition, resting on theorists' conception of play as important for children's development. These theorists have paralleled human development to the evolutionary perspective of animal play.

The basic assumption in evolutionary play theory is that, through play, we have a chance of exploring and training in areas that are relevant in our everyday life. Through framing something as make-believe, we can engage in activities that are normally not acceptable, potentially dangerous or completely unknown. In this way, animals (and humans) adapt to the surrounding environment and, through play, ultimately get a better chance of survival (Fagen, 1995). The evolutionary perspective does not see animal and human play as qualitatively different, but as lying on a continuum. Most basic human play forms mirror animal play, but humans are capable of performing more complex forms of play. The same rationale that works for animals applies to humans, and from this perspective, play is well suited to allow humans to engage in new activities and to learn about these activities (Fagen, 1995; Sutton-Smith, 1997). The developmental perspective on play in humans has been the object of study especially in the twentieth century. It has roots in the Enlightenment with its romantic perception of childhood, like the one represented by Jean-Jacques Rousseau in his book *Emile* (1762/1993). Play continues to be an important element of pedagogy theories with significant theoretical work picking up in the 1960s. The development perspective, championed by Jean Piaget, Lev Vygotsky, Donald W. Winnicot and Erik E. Eriksson, also has strong roots in psychology and education. They all saw play as a central part of development and stressed different functions of play (Bruner et al., 1976; Corbeil, 1999; Makedon, 1984).

The overall idea of play as a safe area for exploration is central for the above perspective, but we have yet to explore the ability of play to paraphrase certain actions. We will, therefore, take a closer look at Gregory Bateson's (1972) theory on meta-communication that describes the characteristics of play as the framing of a context. He convincingly argued that play is capable of framing a situation differently so that participants negotiate how actions within a certain context should be understood. Huizinga (1986) called this the magic circle that shelters play from outside interferences and repercussions. Bateson called the skill necessary for play meta-communication and stressed that this ability is widely used in all encounters in society, but is first developed in play.

In this perspective, play can be seen as the basis for engaging in social encounters, where we have different expectations and conventions in different settings. Through play, we learn to appreciate that actions within different contexts do not hold the same meaning. The following situation illustrates the communication in a play situation. Two boys are engaged in rough-and-tumble play. On one level, the boys communicate to each other that they are fighting in imitating the movement, noises, thoughts and feelings of a fight. On another level, they are also communicating that it is not really a fight. When they throw a punch, it is a punch, but still not really a punch. They communicate that this is a play frame and that special rules apply. This makes it an obvious place for exploring new ideas and concepts that may otherwise be threatening or beyond the immediate reach of students.

The real significance of the above discussion is in the perception of play as one of the first areas in which we are able to construct a fitting context around our actions. We can do something without meaning it or do something so it means something else. Play is important for the development of communication and especially meta-communication. But play is also the place where we can actually engage in new, strange or dangerous activities with different consequences from usual, as the evolutionary perspective argues. In play, we are allowed to change rules and consequences within a given frame to explore different alternatives in a safe environment. The safe environment is even truer of computer games, where the player explores representations that are more flexible and open to our manipulations. One can set up more realistic situations in computer games, like mountain climbing, racing, martial arts tournaments or huge battles than would normally be impossible in play, through the use of a number of props at one's disposal. 'All of the power, none of the responsibility,' as the commercial for the computer game *Red Alert* reads. At some level this reduces the fantasy necessary for playing, but at another level it extends the need for being imaginative. At the initiation of a play setting the computer game takes over a part of the fantasy with its building of a representation. This implies a play experience that brings you closer to a topic by providing a more demanding and responsive universe than your own fantasy is capable of. The game representation will be more extensive, complex and unknown, and this requires an even greater extent of fantasy and creativity on the player's part. The player's fantasy will be stretched to find ways to explore and challenge this richer representation of the computer game's topic.

The important thing to take away is that play relates to learning primarily as a setting, where it is possible to safely explore ideas, concepts, experiences and sceneries. As discussed, computer games provide play with a number of unique capabilities in terms of representing a safe environment and the props available. The significance of the extra props will be discussed in the following.

BUILDING BLOCKS FOR A THEORY ON EDUCATIONAL USE OF COMPUTER GAMES

When approaching educational use of computer games, one should be careful not to confuse the merits belonging to the domains of, respectively, computers, games and play. It is obvious that playing a computer game will share some similarities with the activity of playing – in the framing of the experience with the computer platform as the tool used and the game as the representational form. Here the aim is to understand the manifestation of the latent potentials that in combination make up a computer game and how this connects with educational use. A first natural step is to start with the characteristics of the computer medium, which we have so far neglected. Many of the characteristics we ascribe to computer games are general to applications using the computer medium.

The charateristics of the computer medium

> Computers can 'only do what they are programmed to do,' but the same is true of a fertilized egg trying to become a baby.
>
> (Alan Kay, 1999: 46)

Drawing on the work of Alan Kay (1999) and Niels Ole Finnemann (1999), we can think of the computer as consisting of an infinite number of 'atoms' or as a new alphabet that we can use to make different forms of representation. In a computer, the manifestations of atoms into different forms can be chosen freely compared to the limitations of traditional artifacts. What is really interesting is what form or architecture we use for shaping the atoms and what implications the exact form of computer programs may have for the actual use.

Finnemann (1999) provides a thorough attempt at describing the computer with a terminology that has little preference for a specific use of computers. He outlines three constraints for use of computers:

- **Informational alphabet**: This refers to the computer as relying on a notation system consisting of units emptied of semantic value that are layered into a sequence. It is possible to manipulate the physical operative unit, which provides us with a high degree of freedom.
- **Set of rules**: Any computer process is controlled by a set of rules, which is systematic. We are capable of manipulating these rules in any way as long as the syntax remains consistent.
- **Interface**: We determine the content of the processes controlled by the rules on the semantic and the rule level through an interface.

Overall, this implies that we can manipulate the computer on the lowest level – below the semantic content and below the rules level. We can, in principle, change any process in any way at the time when it can initially be represented in the computer.

> The notation system (and the presence of the computer) represents the only invariant constraints for any computer process. If something can be represented in this system it can be processed in a computer and thus we can say that the computer is basically defined by a new kind of alphabet.
>
> (Finnemann, 1999: 145)

Finnemann goes on to argue that the computer with its new alphabet is capable of representing a multitude of semantic regimes (e.g. linguistic, auditory, pictorial and logical). The informational alphabet can represent an infinite number of linguistic alphabets while a linguistic alphabet only works within its own limits. Finnemann points out that it is possible to use different semantic regimes for controlling the machine. However, one would inherit the restrictions of the semantic regime in interfacing with the computer. The important point is, however, that the computer is a 'multisemantic machine', which makes it capable of combining a number of previously unrelated representation forms. Finnemann (1999: 146) concluded with what he calls 'a whole range of "first-time-in-history" features'. These features imply that the computer provides a new way to represent knowledge by integrating a variety of previously separate knowledge areas. The computer is characterized by:

- Medium for producing, editing, processing, storing, copying, distributing and retrieving knowledge by integrating processes earlier separated. Similar to writing a book, publishing it and selling it.
- Medium for representing linguistically, formally, pictorially and aurally knowledge while integrating these in the same system.
- Medium for communication, making it possible to integrate earlier communication forms.

With a computer, one can manipulate the information in ways very different from other representations and one can combine these different areas because one has direct access to the underlying alphabet. This also entails a rearrangement of the sender and receiver relation, where they become interchangeable and the receiver can gain access at the level of the alphabet at any time. The representation of knowledge is not hardwired into the book, picture, artifacts or environment in the computer medium. One can make changes and this is the constituent of what has often been labelled interactivity, which I will return to more specifically in relation to computer games. It should be stressed that interactivity is not an exclusive feature of computer games (Jensen, 1999), but it is often used to describe the uniqueness of computer games.

Understanding the nature of computer games

When we look to computer games research, there have been several attempts at describing what characterizes these games as suggested in the Introduction. In general, theorists have a hard time defining games as such, including a distinction between traditional games and computer games. It is argued that the form of games is quite suitable for the computer platform, due to the focus on rules that are a basic trait of both computers and games, which makes it possible for games to make different kinds of representations from most other media forms. This ability is further enhanced by the computer platform as described above (Juul, 2003; Salen and Zimmerman, 2003).

When discussing computer games in the Introduction, I was a bit dissatisfied with Juul's initial somewhat formal definition. A game was defined as a rule-based system with variable outcomes that the player is attached to. This definition of games does not grant full justice to Juul's (2003) work that included a discussion on the importance of the fictional world in computer games, which is really the semantic content of the computer game in Finnemann's terminology. Juul saw the fictional world as important for the player's actual game experience even though this world in most game genres slowly recedes into the background in favour of the rules. The fictional world provides the setting for understanding the game rules, making the outcomes meaningful and attaching the player to the outcome. A computer game designer cannot assume the player has a lot of previous experiences on a topic, so a well-established setting and genre is usually used. The design of computer games relies on a fictional world and rules that are introduced to the player, who can then manipulate the rules to gain different outcomes. A computer game can become complex, but it is, in principle, always possible to deduce back to some rules that guide the outcome and an overall setting. Although a random factor is often built in, things don't just happen. You as a player make things happen in a very concrete sense. You will do something and see the consequences in the game universe. Engaging the student in manipulation of the rules is combined with strong audiovisual cues that surpass most books.

The basic definition of computer games does not demand a fictional world because we can have almost entirely abstract computer games like *Pong* or *Tetris* with no fictional world. However, the fictional world does make it easier to play the computer game and proves to be an important ingredient in creating rich game experiences. In providing a fictional world, the player gets a handle on the computer game. The advantage of using a fictional world is obvious when we are talking about stereotypical universes that most players will have knowledge of and can use as a handle on the game experience. It provides a variation of starting points for different players, clearing the way for understanding the game universe. The most popular computer games will initially be those that can set up an interesting fictional world for players to recognize and understand. The success of *The Sims*, *SimCity* and the horde of Second World War games fit nicely into that argument. Also, the continuing success of dragons, goblins and trolls in computer games is understandable, providing a strong fictional world for the teenage-minded game population.

However, the actual balance between rules, outcomes and consequences is critical for going beyond the initial interest in the fictional world. We can refer to the diffuse balance as the gameplay, which in combination with the fictional world facilitates the game experience. Gameplay is the important ingredient for creating engagement in computer games as it provides the set of rules for interacting with the fictional world and the outcomes from the interaction. The design of the gameplay that draws on other computer games can also serve as a handle for the player so the ways to interact with the game are not entirely unknown. Until now, computer games have been described as a combination of rules and fictional world, or game universe, that the player interacts with. The interaction has often been called interactivity.

Interactivity is often used like a magic wand that can clarify the very nature of computer games. However, we need to get past the vague concept of interactivity, as Espen Aarseth has argued, and find a more precise definition that differentiates computer games from other media. According to Aarseth (1997: 1), a more appropriate description would note that a 'non-trivial effort is required to allow the reader to traverse the text'. This description testifies to the engagement of the player in computer games and the ability of the game to appreciate the engagement. The player makes a difference since the scenario is changed in accordance with the relation between player and game. Interpretation of the fictional world is not only latent in the player's mind, but also manifests itself on the screen. This is not to say that computer games are capable of expressing all feelings, desires and needs of the player, but it comes further down that road than most other media. The player interprets the game universe differently depending on mood, which will lead to a different game experience unfolding. The player may also interpret a movie differently depending on mood, but the same movie still unfolds on the screen, although the experience may still be radically different for the viewer (Egenfeldt-Nielsen, 2003c).

Students have very concrete experiences while interacting with the computer, especially when the game universe responds immediately to the manipulations. This is quite different from traditional teaching, where students are told about other people's interactions with a universe or, in other words, other people's experiences – indeed, not often other people, but other people's abstract take away from experiences. The student may think about these and may connect them with existing concepts and experiences, but it lacks the richness and variation that are part of any concrete experience. This richness is supported by the engagement, but also by the modal expressions of computers, particularly since computer games have a preference for audiovisual orgies. In computer games, the combination of different modalities is among the most powerful of experiences since computer games are constantly pushing the limits of the computer in terms of graphics, sounds, animation and artificial intelligence.

In line with Finnemann's theory, the computer as a medium is especially capable of bringing to bear a number of different modal expressions. On a computer, the visual appearance, audio use and actions performed open up for different learning experiences. The classroom has, of course, always involved other modes than language, such as gestures, models, movement and gaze, but increasingly other modes are finding their way into school (Jewitt, 2003). It has been found that combining different representation forms (audio, visuals and text) results in better learning outcome, especially if these are presented simultaneously, supplementing each other. When we are involved in learning about a topic, we benefit from pictures or animations in combination with hearing. These multimedia effects are especially strong for students with less prior knowledge of a topic and other individual differences, like spatial ability, may also apply (Mayer and Moreno, 1999).[5]

Next, I present an integrated theory of computer games aimed at educational use of computer games and a number of relevant topics to understand what happens in the game course discussed in the following chapters. The theory draws on the discussions above, but also links back to previous discussions in the book.

AN INTEGRATED THEORY OF COMPUTER GAMES

To understand computer games, we can approach them at three levels: player, representation and system (Figure 6.3). On the system level, we have the computer that consists of a notational system that we can manipulate in a number of ways. This notational system is used to create a set of rules and a fictional world providing a representation, i.e. the game universe. We can create a shed with a hammer (semantic content) and a rule saying that the hammer will change colour when clicked on (algorithm). This representation can ultimately be described as information marking relevant differences. Thus, a computer game is a fictional world with rules represented by marking the important difference through semantic content (fictional world) and algorithms (rules). The player level addresses how we actually approach the computer game, stressing the necessity of the player's interpretation of the differences that make up a game. Through interpretation, we can come to understand the information in the game universe and construct knowledge based on this process. The knowledge is the player's active transformation of information attaching it to previous experiences and concepts with or without instruction. The uniqueness of computer games lies in the ability to combine interesting fictional worlds with rules that make the player's process of understanding active rather than passive. This engagement is crucial for understanding the educational potential of computer games.

One could say that computer games differ from other media in offering a new way to appreciate students' ability to understand what differences make a difference. The ability to *appreciate* and *create* differences that make a difference is ultimately what constitutes knowledge. When I learn to read a map, I learn to appreciate the differences that make a difference. I will not look at the quality of the paper, the colours used or the aesthetics in general (Bateson, 1972). Rather, the borders or terrain are the differences that make a difference. The interesting difference between the paper map and the map on a computer is that one is capable of not only appreciating the differences that make a difference, but also creating differences that make a difference. One can move the borders or change the terrain, but only if one appreciates the differences that make a difference. This results in a reinforcing loop driving the student toward understanding and mastering the map. The appreciation involves a process of exploring and linking concepts as described by Kolb's cycle.

An example is useful for showing the important implications from the above perspective that has repercussions for the educational use of computer games. In *Europa Universalis II*, the player starts with a historical map, where there are a noticeable number of borders. This map is constructed

Figure 6.3: Model showing how to conceive computer games by incorporating both a player and a system perspective that tracks the different forms of knowing, the process to make this transformation and the manifestation of the knowing

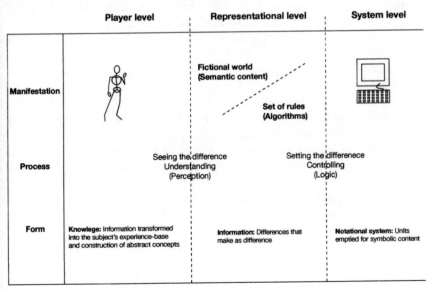

through the notational system complete with semantic content and rules for engaging with the map. Students will initially try to get an understanding of the map based on previous experiences and concepts, eventually moving on to actually challenging these borders. Students can change the borders by invading other countries and they experience the implications of such a change – which again reinforces the understanding of the initial difference in borders. Initially, the students may merely appreciate the borders as showing different countries. However, as players get further into the game, they will see new important characteristics like strategic importance, economic importance, terrain, and cultural and religious variations.

In this sense, the game process is one of constantly appreciating, exploring and linking differences, i.e. setting new differences while understanding the implications of these. This means that the fictional world is necessary for building the differences that make a difference and the rules make it possible to challenge these differences while the rules are also a part of the fictional world. The chance to conquer a French province, explore America, colonize West Africa or convert Poland to a Protestant country in *Europa Universalis II* is not really meaningful without the fictional world nor is it interesting.

A number of important implications for the educational use of computer games emerge from the discussions above which will play a crucial role in the following chapters on theoretical work.

- Students are actively engaged in constructing the differences that they find meaningful with a clear purpose in mind and these are laid out for all to see and comment on.
- Students' understanding of the differences is crucial to move the game forward and the understanding has a direct bearing on the following representations. Misinterpretations tend to be explicit rather than implicit.
- Students do not start from scratch with computer games, as they will use previous experiences connected to the computer game for playing.
- Students playing can continuously be tracked as any student action is represented in the notational system and these actions can be transformed into any representation during and after playing.
- Students can always question the validity of the representations, as it is constantly possible to manipulate the representations, in principle for any user.
- A computer game can represent anything one wants it to as long as one can formally describe it, and any representation should in theory be able to make up a computer game.
- The representations can draw on all semantic regimes providing experiences catering for all modalities. This ability provides richer and fuller concrete experiences with different handles for different students.

- The same semantic content can be re-used with the same underlying rules or minor adjustments. This implies plasticity in adjusting the educational experience compared to the majority of other educational material.
- Students can safely explore the fictional world with few real life repercussions, sheltered by the magic circle.

Reading, hearing, seeing or playing are all equally valid concrete experiences, but as described above differing in form. The computer game lets a player hear, see, observe, do, perceive and feel in a richer universe than most other media, while allowing the player to build and test concepts to understand the game universe. These concepts will without instruction become spontaneous concepts, but with guidance the experiences can be transformed to scientific concepts. With the right balanced instruction, the introduction of scientific concepts can be grounded through experiences in a game universe. This differs from when a student hears a lecture or reads a textbook. In that scenario, the scientific concepts are introduced without any explicit grounding in experience unless the student by chance has some experience to bring into the equation such as something that can serve as an example, a metaphor or an experience that can crack a hole in the scientific concept to let the student invest something of himself.

CONCLUSION: EXPERIENTIAL LEARNING AN ALTERNATIVE TO EDUTAINMENT

Overall, I have argued for an approach to learning, education and teaching that extends from dissatisfaction with previous generations' approach to educational use of computer games manifested in edutainment. To provide an inclusive perspective of player, computer game and context, I took experience as a starting point. This led me to stress the importance of concrete experience for building abstract concepts while maintaining that our concepts will also form our future concrete experiences. I found computer games to be a potentially valuable tool for providing such concrete experiences as they present a rich, engaging universe, where students are performing actions and gaining concrete experiences that are self-sustaining and can be used to build concepts.

Next, I will explore the actual use of educational computer games in a school focusing on what experiences computer games provide. The course provides the last piece in the final puzzle, that is, a theory on educational use of computer games, and will hopefully also be useful for people interested in designing their own course.

NOTES

1   This is also supported by more recent educational research (Schank, 1999).
2   This assumes that in principle any object holds the same interest for humans. One might as well be a top history student as a top maths student, although recent research suggests innate topic preferences. History, culture, evolution, situation and predispositions make some paths easier to take (Bransford et al., 1990). However, the point is that beyond the initial curiosity, one needs to invest in a topic to continue learning about it and this often depends on linking it to some previous or future experience.
3   This is also the focus of Wenger's later work that examines how knowledge travels in a community (Wenger, 1999).
4   It should be stressed that blaming the school for the ever-increasing curriculum is hardly reasonable as external groups in the form of policy-makers and parents have a large part of the responsibility.
5   Many game companies are supported by makers of graphics cards to ensure that the development moves forward (e.g. BioWare, 2004). Computer games are the first place where a new generation of graphics cards will make a difference.

7

Initial Preparation for the History Course with the Strategy Game Europa Universalis II

As I looked over my empire, my sense of fulfilment grew. Instead of betting on costly European wars, I had early on expanded my colonial empire. The strategy was a success. In the early eighteenth century, Denmark controlled most of North America and most western and southern parts of Africa. Wars had been swift and usually to my advantage without becoming a real burden on my economy. I had successfully kept out of the major European wars.

Before getting to the actual course, one should go through a few preparations, which I describe in this chapter. As the quote above indicates, I enjoyed preparing for the game. But to what extent was *Europa Universalis II* useful in an educational setting? This was primarily considered in relation to teaching history in secondary school, but it does have some cross-curricular potential especially in relation to geography. Furthermore, the steps in the analytical process should not be limited to this course in terms of either subject, genre or age group.

The computer game *Europa Universalis II*, published in 2001, was made by Peter Kullgard and Frederik Malmberg. One can play against the computer or challenge up to eight other players. I chose to concentrate on the single-player experience to reduce technical problems. *Europa Universalis II* was one of the most celebrated strategy titles in 2001 winning several awards, as indicated by *GameSpy's* review: '*Europa Universalis II* is possibly the best historical strategy game there is. That's not an exaggeration.' Today, the game still enjoys a huge following with active forum discussions of history related to the scenarios in the game and the game in general.[1] The active community was initially a strong argument for choosing the computer game because the forum discussions proved that it could inspire discussion of both historical events and problems with the game.

Europa Universalis II makes it possible to experience history in a new way. It is not about the facts of history, but instead, the player engages with the underlying historical dynamics from 1419 to 1820 to change or enact the course of history. As a player, I can try to maintain Danish dominance around the Baltic Sea or uphold English supremacy in France. The player has many options, some much harder than others. It is hard to avoid the consequences of history and to do so, the player has to use historical knowledge to prevent historical failures. The game has some major historical events that need to be addressed, such as the rebellion in England in the seventeenth century, the Thirty Years' War, and Spain's bankruptcy due to the overflow of gold from the New World. Usually, one can influence these situations and choose between different options, but the events will still occur. If the player were representing England in the seventeenth century, one event would be:

> In 1628 the English Parliament passed the Petition of Rights. Under its terms, the King could not levy any new taxes without the consent of Parliament. Furthermore, soldiers could be billeted in private homes. Martial law could not be imposed in time of peace. Finally, the Petition of Rights forbade the imprisonment of individuals without cause.

The player can then choose to sign the petition or reject it; in any case, the decision would have long-lasting consequences on many variables, such as the country's degree of centralization and internal stability. The attraction of the game lies in its ability to live up to the strategy genre's principles. The player can build up a nation, plan a strategy for several years, and then suddenly see those plans shattered by unforeseen events that demand a new strategy. The game is capable of entertaining the player at several levels, from the first layer of military conflict to the deeper layers of culture, religion, economy and policy. The exploration of the game universe never quite seems to end and the player constantly experiences new connections or options that make decisions more complex. More and more variables need to be taken into consideration.

The game features more than 180 countries and it is possible to play them all spanning the period from 1419 to 1820. Among these are many non-European countries such as Manchu, Shawnee, Zimbabwe and China. It is possible to design new countries, scenarios and events. There are currently several examples of this online. One of the most interesting initiatives is the EEP project, in which historically interested volunteers around the world add data and events to the game to make it richer. Another interesting example of a modification is the *Europa Universalis II – Asia Chapters*, which uses *Europa Universalis*, but hugely extends the Asian part of the world in collaboration with historians (Typhoon Games, 2003).

Overall, the game has different dimensions, which the player can control. The game universe encompasses a broader part of history than is usually the case in stereotypical historical strategy games, where the gameplay tends to centre on the Second World War. In the following section, the different areas are described along with some of the questions and variables relating to each area. However, it is hard to present the relations between the different areas. One of the most important overall variables is the stability of the country.

The stability is altered by major decisions and numerous events more or less under the player's control: waging war, changes in domestic policies, diplomatic moves, rebellions, bankruptcy, religious turmoil and culture clashes, to name a few.

THE ROLE OF THE MILITARY

The military conflicts in *Europa Universalis II* are often dangerous and one can never quite be sure if they are worth the risk. When one decides to enter into a war, this provocation will have consequences for years to come and one should (if possible) prepare for the war years ahead. One needs to consider a lot of other factors than merely the number of troops. For example, geography, attrition, leaders, technology, alliances, current wars, fortifications, stability and domestic policy all play a role. Often, knowledge of historical events and the problems nations faced historically can be a great advantage in planning.

For example, it is not a good idea for England to enter into the Thirty Years' War (1618–1648) at the start of the seventeenth century because there may be instability due to religious and political conflicts during this period. Likewise, it is a very good idea for Denmark to quell Sweden at the beginning of the seventeenth century before the warrior king, Gustav Adolph the Great, claims the throne and the Swedish battle machine gets into gear. Likewise, Russia probably should not expand with colonies into the New World in competition with other European powers, when it can expand east in Siberia. It should be stressed that the historical awareness does not limit itself to geographical knowledge as to what areas to explore and colonize. An insight like keeping inflation at a reasonable level is very important and can be used in the game, and indeed the problems with controlling inflation also relate to some of the returning problems in medieval Europe.

THE IMPORTANCE OF THE FINANCIAL SITUATION

A country's financial situation is extremely important in the game and is probably as important as the military acts. However, it requires a deep understanding of the game to appreciate the financial implications. One needs to constantly watch out for inflation as one raises armies, embarks on war and improves infrastructure. The player must avoid bankruptcy and be careful with the war taxes, all of which interact with the country's stability.

When I tried to play Byzantium in the fifteenth century, I actually managed to fight off the Ottoman Empire through loans, war taxes and alliances, but my economy was completely shattered and it was impossible to recover from the inflation. In the end, I had to give up. In a later game I managed better by keeping a close eye on inflation. The game distinguishes between income and expenses. Expenses will explode with involvement in war and income will decline due to ravaging armies. This will force the player to 'print' money or take loans, which will result in inflation and make it even harder to raise armies and improve infrastructure the next time. The game keeps the fixed expenses relatively simple, consisting of maintenance of the military forces, interest from earlier loans and a number of random historically related events. Income comes from trade, goods, production and gold mines, which all depend on the different regions of the country, technology level, available resources and the world market in general. Income can also be supplemented from random events.

POLITICAL ASPECTS OF THE GAME

In *Europa Universalis II,* compared to its predecessor, the player has more control over what direction a country will take politically: will you encourage mercantilism in your nation or bet on free trade? Will you centralize or decentralize the government? Can you still defend having serfs? Alternatively, will you free your subjects? Of course, all choices have both disadvantages and advantages relating to previous game choices, the precise country and future plans. You can influence your domestic policies in ten different areas and slowly form your country, but historical events will still make it hard to alter a country's course completely. Will you bet on stability or nurture innovation and be leader in technology? Will your country rule the seas or will you maintain strength on land?

A situation from a game I played myself provides an example. In the fifteenth century, north of the later powerful Russia lay the small trading nation of Novgorod, which I tried to keep independent through history starting in 1419. This was extremely hard. Although I won over Russia, Poland-Lithuania, Prussia, Sweden and other smaller nations by continuously exploiting the weather conditions, I could not keep up in technology and internal development through the eighteenth century. This was because I had failed to modernize my domestic policies and therefore had a conservative, old-fashioned nation, where development of new technology was slow and expensive. Furthermore, Sweden was growing stronger with the warrior king and Russia had expanded into Asia. So while I held my own the other nations developed beyond me.

The country's geographic and cultural composition also influences politics. A country with a variety of cultures and opposing religions should not loosen the grip on the people too much. They will spring liberation movements if given too much freedom too fast. Prussia would not do well trying to build a large navy and France could not be in a good position to change the state religion to Muslim.

DIPLOMACY – THE GLUE OF THE GAME

Europa Universalis II gives many opportunities to use diplomacy to enhance chances of success. Without a firm grasp of how to play different nations out against each other and maintain good relations with others, the game would become a lot harder. Ignoring diplomacy will make a country the number-one enemy of the world, especially if it is just a little too successful. One must also use random diplomatic incidents to further plans for expansion and support relations with other nations through gifts, marriage, trade agreements, vassalization and alliances. It is through diplomacy that the big changes are facilitated. For example, a player can try to establish a strong alliance between Austria and the Ottoman Empire, which would result in an interesting new scenario compared to history.

The game gives good insights into the importance of picking the right allies. In the beginning of the seventeenth century, Denmark and Sweden were fighting for supremacy in the Baltic Sea region. Historically, Denmark was very close to obtaining an alliance with Russia through a royal marriage. However, in the end, the marriage failed due to religious issues. Over the next few years, Sweden slowly took over and became the leader of the Baltic Sea region. In *Europa Universalis II*, one can relatively easily enter into an alliance with Russia (with or without marriage) and this has important implications for the war for supremacy in the Baltic Sea region.

This illustrates some of the problems with the games, as they fail to simulate on a small scale and do not take into account that one person's 'stubbornness' could decide whether Denmark and Russia should enter an alliance and so ultimately lead to a different outcome of war. Here, the game model is built up quite logically, and for both Denmark and Russia an alliance is obviously a good idea. However, this particular incident shows not only the problem with the game, but also a potential learning opportunity if teachers use debriefing appropriately. The incident can serve as a good starting point for discussing different potential outcomes in the game world and in history per se. This opens up a discussion of historical dynamics and variables behind the divergence.

PROBLEMS WITH THE GAME

I have tried to describe some of the areas in *Europa Universalis II* to illustrate the richness and complexity of the simulation. It should be said that I have play-tested this game for well over three weeks of full playing time and have still not mastered it. However, as one progresses, more problems become apparent.

A principal problem with computer games, which is also apparent in this game, is the trickle-down effect. The longer one plays, the further one moves away from historical accuracy. When Denmark subdues Sweden instead of engaging in lengthy wars, the balance in North Europe is suddenly seriously disturbed. The player is capable of making radical changes. There is not really any solution to this problem, and it is both a strength and a weakness. It moves the focus from facts to dynamics, as the computer game does not primarily teach about factual history but how history evolves.

Another major problem is that the artificial intelligence, although improved from the first version, is still lacking in quality and challenge, especially when playing large countries. Using the multiplayer mode can solve this, but this requires that one is able to play with several players simultaneously. Even then, one will still have many computer-controlled countries that act a little oddly. This can also make it hard to discuss the evolution of history in the game as opposed to the real historical development.

The game also seems to crash a little too often, although the game's stability improves once the released patches are installed. The yearly auto-save option improves the situation, but it remains problematic.

The complexity is initially a barrier concerning both interface and gameplay – there are simply a lot of variables at play. It can be quite overwhelming in comparison with other game genres. On the other hand, once the player understands the in-game help and the basics, the player can play the game at some level. Slowly, the player appreciates new features and considers them in decisions. So, the way one plays the game and understands the historical climate becomes even more multi-faceted. This is in line with learning theories on computer games that stress scaffolding, incremental learning and probing (Gee, 2003). The player is able to slowly expand knowledge and constantly test understanding. For example, the domestic policies demand a good overview of the game to realize the consequences. The complexity is also apparent in the messages that pop up, which are initially quite overwhelming. It is possible for some of them to be turned off and the game will remember the selections. Still, it is a problem for most players and especially for players with less game experience. They are not capable of distinguishing between relevant and irrelevant information and often ignore most of it or pay close attention to all of it.

Another problem is the pace of the game. Initially, it can seem slow and with few events. However, this can be regulated by turning up the speed, which is recommended. When events occur, the player then pauses the game. In this way, the game plays a bit like *SimCity*, where one will also run out of money and patience if the speed is on slow. As one learns more about the game, one can speed the time up between events or gather information in peaceful times that will improve one's ability to make the right decisions when events occur. The game has rich statistics with valuable information on other nations and to stay on top of diplomatic relations is quite a task.

Sometimes, it also seems quite odd that nations outside of Europe become part of European alliances. For example, the Creek Indian tribe is at war with

Austria even though it has absolutely no contact with Austria. Although the diplomatic system is more advanced than most strategy games, it is a problem that a country can only be in one alliance and not enter into non-aggression pacts or make minor alliances with Native American nations if playing as France or England. It also seems that the nations outside of Europe are far easier to play than European nations, mostly due to less competition and the possibility of expansion (Bates, 2001).

EDUCATIONAL CONSIDERATIONS

Based on the examinations above, I believe that *Europa Universalis II* has educational potential. Although the game seems very interesting on the surface, there are several problems from an educational perspective. The game is one of the most advanced strategy games and tries to borrow a lot from the simulation genre in which players choose their own goals and the underlying model is quite complex. This means that a lot of time is needed to learn the game. This problem is relieved by the tutorials to some degree, but for students without computer game experience, it is a long road to travel to master the game.

A very important quality of the game is the constant option of getting feedback on the actions, events and status of the major powers within the computer game, including the player's own country. There are tools that support debriefing and after-action reports. For all of the areas described in this chapter, the player can get an overview of the development over the years. In the event section, all the events in the game will be listed. They include declarations of war, peace treaties, marriages, alliances and bankruptcies. Cash holding, running expenses and income split on different key areas can be followed. Another graph shows the player the size of his navy or army in comparison with neighbouring countries.

The description above of *Europa Universalis II* has given an idea of what kind of experiences I envisage a commercial computer game can facilitate teaching history. The content of the game is a prerequisite for using the computer game in history but, as I will argue later, not by itself the source of the most interesting learning experiences. In order to succeed, the game must connect with surrounding activities such as lectures, student discussions, assignments, reading material and debriefing.

Fan interest in discussing historical elements in *Europa Universalis II*

Europa Universalis II sparked quite a lot of historical interest among players, which was apparent from the release. The official game forums bolster a rich discussion of historical events related to the computer games. These fall into different categories and, although not necessarily representative of general player behaviour, they point to some of the potentials of the computer game. These categories partly mirror the findings in this study with a lot of discussions focusing around technical issues, trouble playing the quite complex game[2] and understanding the game's underlying model. Interestingly, a significant number of the forum posts are on historical topics related to the computer game. The posts especially concern the accuracy of *Europa Universalis II* as a historical strategy game and discussion on countries, regions and events in the game. In one example, players discussed Sweden in an online forum:

> Chaingun: I have always thought that Sweden's income is grossly overestimated. It was a very poor country in comparison to France and Germany and in many respects the EU2 [*Europa Universalis II*] province taxes in Sweden do not represent that.
>
> Varya: Sweden would probably be a bit more balanced with lowered base tax and manpower for many provinces, especially the Finnish provinces early on. The leaders are however almost a more important aspect. I don't remember the exact numbers, but Sweden gets a large amount of very good leaders, which allows it to kick around its neighbours quite a bit. Especially combined with armies that are a bit bigger than they should be.
>
> Prince Eugene: First of all, that Karl XII 10/10/10 leader has to go. A lot of other cutbacks are necessary as well. Was Gustavus Adolphus a hero? Sure he was! Do all 100 of his subordinate leaders that live around the same time as him deserve godly stats as well? Of course not. Let's not even talk about their economical power. Denmark should be able to annihilate them until around the time they broke free and even then they shouldn't be able to seize Norway and eventually annex Denmark like they always do.
>
> (Paradox Entertainment, 2004)

Clearly, as evident from the forum postings, the links in the computer game are well connected with background information, and the players switch between different sources to inform their playing and understand what happens in the computer game. It is unclear how much of this exploration is mediated through a social setting, but *Europa Universalis II* does serve as inspiration for the relevant discussions. In general, the players in the forums seem to be quite interested in history and the computer game mediates this interest. However, it is uncertain to how large a degree the historical interest comes before playing the computer game. As we will see in the following chapters, some of the behaviour expected based on observations from the forums did manifest among students. This was especially the case in the group of high achievers that discussed the game around historically significant issues with parents and other students. However, it was certainly not a general characteristic of the students in this course.

Cross-curricular potential

In most research on educational use of computer games, the focus has interestingly been on one subject. This is despite several factors pointing to cross-curricular potential, which can potentially reduce the high start-up cost for learning the computer game's interface and teaching with computer games. A cross-curricular approach was also initially suggested in this study. However, practical problems made it hard to carry through in this exact study. Still, without the specific focus on cross-curricular potential, the links to other subjects surfaced during the course.

The initial exploration of the computer game *Europa Universalis II* pointed to a variety of potential subjects (history, geography, English, Danish). This was abandoned early on due to the huge coordination efforts on top of the challenges of conceiving educational use of computer games. The integration of the computer game with the history teaching's curriculum proved hard enough without also including three other subjects along with those teachers. There would be less of a problem if one were not bound by the specific curriculum and textbooks of one subject when designing a course with a computer game. This would make it easier to present a breathing universe, where there aren't arbitrary splits between geography, English and history. History uses geography to discuss where and what things happened and this often links back to culture and language. The issue of cross-curricular learning popped up during the course especially with reference to geography and partly to English. It actually seemed that from a student perspective, it was easier to accept that the computer game taught them something about geography and English rather than history. The references to these two subjects were mostly based on the clear visual cues that the computer game presented.

GUIDELINES FOR EVALUATION OF EDUCATIONAL POTENTIAL OF COMPUTER GAMES

The guidelines below describe some of the most important considerations based on my initial thoughts described above and the findings in previous chapters. They are also consistent with earlier reviews in the *Journal of Simulation and Gaming* regarding *Civilization III* (Squire, 2003c) and *Panzer General* (Corbeil, 2000). The selection of the game is only the first step in teaching with computer games. After that comes preparation, implementation and evaluation. Still, it secures a foundation before beginning any major preparation of the course. Here are the suggested guidelines:

- **Commercially successful**: Using computer games that have proven successful in the marketplace solves many problems. First, it ensures that the computer game lives up to the market demands, which include a decent interface, reasonable technical platform, balanced gameplay and other factors that are hard to review without thorough knowledge of computer games.

- **Play, review and discuss the game**: It is quite helpful to start by reading some reviews of the computer game to see whether it fits your needs. After this, depending on the game's complexity, you should spend from 4 to 12 hours playing a computer game to assess whether it is appropriate for your purposes. It is often surprising to most teachers that it demands that much time (Kirriemuir and McFarlane, 2003). Be sure to remember how it felt learning the computer game so you can appreciate the students' initial frustrations. Do also discuss the computer game with other teachers to reflect what would be the strengths and weaknesses.
- **Learning curve**: Computer games differ in how fast you can start playing and generally the learning curve should not be too steep. On the other hand, a steeper learning curve usually comes with a more complex computer game. These computer games are often the most relevant and satisfying in an educational context because they draw on more variables and provide richer descriptions of environments. Therefore, they give a stronger and richer model that students can engage with in different ways and discuss to facilitate learning.
- **Setting, time and technical issues**: A few practical things need to be checked. On a basic level, the technical specifications of the computer games should be well within the range of the school's computer. This is often not the case. The teacher should also make sure that students can save their game so they can continue playing later. The game should be possible and meaningful to play within the span of a normal school hour.
- **The model's suitability**: We have described earlier how computer games represent the world with different degrees of realism and complexity. You should especially be alert to computer games that constantly seem to model the world in unpredictable or superficial ways.
- **Discussions about the game**: How do the computer games lend themselves to reflection, thinking and discussions? You can get a feeling for this by visiting some forums for the computer game to see what people find interesting.
- **Suitability towards novices**: Toward the end, let an inexperienced player try the computer game while you, acting as a guide, observe problems, potentials and barriers during the computer game.
- **Dissect the game**: Take a close look at the computer game's underlying mechanics, interesting dynamics and central variables. Be on the constant lookout for links to teaching and good examples and relate it to students' experiences.
- **Gender issues**: Computer games are far from gender neutral and you should be alert as to how male or female students will receive a potential

computer game. You might want to consider having two alternative game titles. This may be a hard goal to fulfil given the propensity of male-oriented titles (Cassel and Jenkins, 1998).

The points above will give the teacher grounding in computer games, thereby confronting early on the major problem of knowing the computer game. Teachers identified this lack of knowledge of computer games as the most pertinent disadvantage along with the quality of current game titles (Becker, 2005; Egenfeldt-Nielsen, 2005). The above guidelines will also confirm to the teacher that the selected title is actually of high enough value to warrant spending more resources. The initial process of selection and preparation will naturally be higher for the first run of a course.

The extent of the efforts above depends to some degree on the complexity of the computer game and the desired learning outcomes. The example above is on one end of the scale since it is one of the most complex strategy games and because the intent was to use it not only to teach some clear-cut facts and skills, but also to encourage student reflection about historical dynamics. The computer game should extend from the educational foundation that I set up in the previous chapter, where the player through concrete experiences in the game can engage in discussions that will ultimately lead to the formulation of scientific concepts through the teacher's instruction. From this perspective, history is a somewhat fuzzy subject. There is an overarching idea of increasing historical awareness. Overall concepts are established to help understand historical events. In the same category as computer games, there are microworlds inspired by Logo, where the precise learning outcome is also vague. In microworlds, there is also an overarching idea of increasing appreciation and knowledge about maths but to say what an appreciation of maths exactly means is not simple.

At the other end of the spectrum are classic edutainment titles that set up very clear boundaries for their learning outcome and are quite easily reviewed in terms of gameplay. This also implies that it may not be the easiest thing to start with computer games at the more complex end of the spectrum because it requires more preparation from the teacher and more potentially can go awry. In an edutainment title, the teacher can sit the students down in front of the computer game and it should be quite straightforward from then on. They will shoot down balloons with the right numbers or collect the right letters faster than their computer opponent – and in principle, learn arithmetic. In Chapter 3 and 4, we saw that these titles did not really seem to lead to any significant advantages and do not really set computer games much apart from other educational software or teaching. It is simply another way to motivate children in its entirety but isn't much different from existing teaching practice. I previously described how this is still the major use of computer games in educational circles and third-generation use of computer games entails a change of teaching practice. This obviously demands more time on the part of the teacher – time that many teachers don't have.

CONCLUSION: INITIAL PREPARATION FOR A COURSE

This chapter provided the key to a basic understanding of the computer game that will be essential for framing the pedagogical thinking and facilitate the development of an appropriate course with computer games. A teacher will initially need to have the proper grounding to form a course that actually takes advantage of the characteristics of computer games. Overall planning and preparation of the course become considerably easier when the teacher already has a good idea of what examples, topics and issues are interesting in the games world. The concrete experience while playing the computer game will also benefit the teacher because it can continuously be used to make connections between playing the computer game and key topics addressed in parallel teaching.

NOTES

1   The forum discussions can be found at http://www.europa-universalis.com.
2   This guide was pointed out to the students but none really used it.

8
Practical Barriers and Perception of History

He looked for truth in facts and not in stories, that history for him was no more than the pretext for rueful fatalism about the present, that a man with such hair was prone to a shallow nostalgia that would inevitably give way to a sense that life was as mundane as he was himself.

(Flanagan, 2003:20)

As we have seen in earlier chapters, the educational use of computer games is still quite narrow, often caught up in a limited perception of how we make educational use of computer games. The next chapters will take a concrete course with the commercial strategy game *Europa Universalis II* as a starting point for understanding educational use of computer games. This chapter looks at how barriers and structures manifest themselves in the actual educational computer games used in classrooms, and the next chapter looks at the implications for teaching with computer games.

The course ranged over a period of two and a half months with students aged 15–19 years. There were three parallel courses, with two experimental classes using the computer games, while one class, the control group, went through the same course minus the computer game. The didactic set-up was that the computer game provided the concrete experiences about history whereas the teacher's lectures used the concrete experiences to build concepts about history. It was an explicit goal not to change the teaching situation beyond recognition, which meant that the two participating teachers were given quite a free rein to implement the course in terms of didactic approach. They were advised to use examples from the computer game to make historical concepts richer and more concrete, although this never really materialized in practice. In reality teaching practice largely remained unchanged.

Initially, different student groups are described to illustrate the positions that students occupied during the course. The main findings presented relate to the practical barriers in the educational use of computers like preparation time, learning curve, lesson plans, physical space and teacher resources. One unexpected finding was that the use of computer games led to discussions concerning history and learning. Lastly, the strong resistance from some student groups in relation to both the alternative learning approach and history understanding is examined. It is a surprising finding given previous research into the area.

It is concluded that introducing computer games in an educational setting is quite hard due to the variation in student background, practical barriers, the challenge to naïve historical understanding and the resistance from the students who stand to lose from using computer games.

THE USE OF AND APPROACH TO COMPUTER GAMES AMONG DIFFERENT STUDENT GROUPS

In earlier chapters, we touched on the exposed position of computer games when used for educational purposes. We have stressed that the structural setting and the teacher are decisive factors, which was also clear in the educational framework presented in Chapter 6. Instruction was seen as necessary to evolve scientific concepts. However, in this course, another important factor surfaced: the large differences between students and the reluctance among some to use computer games for education.

The students were not a homogenous group but differed on a number of parameters with critical implications for educational use of computer games. The first obvious split is between those who played computer games and those who didn't. This is, however, too imprecise to account for all the students who experienced problems during the course. Practically all the students in the experimental group did play computer games, but this meant very different things. The students, who were what we might call casual gamers, were on uncharted waters concerning the complex strategy game. The term 'casual gamer' does not come with a fixed definition, but with this term I refer to students who usually play simple, easily accessible, traditionally inspired computer games for a limited amount of time each week.

Furthermore, distinct demarcation lines between students evolved around historical interest, gender, academic ability and school interest. Initially, all students were positive about using a computer game for teaching history, which was evident from the questionnaire completed at the outset of the course. However, in the same vein, less than half believed that, in general, one could learn from computer games. This is also in line with a later study performed on the title *Global Conflicts: Palestine* (Egenfeldt-Nielsen and Buch, 2006). This is in opposition to the earlier results presented by VanDeventer (1997) concerning adults' belief that one could learn from computer games. Interestingly, it might actually be the case that students are more sceptical about using computer games for educational purposes than adults, which is also evidenced by the problems edutainment faces as students grow older and gain more control of the titles bought. Children are more avid and knowledgeable gamers compared to many adults, and this may provide a better basis for a more thorough and critical approach to the educational potential of games. However, it would be a mistake to put down all scepticism to more knowledgeable students compared to adults as the scepticism was also marked among girls who didn't play. The initial scepticism among students may also arise from an exclusive focus on the existing commercial titles that mostly evolve around subjects like fighting, shooting and fast cars and are not traditionally related to education. It is interesting to note that only a small percentage initially believed that one could learn from computer games. This challenges the popular belief that teachers are the primary barriers for using computer games for educational purposes. Despite the general scepticism of students toward educational use of computer games, the students in the current study could best be described as curious, confused, sceptical and interested in the course. As one girl stated in her logbook after the first week, echoing many students:

I don't think I have learned anything on the subject. But there are many who are normally not engaged in the teachings who now seem interested. It is also fun with a bit of alternative teaching but I don't really see it as teaching. Hopefully it will come.

(Student 5X, logbook)

This quote echoes the general trend, especially among those struggling with learning the computer game. Mostly, those were the ones with less varied experience of computer games. They continuously had a hard time figuring out what was the purpose of both the computer game and the course; they weren't getting anything out of it. The result was that weak students gave up. Those who were hard-pressed for time and had trouble keeping up in general downgraded the course in their overall school efforts. They quickly decided that the course was not worth their efforts and could not be taken seriously. They had other more important homework to do. The evidence of this retraction was more indirect than direct as few students admitted to withdrawing from the course. However, it was touched on in all the post-interviews and was observed during the course. Clearly, a rather large group had given up on different accounts.

An overview of different groups

Before looking more closely at the barriers in the course, I set up groups that outline differences in barriers but also serve to point forward to the next chapter's discussion of the actual teaching with *Europa Universalis II*, in which different student groups had different experiences. Clearly, some students had a harder time approaching the computer game because they had fewer concrete experiences to draw upon and lacked concepts to group experiences. Weak links to both previous games and history experience become quite explicit in the empirical data among some students because students do not naturally accept the computer game as an educational experience. This is a warning that we should not expect computer games to be an activity that magically all students can approach equally. Especially not if we continue with one specific title being offered to all students who will inevitable exhibit different game preferences. There seems to be some consistency in factors that contribute to forming different student groups. The '+' indicates how important the factor is considered to be for a successful educational experience with the computer game and is a compression of all the findings described in this chapter and the following chapter.

Different groups can be identified based on these characteristics (Table 8.1). Each group had a different approach to the computer game and 'fights' about how the course should be understood were a returning theme for all of the different groups: was the game irrelevant, a waste of time, or did it have some serious merits?

Give-up: Within the first two weeks, this group had given up on the computer game and hence the course. Everyone in this group had little experience with computer games. Some had less overall surplus of energy in relation to school and limited interest in history, adding to the inclination to give up. In this group were also a large number of students who simply didn't see the relevance of investing time in this course, due to the nature of computer games. It seemed that for some the critique of computer games was also a defence of their own position in the higher end of the hierarchy for history in general, which is discussed further later.

Upwardly mobile: These were mostly boys who knew and liked computer games but rarely excelled in school. They liked history in general, but had less liking for history as it was taught in a school context. Through their

Table 8.1: An informal indicator of the factors that were found to be significant for the students' success throughout the course

Factor	Influence	Critical stage
Gender	+	Start-up
General academic ability	+	Start-up + underway + late stage
General energy in school	+	Start-up
Historical general interest	++	Start-up + underway + late stage
Computer game literacy	+++	Start-up + late stage
Historical knowledge	+	Underway + late stage

competence and interest in computer games, they managed decently on the course, but lacked the historical background information and academic ability to really engage with the computer game from a historical perspective. There were few connections of the concrete game experiences with scientific concepts in other parts of the course. They were, however, keen to try on the historical perspective and were interested in connecting the interest in computer games with schoolwork. They saw the introduction of computer games to their advantage. This group was somewhat unobtrusive, as it did not really use the logbooks and seldom asked for help with the computer game.

Runners-up: This group was able to learn the computer game through a lot of homework, observations of others playing and persistence in general. This group was positive toward the computer game but never really got beyond the focus of seeing it as lacking in historical facts. Although they learned to play the game satisfactorily, they lacked the energy and historical awareness to engage with it more reflectively and historically. There were some girls in this group, especially those that ended up playing in pairs with an experienced player, who mastered tutoring.

High achievers: These were generally boys who knew computer games, liked history and had a surplus of energy in relation to school. They were able to approach the computer game from a more abstract perspective, not limiting themselves to the lack of facts and the diversions from factual history quite acutely present in the computer game. They seemed to be able to achieve the best of both worlds. Although in general quite critical towards the implementation of the course, they believed it had potential. In the oldest experimental class, a group of boys were especially clear representatives of this group.

The groups described above made up the majority of the students, with the high achievers the smallest groups and the group that gave up among the largest, including up to 25 per cent of the students. Next, we will look more closely at the barriers present in this study and how they had different bearings on the groups described.

PRACTICAL BARRIERS OF USING COMPUTER GAMES

Teachers often spent more time learning about the game and solving technical problems, than they initially allowed for or found acceptable.
(Kirriemuir and McFarlane, 2003: 3)

In general, the discussion on educational use of computer games still remains on a quite abstract level. There is very little room for research criticizing educational potential of computer games and clarifying their limits and potentials. This is also due to the limited everyday use of computer games in educational settings and the continuing experimental status of computer games for education.[1] It is hardly by chance that most sceptical studies mentioned in the earlier research overview have originated in Australia, a country that made early attempts to integrate computer games into the national curriculum. Nor is it by chance that the few other sceptics have centred on edutainment. For several years, this genre has been successful, especially in the US and UK home-learning market, and there exists a rich experience base to draw upon (and criticize). To launch an adequate criticism beyond technophobia, there has to be an experience base to criticize.

In the following, I will describe how a more critical stance toward educational computer games use can be beneficial. I draw on the limited amount of earlier literature on the subject covered in previous chapters to identify classic areas of difficulty. The barriers identified earlier, especially in Chapter 3, are gender, time schedule, physical setting, class expectations, teacher background, genre knowledge, technical problems, group-work experience, teacher preparation, priority issues, class size and attitude toward games.

Gender differences

Those who struggled with accepting the educational experience with computer games were most likely girls rather than boys. There were several reasons for this. First of all, it was generally agreed that boys had an advantage over girls in approaching computer games; boys especially excelled in strategy games. A girl observed that, 'Boys often play such games and therefore have a great advantage' (Student 15X, logbook). This impression was also supported by the teachers. The gender differences would remain strong throughout the entire course, surfacing in students' approaches to computer games, learning outcome, motivation, and perception of learning history.

Gender distinctions may partly have been an indirect consequence of less experience with playing computer games, as descriptive statistics conducted before the course show that girls do play less. However, it was clear that this was only part of the explanation. More importantly, from quite early on, the girls felt some degree of stigmatization in the course. This was not limited to computer games habits in general but seemed to rest on more specific characteristics of this course. The specifics are hard to outline, but contributing factors were game experience, the selection of the genre strategy, the specific game universe and the subject history. Already at the introduction to the computer game, many girls voiced their concerns about the suitability of the computer game:

> When the question of how to wage war appeared, the boys were clearly excited and wanted to go to war straight away. The girls were quieter. After class, some

girls had commented to the teacher that it seemed to be all about war, with the underlying meaning that this was not good.

(Field notes, week 1)

The computer game was a strategy game, which did not seem to sit well with the girls and they perceived it to be too abstract a depiction of history with few personal stories and too focused on the war aspects. The focus on war partly subsided through the course, but it contributed to initially alienating some girls from the course. The approach to playing the computer game also supported this. Compared to the boys, the girls were more interested in building colonies and in exploring the world rather than in waging wars. Also, despite an overall high use of computers, the girls, when it came down to it, seemed less interested in computers and had more technical problems with installing the computer game at home.

Other important gender variations were apparent in the pairing and access to the computers. The pairing of a girl with a boy who excelled in the computer game often resulted in exclusion of the girl. The boy forgot the less competent girl, which is also an all too common event found in learning with other multimedia in pairs (Littleton and Light, 1999). However, some of the experienced male players were capable of sharing knowledge. The lack of computers also resulted in some students being marginalized, mostly girls who were too slow to get to the available computers in the computer room. They, therefore, had to go to the general computer room, where less help was available and where they couldn't be sure to get computers. The girls who succeeded with the game usually did quite well in history in school and had at least some experience with computer games outside school.

The educational setting

In Chapter 3, I discussed the educational setting, which was found to influence the use of games. In an educational setting, the day is split in small segments with each subject having its own allocated time slot. To learn a computer game, get it started, and get into it requires more than an hour, which also caused problems in this course. It proved very hard to introduce a computer game and then continue the introduction two days later. Most of the students had little recollection of the initial introduction and in the next hour started more or less with the game tutorials from scratch. This was not limited to the first steps with the game, but continued to be a problem in the following weeks. The students played the game on Tuesdays and were then supposed to connect it with lectures on Thursdays. This time gap was not feasible since the game experience was too far away to connect with the lectures and also in opposition to traditional game culture where reflection and discussion are an integral part of playing (Jessen, 2001).

The physical frame also caused problems since the school was not adapted to group work. The computers didn't work and there were too few of them. This happened despite months of preparations in advance, when the computer game had been installed and tested. The limited number of computers later proved to be a problem that could not be solved by simply putting two to four students in front of the same computer. The students did not find the set-up with two to four students per computer to be acceptable, due to computer games' emphasis on an active student role. This is also a central part in my educational perspective presented earlier. In reality, two students per computer worked very well, but as soon as groups went beyond that number, it caused problems.

During the first weeks most students spent the first ten minutes of a 47-minute lesson tied up with login problems, bad CD-ROM drives, incorrectly wired computers, video driver problems, as well as choosing the right scenario, locating a saved game and starting the computer game. These problems could be viewed as temporary and of little relevance if we contribute them to the current limited knowledge and use of information technology in general and computer games in particular in the educational system. It could also be blamed on this specific school. However, the situation found at this school is consistent with earlier research on use of information technology in schools and this suggests that the school's problems are representative. The lack of computer equipment is commonly reported as a problem in research and it doesn't seem to be about to disappear. To view the lack of equipment as a temporary problem is dangerous thinking because the situation will probably remain unchanged for many years to come. Indeed, it may be argued that use of information technology, including computer games, will always create obstacles when one has to coordinate 30 people's simultaneous use.

The lack of computers was just one problem. Perhaps the most severe problem was that computer support was too weak and that during recess, some students vandalized the computers by rewiring monitors, mice and keyboards. It should, therefore, not be forgotten that the technical problems will be an important challenge when using computer games in most schools. However, there are some indications that this may change in the future. A year after this study was performed, the Swedish secondary school Västerås, specializing in information technology, experienced few technical problems when using the same computer game in history teaching (Markgren, 2004).

Preparation phase

From the beginning, the success of this teaching course was hampered by the lack of deep knowledge of the computer game among the teachers, which we have already seen is a problem consistently found in similar studies on educational use of computer games. It was not that the teachers didn't play the game, because they played it for several hours. They simply didn't achieve a deep enough knowledge about the game to help the students later, nor did they acquire enough concrete game experience to use it as fuel for more traditional teaching. The teachers didn't really get into the computer game and failed to acquire the necessary knowledge to integrate computer game, group work and teacher talks. This was very much against the original plan, but the teachers were under intense pressure from other temporary assignments and illness. Hence, preparation was constantly behind schedule. This was problematic because the educational perspective I presented maintained that teachers required quite deep knowledge about the computer game to use the concrete experiences from the computer game in their own teaching to introduce scientific concepts.

The male teacher did have quite an amount of experience with strategy games and was more capable of adapting, but still he wasn't really able to fit the game, group work and teacher talk into a coherent whole. The teachers' approach to the game was reactive rather than proactive. They played and learned the computer game at the same time as the students and it was, therefore, hard to plan the teaching in connection with the game. Both teachers recognized this in the post-interviews as a significant problem.

The preparation phase in this study was also impeded by a general lack of time on the teachers' part for preparing classes, problems with installing the computer games and the allocation of computer rooms. The installation took longer than necessary because a server installation did not work for this particular game. Instead, the game had to be installed on each computer separately. In general, many subjects in the Danish educational system experience cuts into preparation time, which is extremely problematic if one wants to support new teaching styles such as cross-curricular teaching styles where computer games would be particularly constructive.

Also, the coordination between the two history teachers and researcher concerning the content in the teaching was not easily solved. Here, the challenge was primarily to find cases and relevant parts of the history book and match these with the computer game. This was a far from trivial task and it might have been easier to take the computer game universe as a closer starting point than was attempted in this course. As explained earlier, instead it was attempted to fit the computer game with the existing content and material used in history teaching. The attempt to fit existing material may in hindsight seem naïve, especially given the educational perspective outlined previously that one should be very explicit in identifying the important experiences and how these can be linked to students' previous experiences and historical concepts usually taught in school. On the other hand, it was found that if the computer games were meshed in with the existing material, they would have a much better chance of actually being used beyond experimental use in teaching history.

Learning to play the computer game

Computer games were a new tool, which students needed to learn how to use, and connecting it with history turned out to be anything but a trivial task. As discussed in Chapter 6, using a new tool entails both potentials and limitations and this became quite obvious during the study. During the selection process of a relevant computer game for the course, I feared that the computer game would be too hard to learn, and according to many students, this later proved to be warranted. One male student said, 'It went well, I think the game is a little hard, but it will probably become better in time' (Student 37X, logbook, week 1).

The game was as complex as strategy games come, but this was also the strength of the game. This made it possible to have a richer representation of the historical universe and give the students more options for exploring history dynamics. The teachers could also appreciate that this was not a superficial action game or war game only. As the teaching progressed, the teachers pointed to this as important, and in the final evaluation they also found the game to present the historical dynamics in a fruitful way. The delicate balance between presenting complex problems and making these accessible wasn't found with this computer game.

> We didn't really get very much out of the course. You spend too much time learning and controlling the game to also remember the data that sometimes suddenly surfaced in a split second.
>
> (Students, Group evaluation)

In hindsight, I should have chosen a less complex computer game, but looking back on the shortlist of computer games to select from, none of the alternatives seemed to strike a better balance. Most of these computer games involve fewer variables and dynamics and they tend to have a more narrow focus on the parts of history concerned with war. The real alternatives were actually more complex; it seems strategy games are far from becoming simpler. One avenue that might prove interesting is to look at older strategy games, where the complexity is smaller, as players tend to demand still more complex computer games. However, using older games may involve other problems in terms of running on the hardware and destroying the important student engagement through outdated graphics and simple gameplay (Egenfeldt-Nielsen, 2003e; Gee, 2004a).

To alleviate some of the problems with learning *Europa Universalis II*, the tutorials included in the game were used. With the tutorial, the first problems with the nature of computer games arose. Firstly, there was a large difference in how fast the students learned the game. Clearly, the students with computer game experience learned the computer game much faster, especially those with prior experience with the strategy genre. Not surprisingly, most of these were boys. Some students finished the tutorials within the first hour whereas three to four weeks later, others were still struggling with basic concepts from the tutorial and, indeed, some hadn't completed all the tutorials satisfactorily. According to the interviewed students, up to one quarter of the class fell into this group. This group never really got involved with the computer game and didn't get the game to work at home. The students were expected to play at home to increase their skills and reduce the long time span between playing sessions. When the weakest students didn't play at home, the discrepancy between strong and weak students quickly accelerated.

Secondly, a lot of students, especially those less knowledgeable about strategy games, didn't find the tutorials necessary. Contrary to the teachers' advice, they quickly jumped into the scenarios in the game and were quite overwhelmed. This was not like other games they knew in which they could quickly overview the possibilities. A lot of time was wasted. Many students experienced a lot of frustration and thought they would never master the game. It was hardly the best start for a course. It was clear that, at first, experiences of success were too few compared to student expectations with computer games. At a later point, one student noted, 'It has been one of the most amusing lessons because it went well' (Student 43X, week 4). This was one of the first successful game experiences for that student. For the students, success was an important part of the game experience and success was vital for them to continue playing even though it was difficult.

Thirdly, the first scenario was constructed in a way that went contrary to normal game experience. The first scenario was intended to show the students that mindless war wouldn't work and, of course, they threw themselves into fierce battles instead of careful diplomacy, trade and development of their nations. Therefore, most of the students lost with a big bang. This made them very frustrated and unsure of the game. Normally, a game is constructed so that the difficulty slowly increases to match the player's increasing skills (Rollings and Morris, 2000). In this case, however, the players did not experience a slow increase in difficulty, but a very steep learning curve. The time period the students were placed into was a rather difficult historical period for Denmark. It was chosen for its familiarity, relatively low number of national provinces and bad fit with warmongering.[2]

We wished to make the students go through a historical learning process where they came to appreciate other important historical factors than war. This was done through some initial scenarios where they would experience the limits of war. This was somewhat naïve and counterintuitive to the computer game. In the game, the player would normally start by learning how to wage war, and as the challenges grow the player learns to take other factors into account to overcome even greater challenges. This is sometimes called a layered approach and is a characteristic way for computer games to present information to the player. In a layered approach, the player is presented with the necessary information and the game gives the player more options as the player's skill increases (Egenfeldt-Nielsen, 2003e). In this course, the student started with a challenge that was too difficult and never really learned to wage war. The course tried to place students on too high a level by progressing too fast, which showed how education may obscure the natural exploration that is inherent in many computer games.

From the perspective of the teachers, this was the natural way to go since the experiences the students had could be controlled within the game. After the first hours, we knew they had tried to play a small nation and had experienced defeat in war. This fit best with the weekly teacher talks, which were to match the game scenario. If the students were in completely different places in the game and had experienced completely different things, then how would the teacher be able to make a meaningful and relevant talk aimed at all students? That was the assumption anyway; looking back, it would have been more appropriate to stress playing the computer games first and then slowly increasing the reflection, discussion and teacher talks. This was especially telling since we wanted students to find their own handles to ground the game experiences in previous experiences and extend the scientific history concepts from this. The historical knowledge among students was also less than expected given they had been taking history for the last three years. After the initial failure with war, the students weren't interested in the more subtle features in the computer game or what the teacher could offer, and instead concentrated on understanding how to wage war and the dynamics in this process. It is highly likely that lectures on the particulars of waging war in medieval Europe would have drawn the students because this related to playing the game. As the best students mastered the waging of war toward the end of the course, more layers were added in the playing of the game. This could have been a natural way to extend with other teacher talks. Quite naturally, students discovered an interesting part of the computer game that they considered as relevant and thus chose to engage with and invest time in that part.

The problems with teachers and students learning the game at the same time is also stressed by Kirriemuir and McFarlane (2003) as a common problem. The immediate access to computer games is quite important and they also suggest that support material could ease this and some of the problems described. An interesting recent example of this is the two teacher packages produced as an extension of Kurt Squire's dissertation. They both use *Civilization III*, but with different historical periods and focuses (Squire, 2003a, 2003b). I am doubtful that this will do the trick. In fact, my course did include a sheet with hot tips, hints and breaks to encourage students to help each other, but mostly it wasn't used and it didn't seem to make a difference. The material by Kurt Squire is somewhat broader than just providing support material for students, and the general idea of teaching material is definitely an important step to help teachers appreciate the difficulties, challenges and possibilities with computer games in educational settings.

Teachers

The teachers did play a large role in overcoming the practical barriers, as the number of students that gave up was quite different between the two teachers. The male teacher had students who came back from the dark side. A girl in week 4 went from frustration with the computer game and uncertainty of the purpose to something altogether more positive. She wrote:

> In general, I think the game has been much more fun and with more substantial content this week. Earlier we just waged war on the other countries, without considering strategy. I also think we put more emphasis on other things, like trade, technology, points and stability. This makes the game more meaningful and you can do more things. [...] As you learn the game and its features better, you have more energy to notice the historical facts. I have especially learnt something about religion, but I still think I get more out of a normal history lesson.
>
> (Student 5X, logbook)

The older class had few who completely gave up, and this was probably due to the characteristics of the teacher in the class. The teacher had a closer integration between computer game and teaching. He also stressed the role of the computer game more and somewhat adjusted the teaching to match it. He was also more capable of helping the students due to his experience with strategy games. Also, the smaller number of students in his class somewhat decreased the risk of becoming completely lost. It was clear that in the older class, some of the initial misgivings were resolved, though the scepticism toward what history could be learned remained a problem. Also, none of the teachers were really able to get the students to feel comfortable with the tools *Europa Universalis II* offered for supporting the educational experience.

Tools for reflecting on the game

One of the strengths of the computer game as a tool is the option to report and monitor the progression for later discussion and comparison. Too little attention was paid to how students' game experiences could be 'moved' between different contexts by using the reporting system in the computer game. For instance, it was very hard for the students to sit down in groups and discuss the computer game because it took place in a different physical location from the computers. Group discussions in connection with the computers were not possible due to the size of the computer room and a strong demand for the use of computer resources. This gave the students a bad framework for working with the computer compared to the control group, which worked with the cases in front of them. Even without access to the computer games, more could have been done to facilitate the students' discussions. For example, maps of the game world and reports on the game progression could be used to support the discussions.

The students were encouraged to use logbooks to facilitate these discussions, but this didn't really spark interest and discussion. The best functionality would be to have the computer game record and represent play actions, events and outcomes. There was a reporting mechanism in *Europa Universalis II*, but the students never really used it despite encouragement; it was too abstract and hard for them with their limited knowledge of the computer game.

Reporting mechanisms, saved games and possible options for reviewing a game have been suggested by several researchers (e.g. Kirriemuir and McFarlane, 2003; Squire, 2003d; Squire, 2004). It also seemed to be appropriate in this context. Computer games like *Europa Universalis II*, *Civilization III*, and *Age of Empires II* actually have these functionalities implemented to different extents. In the *Civilization* series, a movie can be played after the game is finished to show how the civilizations spread in one's game. This could be very useful for teachers to review and see different students' experiences and to present game experiences to each other. However, currently it is not possible to save these replays. This is possible in *Age of Empires II*, where the movies are actively used by players to learn the game, discuss strategies and document game outcomes.[3]

Next, I will take a closer look at a more abstract cultural barrier to using and thinking about computer games in an educational setting. I have earlier hinted that the students were reluctant to accept the computer game, but how exactly did this take place?

THE FIGHT OVER WHAT IT MEANS TO LEARN HISTORY WITH COMPUTER GAMES

Discussions with friends whether we learned anything.

(Student 33X, logbook, boy)

Before really engaging with the computer game from an educational perspective, students discussed whether this was a valid history approach. This was a serious barrier that arose early on and continued to influence the students' learning experiences throughout the course. The discussions among students about what constituted learning and history basically took as a starting point history as concerned with facts and events since ancient times. This quite conservative approach to history among students has also been observed by other researchers. Stearns (2000) finds that students bring in quite naïve understandings of history, influenced by a rich number of sources. Schools don't have a monopoly on history.

In this study, most students constantly stressed how computer games did not live up to the standards of traditional teaching despite the continuous emphasis on the interaction between computer game, group discussions and teacher talks as the important element in the experience. The intention of the course was not to replace teaching with computer games. Rather, the computer game was to supplement teaching. Nor was it the plan to replace one learning understanding with another, but to promote a balanced approach. This was probably partly misunderstood due to the computer game standing out as the experimental part and thereby attracting most student attention. When students in post-interviews were confronted with the underlining course set-up, more than one looked puzzled and surprised.

The question of the merits of a more counterfactual approach to history was much discussed and commented on by the students who were constantly questioning and evaluating the educational use of computer games. In that sense, they were extremely critical and reflective. However, this reflection and critical sense were seldom used to discuss the experiences in the computer games and to compare them with the teacher talks, readings or previous historical knowledge.

Few students really appreciated history as something other than facts. Those who did see some merits to a more counterfactual approach didn't really think it worked in the course. Still, they had great sympathy for the idea when discussing it. The discussions on learning with computer games are reflected in a number of comments by students and were also constantly experienced during the course. Notice in the quotes below how the new approach to history is constantly devalued or actually denied (marked with bold). This was typical of the attitudes of most students.

Regarding learning, I **only** think you learned the consequences of what happened when you did different things, but historical facts were in short supply, you only acquired this knowledge from the book.

(Student 21X, logbook, boy)

The outcome of the game and group work **limits itself** to a general understanding of the time period. Which is also fine, but there are not enough facts.

(Student 27X, logbook, boy)

It was exciting to play the computer game; this is not something I do that often. But I think I had **less benefit** from it regarding history than expected.

(Student 38X, logbook, girl)

It was good that we were allowed to learn in a different way. But we had too hard a time getting started with the game. We are not many who think you learn **anything** from playing.

(Student 40X, logbook, girl)

There existed an invisible schism between the objective and subjective world in students' approach to history. Apparently, it provoked a lot of students that the computer game to some extent disregarded historical facts and changed the events of history, presenting a subjective view on history. This discussion mirrors the battle fought between counterfactual historians and more traditional historians (Ferguson, 1997). Students found the lack of facts to be completely inconsistent with history teaching and rejected that they could learn anything. There was a constant call for more historical facts, especially supported by the students who had limited success with the computer game.[4] The scepticism toward the history the computer represented was aggravated by the cultural standing of computer games and a general resistance from students as newcomers to the community of high school.

Resistance to educational use of computer games from the emerging community of students

Computer games have links to popular culture, gender roles and violence discussions, which currently seem stronger than other media forms. It is rare to see a newspaper dedicate entire columns or even front pages to describing violent television, problematic board games or excessive outings to the cinemas. When other media problems are described, it is certainly with less explosive material and reactions. You will not have worried parents, psychologists and politicians engaging in discussions through the public press (Beavis, 1999b; Egenfeldt-Nielsen and Smith, 2004).

In other media forms, the low and high culture parts have successfully been split into separate spheres. We have great movies accepted as art, but also popular movies that still venture poorly in educational settings. One can argue that the split between movies of low and high culture has given television and video an easier way into education. This has still not happened with computer games despite attempts to elevate them to the status of art.

In that sense, it may be challenged if it even makes sense to treat computer games as a neutral medium, as it has frequently been considered. A medium does not imply neutrality. Camera angles, edits and voice-overs influence the impression a programme leaves. Content in documentaries is influenced by the way it is presented and what is presented. For the majority of media, the critical awareness of the platforms' impact on users' perception is still neglected. In this book's perspective, I will maintain that there is a degree of 'mediumness' to computer games, as we want to use computer games as a platform for delivering educational experiences and content. This platform is, however, not neutral in terms of values, props, culture and teaching (Buckingham, 2003; Newman, 2004).

The cultural position of computer games makes it hard to draw directly on findings from the introduction of other media in school. Television, radio, video and computers may in general have fought hard to be integrated in schools as we saw in Chapter 2. However, compared to computer games, they have a strong push from governmental authorities and these media are to a lesser extent perceived as leisure, fun, popular, juvenile, dangerous and a waste of time. (The opinion of computer games has improved over the years [Buckingham, 2003]). From a teacher's perspective, computer games are strongly culturally loaded and completely alien.

However, it was not only the teachers who opposed computer games in an educational setting. It has not earlier been suggested that students themselves would be a barrier with their understanding of computer games, learning and history, but this was certainly the case in this course. This lack of reference to student misgivings about computer games for education may be a consequence of a somewhat optimistic approach to computer games, resembling some of the early experiences with computers and subsequently the internet. Computers, the internet and computer games are seen as the true learning form of the new generation, forcefully claimed by Prensky (2001a), Tapscott (1998) and, to a lesser extent, Gee (2003).

Some of the unexpected strong resistance might also be found in the students' newly begun road toward an academic career. The students' approach could overall be described as conventional and Wenger (1999: 154–7) would characterize the students as being on an inbound trajectory. He points out how newcomers are often less progressive than established members of a community, due to the general uncertainty of how to act in the community. On an inbound trajectory, members are struggling to find their place in the community and invest a large part of their identity in the enterprise. Unsure of their position and the boundaries, they are inclined to seek continuity and security rather than discontinuity. This may become even more marked since the engagement of students with the academic community is quite unequal, artificial and detached as they are split off from old-timers. They have a distant contact with teachers who present material to them and hardly explore the more subtle and tacit assumptions inherent in the academic community.

This is supported by the youngest class, which is just entering the academic community. They were the most critical, though the tendency was also clear in the older class. The emerging consciousness as serious academics may have led to a stronger rejection of the computer game. The initial interest and motivation was calmed when the students realized that this did not involve the usual kind of history that they knew, and, for many, the computer games were not what they expected. They couldn't really connect the experience with any relevant area in their current school practice and identity.

In Gee's (2003) perspective, identity is inherently linked with learning and people cannot learn without being able to see learning as relevant and desirable for their identity, which extends well from my educational theory. Gee (2003) finds identification to be present in computer games both on a structural level and in the domain of computer games. He states that deep learning:

[…] is inextricably caught up with identity in a variety of different ways. People cannot learn in a deep way within a semiotic domain if they are not willing to commit themselves fully to the learning in terms of time, efforts and active engagement. Such a commitment requires that they are willing to see themselves in terms of a new identity, that is, to see themselves as the *kind of person* who can learn, use and value the new semiotics domain. In turn they need to believe that, if they are successful learners in the domain, they will be valued and accepted by others committed to that domain.

(Gee, 2003: 59)

Clearly, these factors were not present in this course on computer games for students in the group who gave up. The students prioritized other school areas higher and didn't really see the computer games as worthy of academic attention. This poses a considerable problem, remembering Dewey's description of the quality of an educational experience, where relevance is very important. You might also see it as a clash between adults' tendency to rationalize play in a progress rhetoric opposed to a frivolous rhetoric as they are described in Chapter 6. Many students did not buy the rationale that play was potentially able to teach them about history. Convincing them of this took the rocky road over changing their entire notion of what history meant to them, but it also challenged their perception of what the academic track was. The alternative to the safe, mundane world of history as facts seemed too exotic and uncertain and it was in opposition to the general school culture. Looking back, it is hardly surprising that the students resisted being caught in this limbo. A computer game that tells me about history that really isn't history – but rather stories about history – surely this must be a joke. However, it can be argued that engaging in exactly such discussion about the nature of history, education and identity is an extremely valuable educational experience that will move students beyond merely being passive receivers of content.

It is somewhat absurd that one of the most important entry points for using computer games becomes its main Achilles' heel: namely, a closer relation to students' identity and a different approach to history. The students were supposed to appreciate a well-known media for exploring a more modern version of history, but this clashed with their in-bound trajectory to academia. These findings have critical implications for how and when to introduce computer games, as it tends to challenge existing notions of learning, teaching and student identity, which requires some self-confidence and risk-taking on the part of the students. It would probably have proved easier to introduce computer games towards the end of primary school, when students are well established and looking for new ways to explore a subject. The use of computer games should probably also be presented more forcefully as a real alternative instead of a shaky, uncertain, experimental teaching style, which was the impression students were given, especially since the teachers and researcher were quite uncertain of where the course was going. The facilitation of change and new thinking again stresses the role of the teacher as a facilitator of computer games as an acceptable academic tool. This also explains why the teacher who was more competent in computer games had fewer students who completely rejected the computer games as historically relevant.

CONCLUSION: BERMUDA TRIANGLE OF INCOMPETENCE, CONSERVATISM AND LIMITED RESOURCES

This chapter has highlighted the particular problems with introducing a highly successful leisure activity into the educational system, where it becomes caught between heaven and hell. It is not really able to live up to the expectations normally entertained toward leisure computer game experiences and it is not really able to present itself as a trustworthy addition to the life of a student. This is aggravated by a range of practical barriers.

We have examined the problems that computer games trigger by looking at how the course was marked by different groups' very different resources for participating in the course. All these groups were affected by the numerous practical barriers experienced in the course, but with very different outcomes. Interestingly, it seems that although some of these problems were partly triggered by the complex nature of computer games, none of them were qualitatively different from what would be generally experienced in a course using computer games in a third-generation perspective. Instead, the problems were aggravated and presented themselves more clearly. The barriers described above fall into the following three categories:

- **Practical/structural**: The technical limitations, the limited space, the time slots for lessons, etc.
- **Game-related**: Learning how to play the game, the complexity of the game, the balance between playing/learning and integration of computer games with teaching.
- **Expectations and culture**: The students' and the teachers' initial way of thinking about computer games, history, learning and teaching.

The confusing start with technical problems and a steep learning curve alienated some students who normally did well in school. They were inclined to feel that the computer game was irrelevant to history. Furthermore, the position of the students as newcomers to the community of academia may also have led to stronger reactions. Computer games could not be seen as acceptable in academic work on the road to university. The normally high-ranking students in history were not inclined to accept the computer game course as reasonable for accessing their historical knowledge as this would undermine their position in the hierarchy in the subject of history.

The course also ran into a variety of problems that made it very hard to get to the essence. The computer game proved to be quite different from traditional teaching. The practical barriers were overwhelming and this was clearly also a warranted reason for the criticism. It is hard to settle on just how large a role the barriers played, but they definitely didn't account for all the scepticism. Finally, the computer game represented history in a way unknown to most and they were unsure of how to treat conflicting views. Despite good intentions, history teaching is still mostly taught from a textbook which hands down the 'undeniable' truth.

NOTES

1   Recent research suggests that this may be changing with around 25 per cent teachers in Canada and the UK actually having experience with using games in education (Becker, 2005; MORI, 2006).

2   The first scenario starts in 1492 when Denmark is quite strong and in a position to expand. However, if it depends on too many loans and war taxes, the country destabilises.

3   The websites with these saved games can be found in several places. Among the biggest are http://aok.heavengames.com and www.mrfixitonline.com

4   The focus on facts in history existed despite the absence of an initial factual test, which would probably further have supported a traditional understanding of learning by showing what was important in the course, namely historical facts.

9
The Balance Between Play and Learning

There should maybe have been somewhat firmer settings around the whole project.
People have been committed, but at the same time frivolous. It is just a game.
(Student 5X, logbook, girl)

Fundamentally, most researchers in educational computer games expect that learning and playing can enrich each other, but in this course, it became quite clear that the enrichment might turn out to be more accurately described as a conflict if one is not careful. This is not necessarily due to an inherent conflict between learning and playing, but more likely a consequence of the existing approach to learning practised in the educational system. Education and learning are seen as work, which is opposed to play in modernity (Mouritsen, 2003).

Education and play are two modes that we may want to combine, but to some degree we also feel guilty about combining them. More than one student questioned whether playing the computer game was schoolwork, based on the simple premise that it was play. Even though habits and expectations may give some explanation of the resistance toward combining play and education, the resistance also displays fundamental differences relating to learning and play. Play differs from learning as it abides less by specific rules; it also has a more voluntary nature than learning. The student engaged in playing a computer game will expect more autonomy, though it may later be criticized when the learning part of the experience is evaluated. Earlier research points out the advantages of supporting features for educational use of computer games like guiding, supporting, scaffolding, introducing and debriefing the experience, all of which are partly in opposition to play. All of these interventions present demands on the game experience and constrain the perceived freedom in play unless you find creative and meaningful ways to integrate these in the game universe. However, opposition against such interventions relates more to an idealized understanding of play rather than play per se.

There are other more fundamental differences between play and learning, which Andersen and Kampmann's (1996) account of play can help clarify. They distinguish between deep play and social aspects of play. Deep play is described as the complete absorption with play, in which the player forgets about time and place. On the other hand, social play is the surrounding activities that support and facilitate the deep play. According to Andersen and Kampmann (1996), the scope and importance of social play is often underestimated even though it actually seems to be one of the main elements in play. Social play is the place where one learns about power relations, social conduct and identity. What I find worth noting, after drawing on both play culture and research on fan culture around computer games, is that social play is necessary to frame and reflect the game experience. Deep play is the player engaged in the computer games whereas social play represents everything around this gaming experience. When students play *Europa Universalis II*, they are engaged in deep play. This deep play is framed, broken, nurtured and changed by group discussions, teacher talks and other students. This gets at the quite engaging nature of most computer games, where the concentration and required attention are similar to those of deep play. One loses sense of time and place while totally absorbed in the game universe.[1] However, most genres do not leave time to reflect and evaluate the efforts. It happens very much in a continuous state drawing quite automatically on previous experiences. There is little time to stop, reconsider and reflect. Indeed, observations of game players will show almost complete absorption (Jones, 1998).

In this course, each student's exact balancing of playing and learning seemed to be individual and it was not possible to dispense the same verdicts for different student groups. The supporting features were positioned differently for the groups participating in the course, but in general, most students had problems stepping out of the deep play mode. The high achievers wanted little introduction and scaffolding concerning the computer game and history in general. They played around and were able to learn the computer game without formal help. After the initial learning of the basics of the game, they were quite interested in extra material, linking the computer game with teaching and working on their own. They did not see the great benefit of group discussions because they often found these to be irrelevant to the game experience and a waste of their time learning wise. The give-up group was, of course, in extra need of an introduction to the computer game, but they also needed a basic appreciation of the relevance of the course, perhaps even to conceive the rationale for spending time on history in general. The students in the give-up group had a much harder time finding the line between play and learning compared to the high achievers. The runners-up were somewhat strong in all areas and benefited from most of the supporting features introduced in the course. The upwardly mobile did not need help with the computer game and they were eager to go off on their own. They did, however, need guidance to engage with the learning perspective.

The different groups were more or less in balance concerning the play and learning. For most groups, teacher interventions were needed to actually turn the course from a play experience into an educational experience. In general, the students used either play or learning as their handle on the course. For the students missing historical awareness, play became a way into the computer game, but it remained hard to expand the play interest to history. For the students with less interest in the play part, history could be a way in. The give-up group had no handles and therefore did not really engage with the course, whereas the high achievers were able to connect the two experiences based on previous time spent both playing computer games and learning history.

An unfortunate consequence of the course conceived as play was the frivolous approach taken by some students often and by most students at some point. Although the teaching with computer games was perceived by most as characterized by high engagement, this was not the whole story. The engagement was mostly linked with the deep playing of the computer game and the blending into the learning part was limited for most students. Furthermore, the playing part led some students to take a laid-back approach to the course. The laid-back approach did not seem to be a constant phenomenon, but rather varied. Students were more inclined to drift toward their desires. In one lesson, they were quite interested, while in another, marginally interested. This seems natural from a play perspective, but of course problematic from a teaching perspective, where more continuity is expected. There was no stabilizing factor, like a feeling that this is schoolwork and one should work seriously with it. This is not necessarily a reaction that will persist if computer games are integrated more into the educational system and obtain more legitimacy.

The supremacy of playing over educational experience was also apparent in the cases where history set some gameplay limits in the computer game. The criticism of the computer game's failure to adhere to historical facts and events did not stop students from heavily criticizing these limitations in the next instant. In fact, the student who saw the link to real history in the in-game exploration of the world criticized it in the next breath for limiting the gameplay. On one hand, students felt that the computer game should reflect history, and in a number of areas, it did. On the other hand, they criticized the limits this historical reality imposed on their gameplay. Many didn't want it to be that rigid.

Although play and learning did not blend perfectly, it did give the course a progression with more student engagement. However, this engagement was not always educationally relevant. The next three examples show learning experiences at different critical points in the teaching with *Europa Universalis II*: appreciation, exploration and linking.

THE PROCESS OF APPRECIATION, EXPLORATION AND LINKING

The focus in the following examples from actual school use is on the transformation of the concrete experiences into abstract concepts through the experiential learning cycle, as discussed in Chapter 6. The student starts by appreciating the differences that make a difference. Then, the student explores and reflects on these differences found in the concrete experiences, ultimately linking them to other experiences. In this process, the student will revisit concepts and, through instruction, construct scientific concepts.

First example of a lost learning opportunity: no appreciation of historical information

The example below shows the *lack of appreciation* of the simple historical information that students yearned for. When historical principles and limits were at play in the game universe, the students were mostly ignorant of these sound limits.

For example, in an interview, one student complained that it didn't make sense that in one province, a player could raise a meagre 1000 men while another province's player could boast 8000 men. He didn't explore the reasons behind this limit and failed to recognize the historical information in the experience. However, there are relevant historical reasons for the differences that are mirrored in this student's game experience. Not all provinces have the same capacity for raising troops due to population size, loyalty to the crown, cultural background, religious beliefs and infrastructure. Furthermore, troops can't be continually raised in a country. Only so many men are capable of bearing arms in one country.

The student in this example didn't seem to understand that the game's historical universe was made up of a lot of the important actions that history has at its disposal and that the computer game was built on quite a detailed model of history. Many students couldn't really appreciate the historically correct factual information, background, dynamics and events even when they were right under their nose. This was not related to scepticism toward the entire enterprise described in the previous chapter, but rather to a missing historical and game awareness. Clearly, most students lacked the historical awareness and game insight to appreciate the detailed model and the historical information at play. We may find a remiscence of the same problem in the quite ambitious and successful educational strategy game *Making History: The Calm and the Storm*, about the Second World War, developed by Muzzy Lane.

Second example of a lost learning opportunity: appreciation of historical facts but no further exploration

This example shows the *lack of exploration* despite the opportunity to explore. The students have already appreciated the presence of historical information, dynamics and events. The students recognized the historical information but failed to engage further with it.

The students were playing Denmark and were in a war against Sweden. After a series of wars, they managed to get the upper hand over Sweden, which they knew was against the historical realities. Even with this result, the students did not ask questions as to why that happened. They were too busy playing the game. The students found the non-historical victories over Sweden rejuvenating, but they failed to ask what accomplished the victory and neglected to engage with the game's historical representations, viewing them as subjective descriptions of history with little relevance. The students simply noted that winning over Sweden was not in agreement with history as taught by the teacher and the textbook and they dismissed this game experience as irrelevant for teaching history.

Third example of a lost learning opportunity: exploring historical connections but no linking

The *incapability of extending* the game experiences beyond merely exploring the game is demonstrated quite well in the following example. There is potentially a connection between game universe and historical thinking but it is left hanging in two boys' description of the proper strategy for Napoleon to bring England to its knees:

> Napoleon's ambition: Recipe for beating England. 1) Secure the borders against Spain with a peace treaty to disengage troops. In this case it is done by conquering a province in North America and then making peace. 2) Destroy the British fleet by attacking small groups of ships with superior forces. 3) Leave a considerable force to fight off sporadic attacks from Austria. 4) Collect all troops from France and send them over the English Channel. 5) The British will face a force five times their size. 6) Therefore, it can't go wrong. It was surprisingly easy to beat England. It was impossible to defend the [newly conquered English] provinces.
>
> It was surprising that England had so few men in England. The reason for this might be that they felt secure against invasions as long as they controlled the British Channel. They didn't have resources after the Independence War.
>
> (Student 21X, logbook, boy)

In the plan, there are elements of historical relevance though they are not consciously exposed. They are aware of the geographic elements, the threats from Spain/Austria, the importance of outmanoeuvring the enemy, the importance of the British fleet, Spain's vulnerability in the colonies, the

British ability to intervene at their discretion on the continent through their superior navy and the importance of gaining the upper hand through sheer size.

The problem is that nobody really exposes potential concepts and connects the experiences to history teaching in general. The students conclude that this is merely part of playing the computer game and that it has little bearing on history in general. They do not use their curiosity to dig deeper. Indeed, most of their thinking and historical knowledge is quite relevant in regards to European history.

The students' main comment is how they found it surprisingly easy to pull off their plan, beating history. But in fact, a number of things could go wrong with their plan, reflecting historical dynamics. A new enemy might show up or internal rebellions break out. In the late eighteenth century France was strong, so gameplay actually resembled the historical situation quite well. The two boys were surprised at the resilience of the rebellions in the newly conquered British provinces, but this is also historically relevant since one of Napoleon's greatest problems was indeed keeping peace in his new conquests. Rebellions were often triggered by differences in culture and religious turmoil. The problems the boys experienced could have been explored by discussing the problems of occupation in history and by relating their strategies to Napoleon's problems with occupying Spain and Italy. However, the teacher didn't pursue this angle and the students didn't take up the challenge themselves.

These boys had quite elaborate reflections and discussions about the game experiences and they achieved a good general insight into the historical period, but they did not obtain what they really desired, namely historical facts. They were able to draw some of the historical connections above, but others escaped them because they lacked the options for exploring them further in the course and they were not given much support for further exploration from the teacher. This example shows that the computer game can certainly provide relevant concrete experiences, thinking, student engagement and investment, but without the teacher to facilitate it remains a game experience and one with low educational quality.

An example of a strong learning experience: linking

There were few examples of learning experiences that arose from the game experiences, even when the exploration of the game was quite deep. The few successful learning experiences support the claim for using concrete game experiences as a starting point for building concepts about history and show that deep explorations of the game can lead to interesting learning opportunities. Students were interested and engaged when history could be tied into their specific game experiences, especially when links could be made from the game to history.

In one example, a student constantly experienced problems in southern France due to religious turmoil between the Protestant sub-group, the Huguenots, and the state religion, Catholicism. The student perceived the historical reasons for this conflict to be most interesting. In particular, when it was suggested that the downfall of the heretics was paramount to France's success, the student saw how he could send missionaries to the infected provinces to change their state religion or the tolerance towards different religious groups. The student remembered the importance of religion in later games and was interested in exploring the reasons behind the turmoil in his beloved France, both in the game and in history. He engaged with the computer game and invested in it. He was more than ready to expand on his knowledge when he got the chance with the teacher. The student could actually recognize the relevance of some of the material from teacher talks and the textbook on the religious unrest during this historical period. In a very concrete sense, he could see that religious differences led to rebellion, financial losses and domestic problems.

WHY THE TEACHING WITH COMPUTER GAMES FAILED

In their study of the area, Kirriemuir and McFarlane (2003) are disappointed that educational use of computer games does not seem to expand beyond short experimental periods. In that sense, they find that educational use of computer games remains experimental rather than pilots for broader use in the future. Disappointment will probably not get us far. To see computer games as 'merely' a neutral medium we can use for delivering content, skills and attitudes is lulling ourselves into dreamland. We can shape the teaching with computer games but they also bring baggage. Indeed changes in teaching practice are far from unproblematic and not without cost. While small changes and adjustments are a constant part of a community of practice, major changes on both the individual and the group level require an extra effort (Wenger, 1999). Several challenges to the teaching practice are apparent from the examples above. Basically, there are three apparent problematic areas from the examples above, indicating that educational use of computer games can work well, but it requires the right balance on a number of axes:

- **Appreciation of historical elements**: Students are not always capable on their own appreciating relevant historical information, events and dynamics.
- **Exploration of historical elements**: When historical elements are identified, students are not exploring the historical implications. When they do, they tend to focus on the factual information and not the larger picture.

- **Linking of game experience**: Students are not capable of connecting the concrete experiences in the computer game with teacher talks, history in the textbook, or other spheres of life.

It is worth noting that most students did not have a problem with the engagement and motivation. They invested in the computer game and were interested in learning more if it was relevant to playing the game, but this wasn't true for all the student groups (see Chapter 8).

Appreciating the historical significance in the computer game

The ability to distinguish the relevant from the irrelevant is recognized by Wenger (1999) as one of the important characteristics of being a member of a community of practice, and it also fits well with Bateson's approach, where the ability to see the right difference is crucial. From Wenger's perspective, this would imply that the teacher must teach students what differences make a difference in the community of playing historical computer games in school. This includes the ability to recognize the relevant elements in a computer game history course in both historical information and computer game representations. Indeed, these were the characteristics that most of the high achievers demonstrated. There is quite a thin line between what counts as relevant history information and what features are merely part of the game universe. In *Europa Universalis II*, interpreting the game experience demanded more intimate knowledge of history and the computer game than was initially the impression when planning the course.

In Chapter 4, this was discussed as an area still vastly overlooked. When the information is appreciated in the game universe, it is often taken at face value or simply dismissed. Grundy (1991) finds that many students have an almost blind trust in the computer game's ability to tell the truth, despite other opposing sources. In my study, some students supplement this with an almost automatic rejection when the trust in the game is broken. My study paints a more fine-grained picture of what students relied uncritically on in the computer game and why this was the case sketched in the group descriptions in Chapter 8. There is an automatic rejection in the give-up groups whereas the upwardly mobile took the history at face value. The runner-up students were struggling to find the balance whereas the high achievers were actually able to find the right balance, appreciating the right elements. This ability points to highly relevant skills like critical sense of sources and ability to analyse a given system – an ability that some students master more than others.

Despite the outspoken criticism of the historical facts and inconsistencies concerning the game, the concrete criticism was not very elaborate and appreciation of historical elements was quite superficial. The problems that did get mentioned were the most obvious, but also the least interesting. They included winning a war, declaring marriage, shift in ownership of provinces or outcome of battles. Often, the criticism was quite misguided and lacked appreciation of finer details in history. It took as a starting point contemporary borders and other historical periods. For example, Denmark's continuing struggle in the game to overtake Schleswig-Holstein in the sixteenth century was sometimes successful, but not permanent. Students viewed the conquest of Schleswig-Holstein by Denmark as completely non-historical because students tended to see Germany as a unified country, despite the fact that unification only began during the mid-eighteenth century. For most students, it became quite apparent that marriages, wars and other events did not always reflect real history since they changed when they replayed the scenario. This led to the critique that the computer didn't teach them any history. They wanted facts and the real events.

Usually, the girls were more sceptical toward the different learning form of computer games and more prone to see history as learning about facts and events. They were the strongest critics as to the lack of correct facts and events, whereas it seems the boys were more capable of abstracting from this and identifying the relevant areas. This was probably also a consequence of the boys' more extensive experience with computer games. They knew how computer games worked and did not expect them to be just like traditional history teaching, which was more often the girls' expectation. You may say that the girls appeared more conservative, but in reality, the difference related to weak versus strong students in the course. The better a student did on the axis of history interest, history knowledge, computer games and academic ability, the more the student could appreciate the alternative form of history teaching. To a large degree, this matched gender.

You might say that the problem is really to believe rather than disbelieve. One does not read a historical novel, play a computer game or watch a historical movie with the expectation of it being accurate. The hard part is to strike the balance and appreciate that some parts are relevant, while others in a sense mock history. In movies, the production team often goes to great trouble to ensure historical accuracy. In *Pirates of the Caribbean*, the pirate ship was built from scratch in a real size model by consulting experts and using old drawings of Spanish ships (Verbinski, 2003). The pirate ship was the setting for the movie and in that way mirrors history. The same desire is obvious in most historical strategy computer games. In movies, novels and computer games, the setting tends to be accurate, but the actions and outcomes are not necessarily accurate. If the pirate captain should be required to climb the ship's mast with a wooden leg in a hurricane for dramatic effect, it is not a problem. However, historically this is highly problematic.

In the computer game, the drama or narrative is not necessarily the main force and the instructor is not in command. Here, the setting is at the player's hand and if the player is compelled to take France out of its neutral policy in the late sixteenth century and declare an all-out war on the major powers, so be it. It comes down to being able to think abstractly and see the larger perspective in an action. You may argue that this seems intuitively easier in a computer game, where the player is aware that he/she is actually choosing an action between different alternatives. This freedom of choice must entail that the outcome from the choices is not necessarily in agreement with history textbooks, but most importantly, the freedom of choice leads to an appreciation of history as more open-ended than factual accounts. Indeed, most students did realize the openness of the game, but they stopped there and did not progress any further. Instead, they focused on what they perceived as the computer game's historical shortcomings.

Just the facts, please!

It was clear from the course that the students had a conservative approach to anything else than history as facts. Clearly, students felt bombarded with historical facts and events especially during the teacher talks and did not really engage with the historical information, but just snatched as much they could. Similarly, students felt overwhelmed by the computer game, but on closer examination, it wasn't due to the amount of facts. Rather, the computer game's complexity was in the connections *between* the information rather than *in* the information. However, these connections couldn't really be appreciated without a proper grounding in history. Most students lacked this grounding and therefore were not capable of appreciating these connections or even exploring these connections. There are good reasons for students' narrow focus on the historical facts.

In the introduction to this book, I presented six levels of educational objectives, which may help illuminate why a deeper appreciation, exploration and linking of history was difficult to achieve. The six levels are knowledge, comprehension, application, analysis, synthesis and evaluation. It was stressed that the first levels are necessary for the following levels to make sense, and that might have been the real problem for the students in this study. Students were still grappling with constructing a foundation of basic knowledge and a comprehension of the massive amount of facts and events that they were bombarded with during history teaching. They felt they needed more facts and events to get a picture of what history was and were not comfortable with seeing or doing anything more beyond facts. To apply the knowledge in a game setting, adopt an analytic stance and evaluate this process was way beyond most student groups' capability.

From the perspective presented in Chapter 6, it may appear that the students lacked a sound experience base for beginning to construct scientific concepts, but for students, the concrete experience in the game wasn't feasible for constructing the concepts. They wanted facts straight out of the textbook. They were somewhat stuck between these two positions. They relied on historical information in the textbook and teacher talks, while any concrete experiences stayed in the game room. In both learning sites, students felt like drowning and resorted to defensive manoeuvres evident in the previous chapter's uncovering of barriers.

In the case of *Europa Universalis II*, the computer game delivered more complexity than the students could cope with, even if some students found the historical facts too limited. Considering the students' level of understanding regarding history, the broader approach to history as a dynamic process with underlying variables that lead to events was premature. During the course, the students were primarily concerned with digesting facts and had little initiative for going beyond these facts. In fact, the very thought of linking these contexts was an abomination for all but a few high achievers. The lack of student maturity may also explain why some suggested that computer games really belong at college and university level. Indeed, Muzzy Lane's, with similar complexity, aim for the higher grades.

Edutainment pop-ups in the search for facts

The inclination to prefer facts was also most apparent when students talked about what parts of the computer game actually worked. Students looked for the computer game to provide facts and thereby link better with other history teaching and their understanding of history, which would unify the learning sites in the course. Given edutainment's dominance in the current market, it is interesting that characteristics from edutainment surfaced as a solution, a way to unify games and facts.

Edutainment's characteristics centre on pop-up boxes, the one element in the computer game that most students consistently connected with history teaching. Pop-up boxes were consistently seen as the most educational part of playing the game and students suggested using more of them for a more educational game experience.

The pop-ups in *Europa Universalis II* actually span a variety of types. In some of the pop-ups, necessary information is given so that the player can make an informed choice in the game. Some students also found these pop-ups interesting. Still, most students were not impressed with the pop-ups, even though they actually provided the facts and events from history they accused the computer game of not delivering. When students had the chance to acquire historical facts in the computer game setting, they didn't find it fitting, as the quote below attests:

Well, when you are playing, then suddenly one of these windows pops up. When there is something about a historical event, for example the French revolution or another famous person who pops up and then dies. For example, this guy Ove Guldberg, I think that was his name, when I played Denmark. He popped up and then there was a long description of him. How it happened, and that was okay, but I mean … I just think it was suddenly a bit dry … It might be educational, but I think it was kind of, dah.

(Students, Interview 2, boy)

The paradox of pop-ups being attractive yet unappealing points to the perceived strength of edutainment. Although pop-ups extended from an edutainment formula intuitively attracting students' educational 'instinct', in reality they had little teaching capacity. Pop-ups were scorned as irrelevant to the game and usually quickly clicked through.

When you are sitting there and playing then you are playing the game. I don't think you really want to take the time to read the pop-ups. There are many, I know we also did, who clicked away from these pop-ups. We didn't have time to read them. We were sitting in the middle of the game and then suddenly came that pop-up. It was kind of an intrusion towards the end that they kept popping up.

(Students, Interview 2, girl)

On the other hand, these very pop-ups were suggested as a basis for more historically correct computer games. By expanding on the pop-ups with movies, sound and more historical information, students believed a higher educational impact could be achieved. On closer examination, students recognized the limits of pop-ups, but were still tempted by the promise of pop-up boxes as a simple way to get historical facts and events. They wouldn't threaten students' practice of learning where facts were in the driver's seat. Pop-ups are basically going down the path of edutainment's sugar-coating of content in picture and sound, introducing information of little relevance to the computer game and changing the game experience to live up to external demands.

The demand for factual information is as strong with students as it is with any parent buying an edutainment title, or publisher living up to the national curriculum. At least, it seemed so when students were asked in this study. However, it also reflected their struggle with fitting the computer game into an educational setting. We should be alert to this tendency in educational settings for preferring edutainment that reflects underlying propositions in education and history. Indeed, edutainment would seem more in line with the history perception found among students in this study. Students preferred the approach to history as facts, both on a didactic level and on a more personal level. History was facts and not much else. This was challenged during the study and caused great commotion and discussion among different student groups. Next, we will look at the challenge of the facts, when students were expected to explore the game experiences beyond their face value.

Exploring the game beyond facts

In general, the exploration of different implications of game actions was not something present in students just starting to familiarize themselves with the game's interface, a new approach to history and deluge of facts from the teaching. Rather, the exploration slowly evolved as students learned to appreciate the finer details of the game universe. Whether the teaching can be described as deep or superficial is a harder question.

A deeper exploration was critical for teaching with *Europa Universalis II* to extend beyond unreflective playing and to offer something else beyond learning the facts of history. Exploration in depth implies a more complex representation of a topic. However, this is somewhat inaccurate. It doesn't fit with the discussions the students had in this course and the observations made during playing. In addition, it is at odds with the structure in most computer games. Looking at the rule-based universe of *Europa Universalis II*, students were far from struck by the complex information delivered. The information represented by historical facts and events was not overwhelming compared to the textbook and teacher talks, which, as documented in the previous chapter, led to scepticism from students. The rules in *Europa Universalis II* represent the most important and interesting elements from the given historical universe. The simple rules were at the centre of the game experience and not detailed information.

The confusion related to complexity arises because we tend to think of complexity as a function of the amount of information. However, any computer game's real complexity arises from the interconnections of simple rules derived from the dynamic relationship and parallel interaction of variables (see Chapter 6). When the students read their textbooks, things happened in a particular order and a more or less linear narrative was presented. This wasn't the case in *Europa Universalis II*, where students' game actions spread out in different directions and students were expected to willingly explore the different connections.

In this study, the complexity was evident several times as students paused or slowed down the game to examine the exact implications of a game event. The complexity was clearest when students in *Europa Universalis II* experienced historical events, declarations of wars, offers of alliances, political crises or discovery of new regions. These experiences forced the students to make important choices, balancing a number of possible outcomes against each other and exploring different alternatives. In these cases, students took a break in the game or at least changed the speed to very slow. The high achievers in particular commented on the role of speed in the computer game. To some degree, the use of speed was a demarcation line between high achievers and the other groups who didn't use the manipulation of time very often.[2] Some students did explore the game in depth, but most perceived the game experience as superficial due to its lack of historical facts.

The exploration depended not only on students' computer game ability, like pausing the game, but also on their historical background information and general historical awareness. Only a few high achievers became capable of seeing the potential of exploring the game experience from a historical perspective beyond facts:

> It is also that even though the history [in the game] doesn't follow what the history textbook says then you are still learning something. What makes a society like it is and what consequences your actions have and likewise.
>
> (Students, Interview 3, boy)

> Good – interesting, but you don't learn that much about events, on the other hand, you learn about the underlying reasons for the events.
>
> (Logbook, 39x, boy)

Exploration really began to show up among the high achievers and partly the runners-up towards the end of the course. However, the students were unsure of what to make of these explorations and they were not sufficiently encouraged during the course. It did not mean that the strong students thought the course had been excellent, but they criticized it for not facilitating a better, different, explorative learning experience and focused less on the lack of facts. In the following quote from a post-interview, you clearly sense uncertainty and vagueness as to the nature of this alternative approach to history. It is hard for the students to formulate the meaning of history beyond facts and events, but high achievers in the end sensed something more than facts were out there.

> I think that this was also something that the game did. I mean it gave a general understanding of the period and that was it. There were some dates, events and similar things but it wasn't something you learned in the games. It was something you knew before, I think. The game gives a general understanding of how it worked. And that was good; it was really good in the way it did it. But I am not sure whether we learned it because of the game or the parallel teaching. I don't know if the game could work by itself.
>
> (Student, Interview 1, boy)

There seems to be an appreciation of the computer game's potential, if only it had been done a bit differently. Although this holds some truth, as there were technical problems, it seems that the problems stem more from the general problems in teaching with computer games, which we will continue to examine. One initial hope was that the inaccurate historical events could spark such exploration. However, in this study it didn't seem to happen.

Linking concrete experience in the game with scientific concepts

The missing links between the different learning sites were constantly noted by students. According to some students, playing the computer game might as well have been a separate subject with no connection to teacher talks on history. This, quite naturally, led to a lack of appreciation of historical elements in the computer games, especially the facts.

> When you sit and receive teaching from the teacher then it is primarily facts that are hurled at you. I mean she really tells what happened in these periods, right. When you sit and play the game then it is not like it happened in reality. So, it is not completely correct how it [the game] follows history. So I don't think you can draw any parallels to the teacher talks, I really don't.
>
> (Student, Interview 2, boy)

The lack of connection is demonstrated in a teacher's quite elaborate description of mercantilism not being accessible in the computer game. Few students, if any, used the knowledge of mercantilism in playing the computer game even though this was central in the teacher talks and the textbook used. Mercantilism was more or less the basic economic model the computer game used. In an interview with a girl, she indicated that she really couldn't use the teacher's description of mercantilism for anything because as she said about the computer game:

> It's not as if you notice it when you obtain a bank loan and then you have some money. Then you use some money to create armies, to build a navy and go to war and then suddenly you don't have any more money.
>
> (Student, Interview 2)

It is interesting that, while not very eloquently, in this short sentence she has described central elements for most monarchs before trade became prominent as a way to bolster the revenues. When you add trade to her description, which she did later, you have some important elements of mercantilism. The reason why she doesn't use mercantilism as support for playing the game points to interesting problems when teaching with computer games. The way the concept of mercantilism is constructed in the teaching consisted of the teacher showing a model of mercantilism, which the students were then expected to memorize. There weren't really any attempts made to link this material to student experiences in general, or to the game experiences in particular. This meant that the concept of mercantilism didn't really link to students' experiences beyond the history lesson. There were no handles other than external tools like the teacher or model presented, which would usually not be available to the student when playing. Most of the students would probably have been able to explain the model when confronted with it, but the students did not internalize it. You can say that mercantilism floated in thin air.

What I argued in Chapter 6 was that mercantilism should have been approached the other way round by using concrete game experiences to build the richness of the concept. This was also what was demonstrated in the example of a strong learning experience earlier in this chapter. The students would have a number of self-sustaining concrete (game) experiences that could be drawn upon in using and understanding the concept of mercantilism. In addition to giving a strong understanding of mercantilism, it would also imply that the core of mercantilism could be recognized in later similar experiences. The next time the student played the computer game, she would be able to recognize that this related to mercantilism, which would again expand the strength and richness of the concept of mercantilism.

As was previously discussed, this approach didn't manifest due to the teachers' reluctance to change teaching practice, but also because it wasn't made explicit during the course preparation. The initial idea of the study was to examine how far the teachers could get on their own with computer games in an educational setting and on the school's premises. Therefore, the course used a normal textbook and traditional teacher talks, which were only partly adapted to the computer game experience. Teachers didn't really change their teaching practice despite encouragement, which indirectly led to the teacher talks and textbook having a less than perfect fit with the playing of the computer game. The less than perfect fit led students to reject the computer game for having no bearing on history because no connections were made. Just like the teacher, the students took what they knew as a starting point and that was the facts in the history textbook. For the students, there was little meaningful transfer of knowledge between the two contexts. This was hardly a conscious choice on their part or the teachers', but more a consequence of little resemblance between the computer games and the more traditional teaching.

It is worth noticing that the lack of connection between the game experiences and the teaching does not necessarily mean that the experiences with the computer game or mercantilism would not be activated in other contexts. The dominant feeling among students that playing the game had little to do with learning history in school may paradoxically make it more transferable to other everyday contexts, because the students construct other handles (Schank, 1999) for these experiences through spontaneous concepts. For example, some students said that the playing of the history game had led to discussions with parents, and some of the male students even played it with their fathers. Such experiences provide quite different handles than normal school experiences, potentially transferring the game experiences to other environments like the home.

THE IMPORTANCE OF THE TEACHER

The teacher is always a significant resource when information technology is integrated in schools and this hold true for computer games as well. Indeed, the findings from this study concerning teachers and computer games mirror previous findings on educational use of information technology even though technical challenges on the surface seem to play a larger role. The continuing prevalence of edutainment stuck in a first-generation perspective shows that teachers so far have not been able to change their teaching practice to accompany the use of computer games. The resilience to change teaching practice is well-known from educational use of information technology in general and was also apparent in this study.

Veen (1995) finds that the teacher's belief about teaching in general steered the way information technology was used. Important elements were whether the content was perceived as relevant, preferred teaching style, the teacher's role in the class and the teacher's broader conception of education. The teacher's skills were also a strong indicator, especially their pedagogical skills and, to a lesser degree, computer skills. It is interesting that the computer skills did play a role but are outperformed by the pedagogy challenges, which also seemed to be the real challenge in this course.

On closer examination, the resilience in teaching practice makes good sense since the change of teaching practice is closer to the identity and practice of being a teacher. Changing teaching practice puts the teacher at risk and it will be easier to stay with the normal classroom teaching. The teachers in Veen's study used the computer game in ways that fit with their practice, and there is no reason to believe this should be different for computer games. Changes in teaching practice cannot be expected to arise by themselves.

Looking more closely at the challenges the teacher faced with *Europa Universalis II*, the variation in student experiences emerges. There is not one solution and the students may be able to win the game through problematic assertions and decisions. One player found that military expansion is the dominant strategy in *Europa Universalis II*, basing this on two to three games, whereas another player saw diplomacy as superior. This calls for a changed teaching practice that engages more closely with students' interpretations and assertions from their learning experiences. The large difference between the different student groups (see Chapter 8) in playing the computer game gives extra support to the importance of the teacher intervention. The teacher needs to facilitate an approach to history that includes historical information, events and dynamics while balancing learning versus playing. Additionally, the challenge of facilitating appreciation, exploration and linking lies with the teacher. The teacher must solve computer problems and help students playing the game. In general, the amount of new challenges meant that teachers stayed with what they knew and this meant staying with a traditional teaching practice. The fact that teaching practice didn't change was not due to lack of will among the teachers. Considering the expected reluctance among teachers in engaging with information technology, the teachers in this study were quite positive. Their frustration and scepticism was not based on a rejection of the learning approach tried with computer games, the content in the computer games or the general perspective on history in the computer game. Rather, it was a quite expected and logical consequence of resource prioritization. Both teachers were interested in alternative ways of approaching history and the students were faster than the teachers to reject the new learning approach inherent in the course's use of a computer game. Despite interest in changing teaching practice, the teachers in the end found it too overwhelming to actually adjust their teaching to include the computer game.

Interestingly, the teachers differed in how far they came down the road of changing their teaching practice or, perhaps more precisely, to what degree their existing teaching practice and background fit with using the computer game in teaching.

Teacher differences

The two teachers were quite different on several parameters (Table 9.1) and this proved to have a bearing on the approach to teaching the course. It is interesting to take a closer look at the two teachers who participated in the study to assess advantages and disadvantages of different teaching styles.

Teacher A was technically much better equipped to approach the game and integrate it in the teaching. He learned the computer game relatively quickly and found it interesting to play the computer game for long stretches at a time. Teacher B took five weeks into the course before saying, 'Ah, I am finally beginning to see how this game can be used in teaching history.' This was when she became familiar enough with the game. This is believed to be the development most teachers will experience. The first time around, they

Table 9.1: The key parameters for the participating teachers.

	Teacher A	Teacher B
Gender	Male	Female
Age	Middle aged	Middle aged
IT experience	High	Low
Game experience	High	Low
Expectations	Optimistic	Wait and see
Teaching style	Overall, general	Detailed, thorough
Ambitions for students	Moderate	High

will tend to learn the computer game along with the students, unless they previously have a private interest in the computer game.

The teachers didn't prepare examples from the computer game that could be used in the teaching. Consequently, teacher talks made little use of events and experiences from the computer game. Ideally, teachers should have played through some scenarios and picked up interesting examples for teaching, which turned out to be too overwhelming a task. This point is supported by Squire (2004) who had some success with just-in-time lectures but also considerable problems. On the one hand, just-in-time lectures seemed to be the only relevant approach to connect computer games with teaching. But on the other hand, the students weren't that interested in engaging with the teacher when playing the computer games. They had civilizations to destroy and wonders to build. Students were only really paying attention when it was directly relevant for playing the computer game.

Teacher B was significantly more worried about whether the students received the historical material on a level that was detailed enough. Her ambitions were higher and her approach more sceptical. This was not in a negative way, but rather a healthy approach to a new teaching style. She was very much caught up in a prioritization problem, where she constantly felt that more time was needed to teach students the necessary history. She also had several problems with supervising the class since she had 28 students compared to 19 in Teacher A's class. Teacher interventions were clearly hard to manage when the students played the game. Some students became stuck in the game and here the degree of familiarity with computer games became apparent between the teachers. The game-experienced teacher could more easily identify problems and pick up on interesting discussions. Students clearly found such interactions with the teacher very worthwhile. However, much of this interaction for the female teacher centred on concerns. The female teacher worried that the students might actually conceive all game experiences as factual accounts. In the post-interview, she mentioned how interventions were important to highlight in the situation when history was incorrectly presented in the game universe. Her wording was interesting because it seemed like she didn't extend history from the game experiences, but questioned their validity. This was perhaps relevant for the less experienced gamers and weak history students, but it also facilitated the 'obsession' with facts that were more evident in her class.

When interaction worked, the students would encounter a problem and discuss it with the teacher. The teacher would explain the background and challenge students' assumptions about events, such as the reasons behind religious unrest in southern France during the beginning of the seventeenth century. Here, the interest and motivation of the students were driven by a concrete experience in the computer game. Unfortunately, these intermezzos were quite rare for both teachers, though the male Teacher A had more instances of intervention. The limited number of intermezzos was probably due to class size and more practical problems that arose while learning to play the computer game that demanded the teacher's time. Furthermore, successful learning experiences required that the teachers had knowledge of the computer game and of the historically relevant knowledge. This was easier to handle for Teacher A because he was more likely to connect history to the computer game than Teacher B, due to more general experience with playing computer games.

The teaching style of the two teachers differed in how well they fit the educational use of computer games into the curriculum. The more general and overall approach of Teacher A was closer to the game and, therefore, this was more easily supported by what was happening in the game. On the other hand, the more detailed approach from Teacher B was a good supplement to the game that presented the larger picture, but the detailed accounts were mostly too abstract and detached. The more detailed account of history in Teacher B's lectures seemed to make it harder for the students. Instead of using concrete experiences, more details were added and this didn't really help students identify the overall important concepts. It is hard to judge one approach over the other, but the students presented with the detailed approach struggled more with the clash between history as facts and history as a process. Students exposed to the general approach were also somewhat more capable of using the teaching in relation to the computer game. The male teacher's focus on providing an overview did not bury the obsession with facts among students, but it did limit the obsession somewhat.

OTHER SITES OF LEARNING SUPPORT APPRECIATION, EXPLORATION AND LINKING

Until now, the student and teacher have been the primary focus for facilitating the transformation of concrete experience to scientific concepts, allowing students to gain knowledge of high educational quality. Squire (2004) suggests that the school setting may overall be described as quite impoverished for learning to play computer games when he refers to *Civilization III*. This also seems to hold true for *Europa Universalis II*. The characteristics of the game culture normally surrounding the playing of computer games are lacking. Although it is hard to specify more closely, it will be attempted below. There were few examples of the distribution of learning. The students couldn't figure out what approach to take in learning the game.

The exploration and linking of the game experience could have been explored further in the social setting around the computer game, namely in the group discussions, teacher talks, teacher interventions and informal peer discussions concerning the game, but there was little surplus of energy for such endeavours as we will see in the following. However, other sites did support educational use of *Europa Universalis II* in this course:

- **Class collaboration**: This includes interactions between the two players in front of the computer game, between different pairs playing the computer game, and in groups discussing the different experiences with playing the computer game.
- **Spark of interest outside school**: This relates to situations and contexts outside school, where students' appreciation, exploration and linking of the game experiences were supported.

Students did little to co-operate beyond the pairs they worked in and the group discussions didn't work. Many students mentioned that discussions played a role outside school but many students also stated the opposite. Even the collaboration between two players was far from unproblematic. This challenges some of the beliefs about the importance of social dynamics around computer games that are becoming increasingly popular (Jessen, 1998; Newman, 2004; Sørensen, 2000). I far from reject the importance of the social setting and its potential for facilitating a richer learning experience with computer games. Rather, I challenge the idea that collaboration will magically appear around computer games in an educational setting and lead to a stronger educational experience.

Class collaboration

Class collaboration happened between the pairs working together at the computer and to a lesser degree between students walking around the computer room. The earlier example with the recipe for Napoleon to defeat the British is based on a quite close collaboration between two students, but another girl highlights the imbalance often present.

> So, then I just actually sit and try to follow what happens. It is someone else who is playing. It has actually been like that most of the time.
>
> (Student, Interview 1, girl)

In some pairs, it worked well with novices and experts together while in others it was problematic. Despite efforts to match those with computer games experience with those less experienced, this was not easy. It was hard to know who the good players were and the students wanted to be with someone they knew. Both experienced and inexperienced players took this approach, resulting in groups with very different combinations. It seemed that often it actually worked better by splitting the experienced and inexperienced because the inexperienced couldn't keep up the pace. They gave up and the experienced players were far too absorbed in playing and raced ahead.

The work by Littleton and Light (1999) on group interaction around computers seems to shed some light on the problems. They find that boys are not good at helping other students and that they tend to dominate the computer, especially if their skills are better than those of girls. This was also mostly the case in this study, even though a few boys were quite excellent in teaching the girls to play the computer game. However, generally the boys were the most experienced gamers and that may explain the less than collaborative atmosphere.

Broader collaboration among students in general in the computer room didn't really happen. The following interesting snippet from an interview highlights the students' perception of the missing collaboration in the class. In the quote, the students struggle to explain why collaboration didn't really work with computer games.

> Boy: Well. You can't [help], it is kind of hard to go and help. If you are sitting and playing, then well, of course, you can, but it is different when you are in a computer game. It is something different with homework. You know, you calculate this by doing so and so.
>
> Boy: The others are sitting in another situation, right. It is not similar to other subjects. It is a different situation and then it is hard to go and help them. You can, of course, try but … First, you have to understand their situation and then try to help them and then [go] back to your own. You can't expect that the solution will be optimal when they are in another situation.
>
> Interviewer: So it is really hard to cross between each other's games because you are in different places?
>
> Girl: The only thing you could help them with was to tell them what different icons were.
>
> Boy: Yes, what the different things did, that's the only help you can offer. You can't just say that you have to build up your country or make it stronger, here you go. There the help percentage was quite low.
>
> Girl: But how do you do that? But you are France and I am Spain. I have a completely different situation here than you have. You just have to do it.
>
> (Students, Interview 2)

Clearly, these two didn't find the help between students very useful, and it was not prevalent in the class. This is also discussed by Squire (2004), supporting the notion that social collaboration around computer games is quite hard. Although socializing between students was stronger in Squire's study, this did not necessarily facilitate learning history and only partly supported learning to play *Civilization III*.

The boy in the interview is among the high achievers and was often asked for help. Although normally used to this role, he found it harder to accomplish it with computer games. Of course, there was some interaction but it was limited and unfocused. Thus, the burden on the teacher for helping out with even the smallest problems was not lessened by experienced players, who were slow to help. Both students are really circling around the student autonomy when playing computer games and the openness computer games allow for. It is hard both for students and teachers to relate to each other's experiences. This was a continuing problem throughout this course with computer games.

The appreciation, exploration and linking was not supported by the group discussions. In these, the intention was for the student pairs to discuss and reflect on differences in their game experiences and challenge each other's decisions and assumptions. The high achievers found these group discussions to be superfluous and a waste of time, whereas the least capable groups treated the group discussions as a free pass. The complete lack of relevance expressed by some of the students may be over the top. There was a lack of understanding of what the group discussions were good for and the less experienced, in particular, were not ready to engage with harder questions concerning the game. They hardly knew how to raise an army, let alone how to discuss the game in relation to history.

The students suggested that the discussions should have been at a much later point and, in general, they found the introduction to the game too short and limited. It proved extremely hard for the students to think beyond the computer game experience and use the historical information in another context. The group discussions were not the answer. As we have mentioned previously, identifying the underlying historical information was cumbersome and this became painfully obvious in the group discussions. Despite ideas for questions to discuss and game examples from each student, the groups seldom got beyond describing what they had done in the computer game on a very concrete level. Experiences were not reflected beyond the computer game nor linked to history, and especially weak students took historical information at face value.

There were, however, indications, especially in the last two scenarios, that as one got further into the computer game it was possible to discuss, reflect on it and possibly relate it to history teaching in groups. Some students did get a feeling for the different outcomes that the computer game offered, and became aware of how the underlying factors interplayed causing different historical outcomes. The lack of success in the group discussions may also partly have been related to the setting. It was not possible to hold them within the classroom or computer room and, instead, they took place in break areas. This hardly framed the experience for the students as serious and, since they were already a bit unsure of the purpose, they slipped into talking about topics unrelated to history.

The lack of class collaboration does not necessarily disqualify the notion that educational computer games are strongly supported by the surrounding social context. It rather stresses that this social context does not emerge by itself and that the use of computer games in an educational setting may not automatically offer the qualities we see in leisure game culture. The theories by Jessen (2001), Newman (2004), Buckingham et al. (forthcoming) and Gee (2003) point to the rich social life and culture around computer games and this plays a significant role in learning to play computer games and the potential spin-off learning often found in game forums. The game culture has a lot of support for playing a computer game and sharing of different experiences. There are the more formalized representations like forums, magazines, modifications of games, elaborate walkthroughs, strategy guides and game-related art to name some. These representations reflect an underlying game culture that thrives on social interaction and the sharing of game experiences. This indirectly makes up a quite interesting learning environment that is automatically often associated with the nature of computer games. However, as Jessen (2001) stresses, computer games are embraced because they live up to the existing play culture among children. The sharing, helping and collaboration is in this perspective more an intrinsic quality of children's play culture than of computer games. It can be argued that the use of computer games in an educational setting is at odds with children's culture and, therefore, the rich social interaction often found around computer games tends to disappear.

In a learning perspective, engagement arising from computer games is highly relevant for getting strong concrete experiences but it also has drawbacks. The players are so absorbed that they will not really connect playing the game beyond the immediate context. Importantly, this short-coming of computer games in a learning perspective is in game culture remedied by the rich social interaction and fan culture. In this course, these cultures weren't really appreciated and built by the students because many lacked the necessary game experience. For the most avid gamers such a shared space was naturally constructed but hard to extend to less experienced gamers, especially for the girls, which is parallel to findings on game culture in general. Many girls feel excluded from the strong male game culture (Jessen, 2001).

Spark of interest outside school

There were indications that among some students the context of learning expanded beyond school, especially among male students. Before the course started, it was also hoped that the exploration and linking of the game experiences would expand beyond school and this partly seemed to happen. It was not possible to observe the exact interactions outside school but students were asked whether the teaching during the course had played a role outside school in discussions in breaks, at home, with parents or others. The student responses below indicate the variety of answers:

> Have discussed it a lot with both classmates and parents.
>
> (Student 39X, logbook, boy)

> My father thinks the game is fun.
>
> (Student 45X, logbook, boy)

My parents were interested in the alternative teaching style.

> (Student 21X, logbook, boy)

It's the only homework (besides French) that I talked about at home. But I have mostly talked about the influence I had on the world.

> (Student, 16X, logbook, boy)

Has been exciting to talk about something at home that they didn't know anything about.

> (Student 40X, logbook, boy)

I don't think it has played a large role outside of school, but we have discussed it a little at recess.

> (Student 24X, logbook, girl)

Discussions about the game itself, but it has been very limited. Sure, we have talked about it at recess, but not a lot.

> (Student 27X, logbook, boy)

Overall, most students indicated that they hadn't discussed the computer game outside of the classroom, but a few very enthusiastic students said that it was discussed a lot and quite a few boys pointed to an interesting connection with parents. In general, more boys than girls indicated that the computer game played a role for them outside the classroom. This is also in line with earlier findings that computer game culture is more in step with boys' culture, in general, and the prevalence of playing computer games among boys (Jessen, 2001).

AFTERTHOUGHTS ON SETTING UP THE RIGHT COURSE USING COMPUTER GAMES

The experiences from the course lead one to consider a number of alterations that would greatly improve and ease the use of computer games in educational settings. However, many of these alterations are problematic. Firstly, splitting the teaching across three lessons during a week didn't work well. At least some lessons need to be in conjunction so there is time to play the computer games and discuss then afterwards. Overall, it could be set up as project work. It would be most effective if an entire day could be set aside for the game experience, when there is necessary time to explore further. This would be preferable in a cross-disciplinary context where different social studies subjects could be mixed. In the case *Europa Universalis II*, it would have been interesting to combine history, religion and geography. Most computer games will have such cross-disciplinary potential due to virtual-world quality. Different subject matters will be encountered in the world very quickly and this is similar to virtual worlds.

Secondly, it is important to create a full educational package that fits well with the computer game and takes some of the burden off the teacher in terms of preparation. Such an educational package would include a teacher manual, relevant background material, lesson plan and relevant assignments. The background material should preferably be tailor-made for the computer game so that it expands from the concrete experiences in the game. The educational package should also contain guidance to tools and functionalities like saved games, event lists and graphs of progression that can extend the game experience.

Thirdly, there is important functionality to consider that is often not supported in commercial computer games. The most important element is that there is an overlap between the educational goals and the game's rules and universe. This implies that a history game should not mostly deal with war but perhaps with economic issues, which is quite rare in most commercial computer games. Also, the need for tools to facilitate the educational process is often not fully available in commercial titles. These tools include recording games and rerunning them for analysis, integration of debriefing and assessment in the game. In addition, very down-to-earth things like installation and update through a server is relevant, so that teachers do not have to individually manage each student's PC.

Fourthly, teachers should be prepared to change their teaching practice so that it accommodates the gaming experience. Teachers should have the necessary time and surplus energy to change praxis, especially for the first course run with computer games. Computer games will not make the teacher's role less critical, but rather more challenging. The teacher has to adjust to specific examples and situations that the students encounter. Teaching should facilitate the linking of individual game experiences with relevant abstract concepts from the curriculum.

CONCLUSION: STUDENTS AND TEACHERS NEVER REALLY GOT THE IDEA

In general, the teaching with *Europa Universalis II* never really reached a level where it could be considered a success because there was too much uncertainty, resistance and difficulty relating to the course. Still, the course did provide a blueprint for some of the key challenges in using computer games. These were outlined as the progression of students from appreciation through exploration to linking, all of these having their own problems in an educational setting. A major challenge when using computer games lies in the linking of students' concrete experiences, which are gained while playing the computer games, with historical concepts. This linking requires an active change of teaching practice coupled with extensive knowledge of the computer game, which will not automatically emerge in most educational settings.

The resilience of the teaching practice is interesting because it points to the potential of computer games. We should not believe that magically computer games will be used differently from traditional classroom teaching. Even though computer games have the potential for facilitating alternative teaching styles and challenge current perceptions of learning with information technology, no guarantees are given. Computer games may have to wait for teachers to change before significant transformations in teaching practice can manifest themselves. As such, computer games are caught in a paradox. On the one hand, they are championed as possessing new ideas and concepts for teaching and learning. On the other hand, it may be precisely this innovative approach that makes it so hard to get computer games through the school doors.

NOTES

1   This argument gains support from the theory on flow (Csikszentmihalyi, 1992).
2   The use of game speed is also a well-known playing style in *SimCity* where the player can regulate the game speed according to the complexity surveyed.

10

A Theory on Educational Use of Computer Games

Colors fade, temples crumble, empires fall, but wise words endure.

Thorndike

We have so far covered a lot of ground in order to get a fuller understanding of the elements necessary to understand the educational use of computer games. The intention has been to build a framework for using computer games in educational settings, in the process challenging the current dominance of edutainment. This chapter fits together the pieces by presenting a theory for the educational use of computer games extending from experiential learning.

The theory presented in this chapter describes an ideal for educational experiences with computer games. This ideal includes both the strengths of computer games and the necessary instruction given by the teacher to qualify the games experience. The chapter starts by looking at the role engagement plays in the appreciation and exploration of relevant educational elements in a computer game. This engagement is driven by the students' perceived relevance of the game activity and is necessary for students' building of an investment in the educational activity.

The chapter concludes by characterizing educational use of computer games as follows: the student is playing and constructing knowledge through interaction with the game universe. The knowledge slowly builds on top of existing knowledge from previous experiences arising from inside the game universe and other spheres of life facilitated by instruction. It is an experience-based hermeneutic exploration in a safe, rich environment, potentially scaffolding the student while maintaining student autonomy and ensuring a high emotional investment in the activity.

ENGAGEMENT IN EDUCATIONAL EXPERIENCES WITH COMPUTER GAMES

I have stressed earlier that it is essential for education to engage the student, thereby ensuring investment in the topic under investigation. The topic then becomes relevant to the student. Engagement in computer games certainly seems to be higher than engagement in most traditional school subjects. In computer games, engagement is closely tied with relevance. When students see something as relevant, they will engage with it and invest in it.

We saw in Chapter 6 that computer games provide a number of advantages in terms of building engagement compared to other media forms, which has also been found in numerous studies. Although these properties are not by themselves exclusive to computer games, the combined manifestation is quite powerful. The ability of computers to combine different semantic areas is well exploited in computer games. When combined with strong audiovisual experiences, the overall manifestation is very engaging. Most game universes are modelled through 3D technology, providing detailed and rich universes that the user can interact with, leading to strong concrete experiences. A game universe can be freely designed so that it allows the players to slowly explore the different layers from their perspective, while not risking major real-life repercussions. Computer games' pursuit of an open-ended game universe is also a strong feature to engage players, letting them make a difference. Despite the constraints from rules offering explicit purposes to the player, the playing of computer games is more open-ended than most other media. Overall, computer games provide strong and rich game universes that are interesting to engage with.

I have argued that computer games provide an interesting game universe, but the actual engagement in an educational setting is still unaccounted for. However, it is well-documented that computer games are seen as motivating and interesting by many students. This is also apparent from their continuous success as a leisure activity (ESA, 2003), most of the studies reviewed in Chapter 4 and the motivational assessment conducted in my own studies (Egenfeldt-Nielsen, 2005; Egenfeldt-Nielsen and Buch, 2006). The commercial success doesn't mean that computer games will necessarily maintain the engagement in a school setting, and engagement as such doesn't necessarily imply a stronger learning experience even though computer games obviously provide an important impetus.

Although many current computer games may not be set up for an educational agenda, the potential is there. In *Europa Universalis II* some students would start by waging huge wars while others would explore the world. Some would convert heretics and others would settle in a quiet part of the world developing their country. This leads to a sense of perceived choice and a feeling of autonomy that strengthens engagement. Students can focus on what they find relevant and invest in that precise area. Also, computer games are built so that they challenge the player and push the students to the limit (Adams and Rollings, 2003). This challenge is direct and requires the student to make the right choices within the computer game. Additionally, the playing of the game happens in a safe environment, where the student can make mistakes without repercussions. The student sees the consequences of actions and changes actions by reloading the game. The group pressure is also considerably less with the computer as the only observer. Many students are not comfortable testing their assumptions in a classroom context, where other students are listening. All of this makes the computer game relevant to students if they can get beyond the initial scepticism of using computer games. However, engaging with a computer game may be more or less relevant from an educational perspective, depending on the game's educational quality that is derived from the curriculum goals, support for learning desire and the ability to point forward in an educational direction (see Chapter 6).

The relevance and engagement of computer games may be challenged by the cultural expectations among students and teachers. When bringing computer games into an educational setting, demons and angels tag on and both influence the game experience. In my course, we saw a strong opposition to and fight concerning whether teaching with computer games was acceptable. Although students liked computer games, they didn't appreciate their educational value and didn't find that *Europa Universalis II* lived up to their perception of history. The relevance of the computer game in the educational context was hard to see for students. Expectations of school as providing serious (or boring) learning were hard to reconcile with computer games. Furthermore, the understanding of history by students differed from the computer game's approach. Despite this, students actually were more motivated, interested and engaged.

EDUCATIONAL QUALITY IN USE OF COMPUTER GAMES FOR EDUCATIONAL PURPOSES

A good computer game provides relevance and engagement, resulting in investment from *players* but not necessarily from *students*. Although a student may be engaged as a player in a school setting, the student may not necessarily be an engaged playing student, as seen from the results in the course, and the quality of the educational experience may consequently be lacking. Computer games should have a universe that aims at educationally relevant actions and goals pointing in an educationally desirable direction. The engagement from computer games will, for most students, result in a stronger learning desire if the educational links are provided. However, few game universes have explicit educational quality.

This was an important problem in the course, where appreciation of historical elements, and hence the exploration and linking, was clouded by students not engaging with the computer game beyond play. The best students were capable of connecting the two modes, playing and studying, whereas the least successful students didn't master this connection. The somewhat successful students were capable of extending from either a student perspective or player perspective without exactly finding the balance that ensured a connection between the concrete game experience and a student's existing experience base while pointing in an educational direction. Such a balance is necessary, regardless of the general features computer games offer for building relevance and engagement. For one student, a computer game like *Europa Universalis II* may link to previous successful experiences of enjoyment with computer games, take place in a medieval setting and support the student's autonomy, but this is useless if the concrete experiences in the game cut the student off from appreciating history as such. Topics can't be understood in a vacuum and although the computer game provides a rich audiovisual base of concrete experiences, these need to be transformed and expanded through some form of instruction. This instruction potentially results in the building of scientific concepts rather than spontaneous concepts.

As indicated in previous research as well as in my course, the transformation of the game experiences relates to a major problem dealing with the clash identified between play and learning. The game experience becomes too strong and closed around itself instead of linking to other scientific concepts. Left to their own devices, students will gain concrete experiences and form spontaneous concepts that will mostly be useful in a game setting. However, they won't connect the game experience with the broader idea of understanding history. The appreciation, exploration and linking of game experiences require an instructor capable of seeing the concrete game experiences as pointing to a broader scientific concept and who continuously attempts to extend the experience beyond the game context. Students will increasingly begin to look for these connections once they experience this as a fruitful and appreciated line of enquiry. However, the appreciation, exploration and linking of concrete experiences from playing a computer game to scientific concepts runs into problems. The play context supports the engagement offered by computer games and provides a safe haven for exploring new experiences and concepts. However, the linking is hampered by the strength of the game as a frame for playing. A play frame clouds student interest in seeing beyond the play frame and ultimately challenges the educational agenda of transforming experiences. Students are only interested in performing well in the game as a play experience and, if the teacher cannot justify the instruction in relation to gameplay, it seems irrelevant. In this way, the initial use of computer games as a way to increase the relevance of a given topic may backfire if not carefully managed. To avoid the play frame from backfiring, we should make sure that the computer game is built so that knowledge of scientific concepts will improve gameplay and we should stress the educational context. When the potential links from other sources and playing the game are present, the teacher should be very explicit about them and should also attempt to link them to broader discussions outside school and the computer game. Also, physical artifacts can, with great advantage, be used to make a link between the game playing and educational agenda. When used correctly artifacts can serve as bridge-builders. An artifact could, for example, be a notebook that goes with the game or a manual with additional information about the game. However, artifacts have to be meaningful in the educational context and not just randomly tagged on. In *Europa Universalis II* it could be historical maps showing how Europe developed or short descriptions of the major countries in the game. In our recent game, *Global Conflicts: Palestine*, we work with the player being a journalist both inside the game and outside. We use artifacts for supporting this experience, more specifically a physical notebook for jotting down observations and thoughts along with a file cabinet covering characters you run into. This works very well for extending the game universe and reflecting on it, because the artifacts are an integrated part of the game experience.

Teachers should stress that there exists a difference between education and play, though not necessarily between learning and play. Certainly, we will learn while playing, but education is a much more controlled learning situation that will steer play in certain directions and make demands on the game experience.

From the above it follows that one should be careful in assuming that appreciation, exploration and linking is an inevitable consequence of playing computer games. Indeed, the quality of the educational experience in computer games is often assumed rather than studied. As the overview in Chapter 4 attests, too many researchers approach computer games as theoretically educationally sound, but most studies will find many problems on closer examination. The educational quality will often be questionable or limited. Unfortunately, the closer examinations are not made, because studies tend to rely on a one-string method approach focused on only testing or interviewing. The limitations of assumed educational quality were encountered when previously analysing the empirical results. In the course, we saw this on the lowest level of merely appreciating history elements in the computer games and even more in the lack of exploring history elements beyond their game context. Even when students appreciated the historical elements and explored these, the linking to relevant historical concepts was hard. This is critical for giving the playing of the game a higher educational quality. Remembering the difference between scientific concepts and spontaneous concepts, we would expect informal playing of computer games to, at best, result in spontaneous concepts. We will usually not reflect, generalize and systematize the concrete experiences into scientific concepts, even though we might make some kind of unconscious ordering in spontaneous concepts. Therefore, the process from appreciation through exploration to linking is critical for using computer games in educational settings. This goes beyond what is traditionally labelled debriefing and after-action reports, because the appreciation, exploring and linking is more closely tied to the game experiences in terms of both content and process. The teacher educates the students to approach the game experiences in a different way, thereby harnessing the full potential of computer games. In this way, the student gains the strong concrete experiences and the impetus to reflect, expand and challenge the concrete experiences by building strong abstract concepts based on this process. This successful process makes great demands on the teacher, both in the understanding of the game and the limitations found in different students ability and approach.

Teachers should be careful not to confuse their own conceptual understanding of citizenship, geography, history or any other subject with the common student understanding. Educators, researchers and parents may be able to appreciate that certain concepts are mirrored in a computer game, but this doesn't mean that they arise automatically from the concrete experiences in the computer game. It would be similar to one expecting that voters with a huge deficit problem automatically have a full understanding of the deficit. However, the experience with the deficit and chance to explore it in a game universe provides the foundation for gaining a fuller understanding of the deficit. Indeed, Vygotsky (1986) stresses that this will not be the case in traditional learning and there is no indication that this should be different in computer games. Bearing in mind that the precondition for scientific concepts is some kind of instruction, the transformation of concrete experiences may happen in game culture through peers, parents, forums or tools. A computer game can be questioned, analysed and discussed with links to more general concepts and relevant issues in society. However, we saw in the course that the strong peer culture around computer games does not necessarily transfer to educational settings (although certainly sometimes they may). Therefore, instruction becomes critical. We can work around instruction needs but there is no substitute that can fully take its place.

INSTRUCTION: FROM IMPLICIT TO EXPLICIT

Of course, I do not contest that we can facilitate educational experiences with computer games, but we often expect too much from the computer games and the student's active knowledge construction. The course discussed earlier certainly did not show a seamless educational use of computer games. Therefore, instruction should aim at making explicit what is implicit. To broaden this discussion let's look at another game. In the quote below about the computer game *Freedom Fighters* the question of ideology of educational relevance is latent and not manifest. This makes it hard for most average students to dig out the ideology question:

Freedom Fighters allows players to live out the ideologies surrounding the U.S.-Iraq war in reverse: Is the difference between a freedom fighter and a terrorist simply that the person using the terms believes, in one case, the cause is right and not in the other? In these games, such thoughtful questions are not abstractions, they are part and parcel of the fun and interaction of playing.

(Gee, 2004b: unpaginated)

The example with *Freedom Fighters* is interesting because it is quite a different genre to *Europa Universalis II* and has been the topic of some debate in research circles. The players of the action game *Freedom Fighters* may appreciate elements of terrorism, engage in an exploration of it and link this to a wider context, but the problem with the above claim is that it lacks substantiation. True, a student *may* engage in such activities, but we have not really examined it. On the contrary, I would argue, extending from Vygotsky and my course, that such reflections require certain student skills and preferably instruction of some kind that may or may not be a part of game culture surrounding *Freedom Fighters*. Some students will benefit more from instruction than others, depending on the difference between the actual and potential zone of development. This was also clearly the case in the course with *Europa Universalis II* and is supported by previous research into educational use of computer games (Grundy, 1991; Leutner, 1993; Wiebe and Martin, 1994).

In particular, if reflections are to have an impact outside the game universe, we need quite explicitly to identify these links and lead the students in that direction. This is not to say that students do not learn anything from playing computer games. They will learn to play the computer game, which can be quite complex. The continuous repetition can also provide them with factual information. In addition, different spontaneous concepts may also arise, though probably only usable to a limited extent beyond the game universe. Certainly, students will learn from computer games, but the question is what, how and whether it is different compared to other forms of learning as previously discussed in Chapter 3.

When thinking about making the educational qualities explicit in computer games, one needs to recognize that computer games differ from other media. Primarily, computer games are about engaging and doing concrete things, which is not much different from any other physical activity, like soccer. When playing soccer, we will naturally draw on a number of important principles in the world, like probability, force, movement, anatomy and social relations. All these elements are part of playing soccer, but during play, we will not really appreciate or explore these elements and certainly rarely link them beyond the soccer field. However, over time we transform our concrete experience to somewhat ordered spontaneous concepts. Although we may gain spontaneous concepts related to soccer and layered into the soccer context, the learning will be narrow, random and fragmented.

An instructor may, however, afterwards try to expand these concrete experiences by generalizing and ordering the experiences, i.e. digging out the important elements that can be transferred to other matches and contexts of life. For example, the concept of weak midfield provides an understanding of what happens in a game. Weak midfield relates to a number of different concrete experiences that explain why the team keeps losing the ball and never gets any attacks, and the opponents seem to occupy their half of the playing field. It is highly unlikely that any of these concepts would emerge among all the players without joint reflection in the community and the active enquiry of the coach as an old-timer in the community. Certainly, the instructor can order and generalize the concrete experiences by referring to existing knowledge that can qualify the recent experiences players had. The concept of weak midfield is certainly a returning topic in books on soccer tactics. It is not obvious how concrete experiences in soccer can be useful in a school setting, since the soccer universe is quite detached from most school subjects. However, even in soccer, an instructor could use the concrete experiences as examples of probability and force in physics or the hierarchy in society. It is important from an instruction perspective to recognize that some elements in soccer as well as in a computer game will typically be easier to appreciate, explore and link to other concepts, which was also clear in *Europa Universalis II*. In the course, students tended to focus on the pop-ups, which did not prove very useful, but at the end of the course, general underlying rules were appreciated, explored and linked, albeit by few students.

In Chapter 6, the formal characteristics of computer games were described as a set of rules with semantic content making up a game universe. This implies that our actions in computer games are guided by rules and our interpretation of the fictional world; to perform actions, we manipulate rules to achieve a certain outcome. The set of rules is typically layered into the fictional world. However, a large part of the fictional world is not really activated and integrated in the game experience. One doesn't engage with a fictional world's setting. The setting is indicated by background history, cut scenes or the semantic content in the game universe, such as the Soviet enrolment posters in the background in the game *Freedom Fighters*.

The playing of the game does not really require an awareness of a large part of the setting. When you are playing a computer game, the primary action is the manipulation of rules. These are the ones you learn to master and constantly engage with to win the game. Appreciation of the setting and the conflict it enacts is only required on a superficial level. When the setting is important for the game experience, it will gain more attention and potentially be part of the concrete experience, available for building concepts. The problems with relying on the setting for learning have been demonstrated in earlier studies (e.g. Malone and Lepper, 1987b).

The overall conflict in *Freedom Fighters* may be terrorists versus freedom fighters, but arguably it doesn't really play a role beyond creating the right setting and a progression in the cut scenes. The primary focus is on learning the rules of playing, and when the setting is not required to achieve this goal, it becomes secondary. Should the rules in *Freedom Fighters* pertain to what leads to the formation of terrorist or freedom fighter cells and not merely to getting the next opponent killed, it would be another case. This would change the focus and facilitate potentially stronger educational experiences on this topic. Also, the houses in *Freedom Fighters* can either be important for hiding and tactics or merely a neutral background. As a neutral background, most players won't really notice or appreciate the significance of houses, but they will be appreciated and explored, and potentially linked to other areas, if they are important for actually playing the game. There will only be a limited amount of engagement in larger discussions of the terrorism question from playing *Freedom Fighters*, which also happens to be evident if we scan the game's forums. Even when discussions surface in relation to *Freedom Fighters*, students will lack the ability to go beyond the game because there are few concrete experiences to work from and students will only have a limited experience base to which they can connect. Students do not have the concepts and the experience base to understand and qualify the discussion that would be considered necessary for educational experiences to emerge (as opposed to *Europa Universalis II* where we did actually see an overlap between game actions and goals, which led to historical discussions). As indicated in the earlier quote, Gee (2004b) may see the potential for educationally loaded discussions from computer games; however, he misses the point. Computer games can indeed provide strong and rich concrete experiences, but we need a context where these can be transformed into something more. We need the coach from the soccer field. It is worth stressing again that this coach may be a teacher, parent, peer or partly even the computer game, but for now I will stay with an instructor perspective. The instructor makes players listen, focus and engage with the experiences.

The elements of appreciating, exploring and linking differ in computer games. As described, the rules often take precedence, but in some games, this is to a lesser degree the case. The exact balance between rules and semantic content in a computer game differs depending on genre. A progression game (such as *Grim Fandango*) will rely more on the semantic content whereas an emergence game (such as *Age of Empires*) is focused mostly on the rules[1]. This makes a difference when we discuss the educational quality of what it is that students engage with. It is a difference that becomes clearer if we look at traditional textbooks, which are usually closer to progression games. In a textbook, some content will, of course, also be more prominent in the experience, but the interaction with the text is the same and there is not such an exclusive focus on the rules for reading. It is seldom the grammatical rules that become interesting when reading a textbook. But in a computer game, it is actually the underlying rules (the grammatical rules) for the semantic content that are dominating and drawing most of the player's attention.

Playing a book could be described as finding ways to beat others by knowing the rules, like students competing to see who can finish the textbook first. Such book competitions are actually quite common in the first school years, where the semantic content is of little interest but the underlying rules are paramount. In such competitions on reading, the focus is seldom on the actual content of the book, but rather on the mastery of the underlying rules that determines the winner.

The instruction in the perspective outlined above can be described as the ability to help the student see the differences that make a difference. This is, however, only possible by referring back to concrete experiences, which give the concepts their substance and make them generalizable and orderable. Appreciation, exploration and linking are tools that the student can use for seeing the important differences. The important point is that the concrete experiences used to build the concepts should not be confined to the domain of computer games. In summary, the educational experiences with computer games face the same challenge as any experiential learning activity: the transformation of the concrete experience to go beyond the immediate context and linking the experience to a broader conceptual understanding by drawing on students' existing experience base and engagement. Computer games can provide rich, safe experimentation through examples from any semantic area, securing student engagement, leading to investment in the topic. Next, we will look at the inherent problem of representation in computer games that challenges the very appreciation of concrete game experiences as relevant beyond the game universe.

THE PROBLEM OF REPRESENTATION IN COMPUTER GAMES

The basic representational and plastic quality of computers is both a strength and a weakness in relation to educational use of computer games. In the most basic sense, a game representation may *miss important aspects* of a topic or *misrepresent aspects*. Some of the substance will always be missing in a representation and the threat of missing parts is enough to challenge the validity of the very representation itself. Furthermore, this can ultimately lead to students learning wrong things if they are not capable of seeing when a representation is skewed. This is true for any representation whether it is a computer game, a Hollywood movie, an interactive story or a television show. The challenge with computer games, inherited from computers, is that in some sense the representations become even more unstable and untrustworthy than in other media due to student engagement in the game. Our illusion and trust in the representation is challenged because we are influencing the representation.

When using computer games for educational use, we have at least two problems related to the representation. First of all, game designers do not know the background of their fictional worlds very well. This was less of a problem in *Europa Universalis II* compared to other commercial game titles since it was designed around a strong awareness and interest in history in the development team (Malmberg, 2002). Even when game designers know a topic well, a representation will always be an interpretation of the world. This leads to fictional worlds that are potentially ripe with problematic assumptions and assertions that students may pick up. Second, some students will be capable of picking up some of the problematic representations, which will make them sceptical of the entire educational experience. Third, the very threat of failure to represent a topic will cause uncertainty among students. They wonder: how can we trust this game to tell us what happened when we are the puppet masters?

This is exactly what happened in the course on *Europa Universalis II* presented earlier, where the insecurity related to the degree of accurate representation in the historical computer games led students to question the value of the entire educational experience. They distrusted the representation of history that the computer game presented. Interestingly, distrust did not grow out of a problematic game universe that didn't really have any historical problems the students could recognize. Students did point to some historical inadequacies that were actually not historically wrong as such, but were still at odds with students' knowledge which was mostly drawn from current times. For example, students would object to Denmark conquering the small German state Holstein at some point in history even though this is in line with most historical accounts. Scepticism seemed to run deeper than what a few factual mistakes in the game could accomplish. The problems related to the very interaction with the fictional world. Students were actually capable of appreciating the fact that this obviously wasn't history since they could change the outcome. However, based on their historical 'superpowers' changing the course of history, they began to distrust the entire game universe. Interestingly, such a critique was not aimed at the traditional textbooks, which is, of course, also a representation. It was the students' lack of ability for abstraction and the actual *playing* of the representation that caused the problems.

It is interesting to consider the above problem of representation from a different angle and remember what students are actually doing with the computer game representations compared to other representations. In reality, the student is setting new marks with every action in the game universe. The student is constantly making new representations and seeking differences that make a difference. When we consider most computer applications like spreadsheets, browsers or archive systems, they are all setting up different universes. They are telling you what the map is, but they are also defining areas within the maps that you can influence. In principle, the computer can set up any options for the user, but this is not really interesting as most computer applications are really focusing on a special semantic regime:

a spreadsheet for calculations, a word processor for writing, an internet browser for seeking information and *Europa Universalis II* for making strategic decisions in a historical universe. The computer is basically setting up a small universe for us to manipulate and this is different from the representations in books, movies or radio shows, where in reality there is no freedom to change the map. Importantly, this is different from the traditional teaching in schools, where there is a canon. Although the authority of teaching is under pressure, the textbook and teacher are rarely challenged on their own turf, which is in reality what students constantly do in a computer game.

When we look at the playing of computer games the challenge of the representation and authority is central. The experimentation and exploration of the differences in a computer game are very much in line with the experiential approach to learning presented earlier, when you are constantly engaged with the topic you are learning. Here the process entails having a concrete experience with a topic, reflecting on the topic and setting up concepts about it, and actively experimenting with the fit between the topic and your concepts. Such active experimentation is typically hard with a textbook because there are not many handles for experimenting. With computer games, it is quite different.

If we are to believe Finnemann (1999), the computer medium, as discussed in Chapter 6, should be capable of giving a richer representation by drawing on a variety of semantic regimes, which *Europa Universalis II* also did (e.g. linguistically, formally, pictorially and auditorily). However, the representation and the potential manipulations may increase the insecurity among students when entering a new semantic regime. A history textbook will have maps that don't change and the history will remain in a fixed sequence until the next time you read it. This is certainly not the case in the most basic way for computer games, where the informational alphabet requires sequences to work and the user is usually actively constructing the application's progress. The computer may run without user input, but this is usually not the case. Although most computer games rely on the presence of a user to move forward, many games also have an on-going progression more or less independent of the user. In *SimCity*, the city will develop when the user is not doing anything and this is the case similarly in most real-time strategy games.[2] The player makes a difference in the universe and the game universe tends to revolve around the player, but the game has a course set that it follows without the player's input. Indeed, one typical criticism aimed at computer games is that the game centres on the player. This was also apparent in this course with *Europa Universalis II*, where the historical processes were increasingly influenced by the player's actions. Playing England would lead to an England-centric historical development. As the students played, they moved away from the historical starting point and Europe was transformed based on the player's actions and randomly influenced decisions by the computer game's AI. The students were quite capable of appreciating and seeing this as a problematic representation and knew not to see it as actual historical events. After all, students could observe how other students in the class had different outcomes. So the problem didn't really lie in actual faulty learning, but rather in a lack of trust in the representations in the very form of learning, which requires more active reflection, experimentation and thinking on the part of the students.

The unstable game universe requires quite a lot of work from the player/ student. Students need to understand how representations are not necessarily the most important aspect of the computer game, but rather the underlying rules. These rules will let the user explore how the representations are created and explore the differences that make a difference not simply by appreciating these but by challenging them in a constantly changing process. When students and teachers fail to appreciate the superficiality of the game representation in *Europa Universalis II*, they run the risk of devaluating the entire educational game experience by making the mistake that the representation is the truth. This happened when students playing Denmark in *Europa Universalis II* conquered Sweden and then rejected the game representation because they knew this wasn't historically correct. This does not mean that the concrete representations generated by the students' interaction with the computer are fruitless. However, it implies that these concrete representations are mostly important in the sense that they allow exploration of the underlying rules and are tools for referring to what might be perceived as important differences. In *Europa Universalis II*, Denmark's victory over Sweden is not interesting as such, but the underlying rules, assessments and decisions that led to the victory are. Still, such a victory will reinforce a number of assumptions and assertions about Denmark and Sweden held by the student.

The student is required to have quite a high level of abstraction, which is supported by the high achievers becoming the only ones on the course occupying the high ground of abstract thinking in relation to the computer game. The focus on the underlying dynamics of the representation is equivalent to the underlying forces that result in historical events. You can say that in computer games, the focus is on what makes $2 + 2 = 4$ rather than the result of 4. One may also benefit from the actual representations in a computer game, but it will always be at the risk of students not really accepting them since they themselves can change these representations. Students will rightfully question whether representations can tell them anything about history, geography, maths or citizenship if the representations depend on their choices and randomly change. To really benefit from the concrete representations in themselves requires an initial understanding to validate the representations. For example, students may reinforce their understanding of Napoleon as a French general and their knowledge about the long history of hostilities with England when playing France in the eighteenth century.

The plasticity of representation in computer games doesn't completely reduce the educational relevance of the actual representations in a computer game, but it tends to require some prior knowledge of the topic the game relates to. This is interesting as many game designers explicitly avoid building games that require previous knowledge (Brake, 2002) and I think we may need to reconsider this if we are to build computer games that are successful in educational use. The question of game design also becomes relevant if we consider the most obvious way representations influence learning. We should remember that all the representations in a textbook, teacher talks, movies and computer games are based on the creators' interpretations of what differences make a difference. Depending on the creators' choice, some things will be stressed over others, like the Second World War, Pythagorean geometry, Darwin's evolutionary theory, the rise of Christianity or the invention of the printing press. A computer game is capable of introducing certain representations and granting supremacy over others, which provides a way for students to appreciate the borders of a topic. Hardly any computer applications will grant the player complete freedom and the game universe's restrictions point to important information. In a word processor and browser, the user works within confined limits. Although one can run macros in a word processor and produce plug-ins for the browser, these are not accessible to the ordinary user. Computer games similarly set limits for the player's actions, based on the game designer's notions of what differences should make a difference. The designer may not have a very complete picture of the important elements of the Second World War, and hence the representations and actual rules the user can change will be quite restricted. Increasingly, computer games, including educational attempts like the titles by the American company Muzzy Lane, want to give the player the ability to change these confinements. On some level, this makes sense in an educational setting because it allows the teacher to customize the game for an individual approach. However, it also makes the use of computer games more difficult and requires a lot of effort from educators and players. Also, the confinements are an attraction of computer games. The confinements produce the challenge and tinkering with the confinements may ruin the game's balance. The question is what confinements are set up and whether these can point in an educationally relevant direction. To bridge the divide between an immediate game universe and an extension for introducing a deeper understanding, we need to understand the role instruction plays.

A THEORY ON EDUCATIONAL USE OF COMPUTER GAMES

The elements discussed above can be linked together to describe the most important elements in using computer games for educational purposes. The model below describes the final theory on educational use of computer games. It consists of an outer and an inner wheel. The outer wheel describes how Kolb's learning cycle can be expanded to more specifically address computer games while the inner wheel is the basic learning process students go through in any experiential learning activity (Figure 10.1).

The left part of the model describes the process from a player perspective. The student perspective is the right part of the model, which looks at how the game experiences are transformed beyond the game context. The starting point is the game experience, which the student has to see as relevant to

Figure 10.1: Showing how we can perceive the learning process for educational use of computer games extending from the concrete game experience

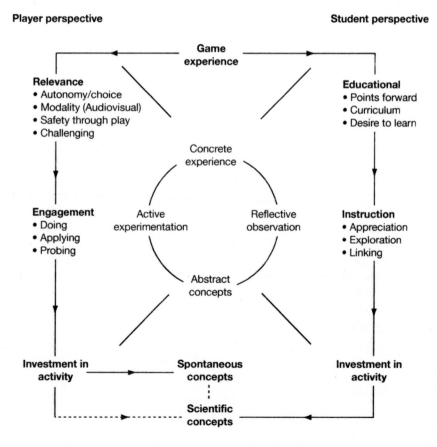

engage with to build an investment in the universe leading to spontaneous concepts. Initially, the student has to see computer games as relevant to make way for an investment in the topic, leading to some concepts representing the concrete experience. However, the formal learning (education) is necessary to take the computer game beyond the informal learning (playing). This makes the concrete experiences relevant in a broader context, through the development of scientific concepts, through appreciation and exploration of game experiences while linking these with other concepts. For this to work, the game experience has to point in an educational direction, implying that the game experience needs to open up for scientific concepts through instruction.

The relevance relating to computer games is increased by the autonomy, choice, audiovisuals, safe environment, playful approach and challenges that are part of game experiences. The perceived educational relevance is hampered by students' perception of school, games and the representation problem. It is, therefore, important that, from the start, the instruction stresses the educational relevance. The perceived relevance leads students to engage in computer games, which we have continuously seen throughout the book. Relating the student side of the model with Kolb's learning cycle shows that computer games are especially helpful for providing the active experimentation that requires active engagement and investment of the students. In traditional teaching, when listening to the teacher, students can appear to be engaged without actually being so. This is much harder with computer games when the game requires the student to interact to continue playing. However, as an activity, computer games often provide little in terms of reflection and observation in a classical sense, which are critical for the educational quality from an experiential learning perspective. Most players will be quite engrossed in the game experience and not retract from the experience and reflect on it. This can happen in some computer games, but most reflection will then be closely linked to the game universe. For reflection and observation to work, we need to introduce some form of instruction, which in schools is obviously given by the teacher (the student perspective in the model). Instruction needs to point forward, include curriculum and inspire a general desire to learn. Computer games are not making the instruction easier; on the contrary, the concrete game experience will be different for each student and the teacher cannot be entirely aware of the different student experiences. It is, therefore, hard to expand from the concrete experience. However, the rich amount of concrete experiences provide students with different starting points more relevant for them, which can spark discussions between students and that can be used for sparking exploration and linking through instruction. The variety in concrete experiences also gives the teacher a chance to differentiate the teaching by drawing upon a variety of game experiences to illustrate important concepts for different students. This requires that the teacher is well versed in computer games, especially the one used in the course. Otherwise, important game experiences aren't recognized and are not used in the teaching. This will result in the game experience staying restricted to the game universe and no construction of scientific concepts that can generalize the concrete experiences.

Overall, my theory extends from an experiential learning approach, where the interaction with the game universe results in concrete experiences that can be transformed through appreciation, exploration and linking. Computer games provide rich concrete experiences that can be manipulated in the game universe, providing more handles for the student, leading to a hermeneutic exploration from the student's perspective. Students' experiences are maintained within a safe environment that is relevant and connects to each one's experience base, which is slowly built up by playing the game. Computer games are not a magic pill that can be used to automatically solve the hard problems in teaching and education. Computer games provide a varied experience base, strong relevance and richness that allow students to engage from their own perspective, but computer games also result in new problems for the quality of the educational experiences especially centring on the representational plasticity of computer games, the stereotypical game universes and the strength of the play frame that has to be balanced with the educational agenda. The fruits of computer games can only be enjoyed if the teacher learns how to harvest the fruits.

SOME THOUGHTS ON DESIGN OF EDUCATIONAL COMPUTER GAMES

Game designers of commercial computer games tend to be interested in designing an immediately recognizable fictional world that will attract a broad range of players. Furthermore, the commercial computer games often have a preference for fictional worlds and confinements that set up a clear conflict. A clear conflict makes it easy to attach a player to the outcome and see the consequences of the player's actions. However, it also tends to paint a somewhat simplified picture of many topics and rely on the same basic confinements. The differences between the real-time strategy games currently on the market are not very substantial on a rules level. The goal is to defeat the opponent by amassing resources and waging war success-fully by adhering to each unit's strengths and weaknesses. Turning to the fictional worlds, the differences between settings are perhaps on the surface larger, considering the variation from *Age of Mythology* to *Age of Empires* to *Command and Conquer*. These games span the last 3000 years of human history. This is, however, done from quite a superficial and stereotypical perspective that does not really push the envelope. The fictional worlds use knowledge most people already have for setting up the conflicts and inter-esting choices:

In a game like Civilization many of the ideas there are important but they are ones that the players are already familiar with. As you start to play you start to run into 'do you want to invent the wheel or do you want to work on currency' – everyone knows those ideas so they feel they understand the decision. We do some historical research but it is not the starting point for a game. We want people to be able to start the game already knowing enough to play. After they play for a while we might introduce a new idea and they might be interested in learning more about that but we want people to feel they are immediately making progress and they are at home in the new world.

(Sid Meier, Brake, 2002)

As the military has recognized, all real-time strategy games seem capable of teaching future generals the necessary skills for warfare, but this is less relevant for fostering knowledge about more educationally relevant content, skills and attitudes. There is, however, not really any apparent reason for the superficial and narrow fictional worlds in current computer games beyond recognizability, marketing needs and the increased complexity needed to get beyond superficial game universes. To go beyond the superficial fictional worlds, educational game designers need to become quite knowledgeable in every topic they use for making a game and find ways to handle the increased complexity. This knowledge can partly be developed by reading background information, talking to students and using subject experts. However, the game designer still makes the actual decisions concerning the game design. These references serve as leverage for the game designer to get a fuller under-standing of the fictional world and what content, actions and potential outcomes are relevant.

A game designer is constantly tweaking game designs by removing and adding elements (Rollings and Morris, 2000) and this will hardly work if the game designer has to consult focus groups and experts every time. On the other hand, game design choices should be educationally sound and this requires the game designer to have a good understanding of the area to work around the problems. A game designer should have a sense of when a tweak ruins the game experience too much and when the tweak is okay to cater for the educational part. Many designers will probably shy away from such an undertaking because it introduces more complexity in the design process and basically makes the game design harder. However, a fictional world that is richer and more elaborate will also provide a richer experience and more progression in the game for the player. It is perhaps not surprising that most successful educational titles beyond edutainment were produced in the 1980s, when game development was less complex. One man could produce the entire game and build more complex and rich game universes that were in line with a topic that the game designer had deep knowledge about.

Perhaps the largest challenge lies in the introduction of an entirely new fictional world that students have little knowledge about. The richer fictional world will increase complexity in general and make it harder to learn the computer game. The initial handle for learning to play the computer game, the why, what and where you play, will also be lost. Students will require knowledge of the fictional world to understand the rules and outcomes. The approach favoured by most current computer games is quite opposed to traditional educational thinking, where the teacher starts off with a topic students know little about. Most education will not worry too much about whether students find it relevant and have a rich experience base to connect it to. Gee (2003) points out that the ease of initially learning to play a computer game is a feature educators could learn from. We should not lose the ability of computer games to be immediately interesting, but in an educational perspective we should consider how to extend the game experience beyond this initial ease of learning to play. In *Europa Universalis II*, the initial learning of the game was probably too hard for many students, but it also offered a richer game universe for students compared to most other games. This balance is hard to strike but it will be easier as students' game skills become more equally distributed and teachers get more experience with computer games so that they can help students learn the game. We need to combine the commercial computer game's ability to create game universes that are accessible, agreeable and relevant to building on students' existing experiences with the educational agenda that facilitates the transformation of concrete experiences and spontaneous concepts into more scientific concepts.

NOTES

1   See Juul (2002) for a disscussion of these two genres.
2   This characteristic is included in a recent attempt to build a taxonomy for computer games (Aarseth et al., 2003).

11
Final Thoughts

Educational use of computer games ... One may ask, is it worth it? Probably not in the short run, but in the long run, I believe that computer games have something else to offer compared to other teaching styles: namely, a dynamic and rich presentation of a given subject that the student has a chance to engage with and challenge through interaction, thereby building a strong investment in the subject. This investment must be guided by instruction from teachers, parents or peers to ensure the educational quality.

Often, the underlying assumption is that computer games have a unique potential for revolutionizing education. Such an approach will paint the area into a corner as it has consistently done with new media introduced over the last centuries. Although computer games have some special qualities, they are more than anything else an extension of other human practices. As a tool, they are formed by culture and history, and although they can inform human action with new potential, these actions still remain guided by a cultural and historical grounding. So far, we have primarily shaped educational use of computer games with conservative practices. However, we are constantly in a position to shape this tool by introducing it in new contexts and by developing the use of such a tool. We should learn from the history of education and the educational use of computer games, but not be confined by it.

Throughout this book, I have gone through quite elaborate descriptions of the conditions surrounding educational use of computer games in terms of practical problems such as the limited availability of relevant titles, the limitations of technical equipment and the few experiences with actually using computer games for educational purposes. We should pay attention to all of these areas. The structural conditions for actually using computer games in schools have been examined extensively in this book and I have no intention of repeating my points. However, the structural conditions are crucial to keep in mind in order to avoid the fantasy that educational use of computer games solely relies on the maturation of the game medium and more research into the area. The following are the most important points in this book:

- *Market conditions*: The market for producing material, support and titles for using computer games in schools is practically non-existent. Publishers have failed to innovate and are trapped in time somewhere in the 1980s.

- *Cultural position*: Computer games have a lot of baggage when they enter schools, resulting in a both positive and negative influence on the educational use. Culturally, computer games are still often seen as entertaining, immature, boyish activities, with violent and stereotypical content, which leads to opposition from both teachers and students.
- *School structure*: The evolution of the school hardly favours the use of computer games, with classroom structure, short lessons, few cross-disciplinary courses, tight curriculum design, closed teaching practice, sparse computer equipment and no budget for software acquisitions.
- *Practical experiences*: We still have few experiences with using computer games for educational purposes and the barriers are substantial for most teachers on the classroom level. We need more actual experiences to see what happens when computer games are brought into the educational setting accompanied by sound didactic considerations.
- *Experiential learning with computer games*: Computer games provide concrete experiences building a strong sense of relevance and strong engagement leading students to invest in the learning activity. Instruction extends from the concrete experiences with computer games and the student's investment. The instruction provides the necessary direction, order and reflection, refining the experiences beyond the immediate student construction.

In conclusion, the structural limitations for educational use of computer games are still considerable on several levels. This should not discourage us from trying to further a deeper understanding of what it means to use computer games for educational purposes. It is important to remember that the educational system has always been 'blessed' with more critics than followers. Also, among a few reformers, there is a recurring fantasy that new media will almost by magic transform the educational system, providing an overall better educational experience for all the media savvy students. However, as has been demonstrated in this book, the truth is more complicated.

One overall trend in the educational system that computer games also adhere to is the individualization of the learning experience through different media and more dedicated time to each student. The idea of media empowerment has certainly not become less pronounced among educators, with learning theories hailing different styles of learning. In some senses, computer games, along with the use of other popular culture expressions in schools, are the final genuflection for this individualization and, as such, potentially an admission of failure for a wider socialization. We attempt to approach new generations with new teaching practice relying on new media that are not our own. The cultural expressions preferred by new media become the material that the older generations feed the younger generation, less interested in a richer socialization capable of building a bridge across generations. This does not necessarily have to be a problem, but quite often it does become a problem when games are introduced in educational settings.

It is somewhat terrifying how computer games fit well within the current trend, where we are paying more attention to what is interesting, motivating and appropriate for the single individual rather than what we as a society wish to convey to the next generation. It is, therefore, not surprising that the immediate attraction of using computer games lies more on the part of the student than on the part of the teacher. This is also an important element in the weak penetration of computer games in schools. It is basically more to the advantage of students than teachers. Hopefully, a genuflection for new generations will not be the sole reason for choosing to use computer games in future education. Indeed, times are approaching when a new generation of teachers will have also grown up with computer games, and this opens up the chance for truly leveraging the educational potential of computer games. Although new teachers will be far from enough. Teachers will not be able to do all the work by themselves, but researchers and developers are already working on easing the task.

To succeed with games we need an even stronger shift in the current trends, where computer games are conceived in a much broader sense. We need not only new games but also new players. This will not happen overnight, and it will not be enough for a few dusty researchers or teachers to engage in the challenge. We need to rejuvenate computer games by making the space outside purely entertainment games attractive to the most innovative and creative people. Those especially that work in the games industry represent a challenge. The games industry continues to be infatuated with great graphics and technology – on a general level the industry still hasn't seen that the challenge of games lies no longer in building the most flashy entertaining titles, but rather in expanding the notion of good games from merely entertainment to include more diverse forms of human activity. Often the argument goes that the educational games built so far have been of poor quality, which I do not disagree with. However, in all fairness you have to consider the limitations of most current educational game projects. They are developed with severe constraints on the game contents and functionality while haunted by small budgets, and can draw on very little actual game development experience. We may stumble over the solution in this haphazard swamp of ideas and projects. However, it may take quite a while, and the entry of more people is badly needed to propel games beyond the limited scope of both entertainment and edutainment.

Glossary

Action: Game genre that focuses on speed and physical drama with high demands on the player's reflexes and co-ordination skills.

Adventure: Game genre that focuses on puzzle-solving within a narrative framework that relies on the player's ability to think logically.

Commercial games: Overall term for computer games that are sold through traditional retail channels.

Drill-and-practice software: Software that primarily relies on training in a number of very specific skills by letting the user repeat the activity endlessly.

Educational computer games: Computer games developed for educational use or titles often used in educational settings, which encompass the fake, bad, ambitious and the superb.

Educational games: Traditional non-electronic game-like activities developed for educational use, spanning board games, simulations, role-playing, etc.

Educational software: All computer programs with an educational aim. Educational software is, therefore, a broader group than educational computer games and the applications are quite different in that they do not necessarily have game elements. When they have game elements, it is seldom an integrated part of the experience, but rather small, separate activities. Educational computer games are often included under the heading of educational software.

Edutainment: Edutainment is a sub-group of educational computer games that is heavily criticized. Typically, edutainment titles are characterized by using quite conventional learning theories, providing a questionable game experience and simple gameplay. They are mostly produced with reference to a curriculum or some quite general overall skills, like problem-solving.

Extrinsic motivation: Motivation that arises due to factors not directly related to an activity.

ICT: An abbreviation for information and communication technologies.

Instructional films: Films produced for teaching a specific subject or topic in an educational setting.

Instructional technology: Instructional technology is an approach dedicated to the solving of instructional problems related to the use of technology. In this book, it primarily refers to the application of strategies and techniques from behavioural and cognitive studies.

Intrinsic motivation: Motivation that arises as a natural part of a given activity.

Logo: A programming language designed by Seymour Papert to teach children maths and science in line with the educational theory constructionism.

Narrative: Organization of elements in a meaningful order that includes the following: 1) A world with characters and objects. 2) Change as a consequence of either user actions or events. 3) It must be possible for the user to 'speculate' around the events, thereby creating a plot.

RTS: An abbreviation of real-time strategy games that refer to a combination of action and strategy, typically involving resource management and the waging of war.

Serious games: The concept serious games is used to describe the overarching perspective of games for something other than just entertainment. The term was coined by the American Clark Abt back in 1968 and is the title of his influential book (Abt, 1968). Abt's book is an important hallmark for alternative uses of traditional games for educational purposes and, in this sense, also leads the way for the later use of computer games for educational purposes. However, the modern use includes more than just educational use of games, including advertainment, edutainment, political games and news games.

Simulation: Games where realism is first priority. The player's ability to understand and remember complex principles and relations is paramount.

Strategy: A game genre in which one needs to maintain an overview and prioritize resources correctly and in accordance with overall strategy.

Resources

There are a number of places where one can find more information on the world wide web, and maybe even get help designing a course using computer games in an educational setting. I have intentionally kept the list short and not included every imaginable website.

EDUCATIONAL MATERIAL

It is still rare to find material that facilitates the use of next-generation educational computer games. There are some materials for commercial computer games, which are listed below.

Civilization III: Kurt Squire has created teaching material around *Civilization* based on his research in the field: www.thinktv.org/education/ntti/ntti/lesson03/squire.html

SimCity 3: There have been quite a few attempts at using *SimCity* in education and these attempts have often been facilitated by the following guide by Margy Kuntz: www.geocities.com/edit6100/Task_4/SimCity.html

CONFERENCES, CENTRES AND INITIATIVES

The number of conferences, initiatives and centres within the area has been growing exponentially over the last few years.

Centre for Learning Games (LLD): www.lld.dk/consortia/learninggames/en
Education Arcade: www.educationarcade.org
Epistemic Games: http://epistemicgames.org
Games + Learning + Society (GLS): http://website.education.wise.edu/gls/index.htm
Serious Games Alliance: www.seriousgamesalliance.org
Serious Games Initiative: www.seriousgames.org
Serious Games Source: www.seriousgamessource.com
Serious Games Summit: www.seriousgamessummit.com

RESEARCH RESOURCES

Here are a few places where one can find articles online within the area of educational use of computer games. Some of them are dated but still quite relevant.

Becta: www.becta.org.uk/research/research.cfm?section=1&id=519
E-GEMS: www.cs.ubc.ca/nest/egems/index.html
Game-research: www.game-research.com
Nesta Future Lab: www.nestafuturelab.org
Seriousplaying: www.seriousplaying.org
Watercoolergames: http://www.watercoolergames.org

EDUCATIONAL DEVELOPERS

Here are a few relevant developers within the field that are mentioned to provide a place to look for products in the future. Some companies have not yet released their first title, but are working on them. I have only included companies that target the educational sector with a third-generation approach.

BreakAway Games
Caspian Learning
Immersive Education
Muzzy Lane
Pixie Learning
Serious Games Interactive

Game Bibliography

Aegis International, *Ports of Call*, 1987. Aegis International (Amiga)

Amusement Vision, *Super Monkey Ball*, 2001. Sega (GameCube)

APh Tech. Consulting, *Electric Company Math Fun*, 1979. Mattel Electronics (Intellivision)

APh Tech. Consulting, *Word Fun*, 1980. Mattel Electronics (Intellivision)

Ascaron, *Patrician II*, 2000. Infogrames (PC)

Atari, *Basic Math*, 1977. Atari (Atari 2600)

Big Huge Games, *Rise of Nations*, 2003. Microsoft Game Studios (PC)

Black Pencil Ent., *Aids Prevention – Catch the Sperm*, 2004. Stop Aids (PC)

Britannica, *Designasaurus 2*, 1990. Britannica (1990)

Brøderbund, *Where in the World is Carmen San Diego*, 1985. Brøderbund (PC)

Chris Crawford, *Balance of the Planet*, 1990. Chris Crawford (PC)

Chris Crawford, *Balance of Power*, 1985. Mindscape (PC)

Chris Sawyer Productions, *Roller Coaster Tycoon*, 1999. Hasbro Interactive (PC)

Click and Health, *Bronkie the Bronchiasaurus*, 1995. Click and Health (SNES)

Click and Health, *Packy and Marlon*, 1997. Click and Health (SNES)

Cornerstone Industry, *Guard Force*, 2002. Army National Guard (PC)

Cornerstone Industry, *Joint Force Employment*, 2000. Office of the Joint Chiefs (PC)

Creative Assembly, *Medieval: Total War*, 2002. Activision Publishing (PC)

Creative Wonders, *Sesame Street Toddlers Deluxe*, 1997. The Learning Company (PC)

Davidson and Associates, *Math Blaster*, 1986. Davidson and Associates (PC)

Deadline Game, *Blackout*, 1995. Deadline (PC)

Deadline Games, *Globetrotter 2*, 2001. Vision Park (PC)

Destineer Studios, *Close Combat: First to Fight*, 2005. Global Star (PC)

DMA Design, *Lemmings*, 1991. Psygnosis (PC)

Dynamix, *The Incredible Machine*, 1993. Sierra (PC)

Edmark, *Millie's Math House*, 1995. Riverdeep (PC)

E-Gems, *Phoenix Quest*, 1994. E-Gems (PC)

E-Gems, *Super Tangrams*, 1994. E-Gems (PC)

Eisenstein, *Global Island*, 2002. Mellemfolkeligt Samvirke (PC)

Electronic Arts, *Scooter's Magic Castle*, 1994. Electronic Arts (PC)

Enlight Software, *Capitalism II*, 2001. Ubisoft Entertainment (PC)
Enlight Software, *Virtual U*, 2003. Woodrow Wilson Foundation (PC)
Ensemble Studios, *Age of Empires*, 1997. Microsoft Game Studios (PC)
Ensemble Studios, *Age of Kings*, 1999. Microsoft Game Studios (PC)
Ensemble Studios, *Age of Mythology*, 2002. Microsoft Game Studios (PC)
FDB, *Miljøstrup*, 1994. FDB (PC)
FireFly Studios, *Stronghold*, 2002. Gathering of Developers (PC)
Freeware, *Lemonade Stand*, 2001. Freeware (PC)
Health Media Lab, *Hungry Red Planet*, 2002. Health Media Lab, Inc. (PC)
Humongous Ent., *Freddi Fish 5: Creature of Coral*, 2001. Humongous Ent. (PC)
Humongous Ent., *Pajama Sam*, 1996. Humongous Ent. (PC)
Humongous Ent., *Putt Putt Saves the Zoo*, 1995. Humongous Ent. (PC)
Id Software, *Doom*, 1993. Id Software (PC)
Ignited Minds, *America's Army*, 2002. US Army (PC)
Impressions, *Caesar*, 1993. Impressions (PC)
Institute for Future Studies, *Brainbuilders*, 2002. Institute for Future Studies (Role play)
IO Interactive, *Freedom Fighters*, 2003. Electronic Arts (PC)
Kræfens Bekæmpelse, *Cell Fight*, 1997. Kræfens Bekæmpelse (PC)
Kræftens Bekæmpelse, *Foodman*, 1994. Kræftens Bekæmpelse (PC)
LCSI, *My Make Believe Castle*, 1996. LCSI (PC)
Learning Company, *Dr Seuss Preschool*, 1998. Broderbund
Learning Company, *Logical Journey of the Zoombinis*, 1996. Brøderbund (PC)
Learning Company, *Math Missions Grades 3–5*, 2003. Scholastic (PC)
Learning Company, *The Robot Odyssey*, 1984. Learning Company (Apple II)
Learning Company, *Rocky Boots*, 1982. Learning Company (Apple II)
Learning Lab Denmark, *Tracks*, 2004. Forlag Malling Beck (Role play)
Lucas Learning, *DroidWorks*, 1998. Lucas Learning (PC)
Maxis Software, *SimCity*, 1989. Infogrames (Amiga)
Maxis Software, *SimCity 2000*, 1993. Maxis Software (PC)
Maxis Software, *SimCity 4*, 2003. Electronic Arts (PC)
Maxis Software, *SimEarth*, 1990. SimEarth (PC)
Maxis Software, *SimFarm*, 1993. Mindscape (PC)
Maxis Software, *The Sims*, 2000. Electronic Arts (PC)
MECC, *Oregon Trail*, 1985. MECC (Apple II)
MECC, *Super Munchers*, 1991. MECC (PC)
MicroProse Software, *Civilization*, 1992. MicroProse Software (PC)
MicroProse Software, *Railroad Tycoon*, 1990. MicroProse Software (PC)
Nintendo, *Super Mario Brothers*, 1985. Nintendo (NES)
Nova Logic, *Delta Force 2*, 1999. Nova Logic (PC)
Ozark Softscape, *Mule*, 1983. Electronic Arts (PC)

Ozark Softscape, *Seven Cities of Gold*, 1984. Electronic Arts (Apple II)
Pandemic, *Full Spectrum Warrior*, 2004. US Army (PC)
Papworth, Nigel, Wallin, Håkan and Frank, Anders, *Foreign Grounds*, 2006. Forsvarshögskolan (PC)
Paradox Entertainment, *Crusader King*, 2004. Pan Vision (PC)
Paradox Entertainment, *Europa Universalis II*, 2001. Strategy First (PC)
Paradox Entertainment, *Hearts of Iron*, 2002. Pan Vision (PC)
Paradox Entertainment, *Victoria: an Empire under the Sun Game*, 2003. PAN Vision (PC)
Pyro Studios, *Praetorians*, 2003. Eidos Interactive (PC)
Quicksilver, *Full Spectrum Command*, 2004. THQ (PC)
Rand, *Monopologs*, 1956. US Army (Mainframe)
ReLINE Software, *Oil Imperium*, 1989. Reline Software (Amiga)
Rockstar Games, *Grand Theft Auto 3*, 2002. Take-Two Interactive Software (PC)
Sculptured Software, *Patton Versus Rommel*, 1987. Electronic Arts (PC)
Sierra, *Castle of Dr Brain*, 1991. Sierra (PC)
Sierra, *Gabriel Knight*, 1993. Sierra (PC)
Sierra, *Leisure Suit Larry 1: In the Land of the Lounge Lizards*, 1991. Sierra Online (PC)
Sierra, *Mickey's Space Adventure*, 1984. Walt Disney Computer Software (PC)
Sierra, *Troll's Tale*, 1984. Sierra (C64)
Sierra, *Winnie the Pooh in the Hundred Acre Wood*, 1985. Sierra (PC)
Smilebit, *The Typing of the Dead*, 2000. Sega (Dreamcast)
Software Toolworks, *Life and Death*, 1988. The Software Toolworks (PC)
Software Toolworks, *Mavis Beacon*, 1994. The Software Toolworks (PC)
Spellbound Software, *Airline Tycoon*, 1998. Infogrames (PC)
Sports Interactive, *Championship Manager*, 1992. Domark (PC)
Strategic Simulations, *Panzer General*, 1996. Mindscape (PC)
Taito, *Space Invaders*, 1978. Taito (Arcade)
TATI Mixedia, *Backpacker*, 1995. BMG Interactive (PC)
Thinking Tools, *SimHealth*, 1994. Maxis Software (PC)
Tom Snyder Productions, *In Search of the Most Amazing Thing*, 1983. Spinnaker (PC)
Tom Snyder Productions, *Snooper Troops*, 1982. Spinnaker (Apple II)
Tool Factory, *Chefren's Pyramid*, 2001. Alega Skolmateriel (PC)

Bibliography

Aarseth, E. (1997). *Cybertext: Perspectives on Ergodic Literature*. London: Johns Hopkins University Press.

Aarseth, E., Sunnanå, L. and Smedstad, S.M. (2003). A Multi-Dimensional Typology of Games. Paper presented at the Level Up – Digital Games Research Conference, Utrecht.

Abt, C. (1968). 'Games for Learning'. In S.S. Boocock and E.O. Schild (eds.), *Simulation Games in Learning*. London: Sage Publications.

Adams, E. and Rollings, A. (2003). *Andrew Rollings and Ernest Adams on Game Design*. Indianapolis: New Riders.

Adams, P.C. (1998). 'Teaching and learning with *SimCity 2000*', *Journal of Geography*, 97 (2), 47–55.

Aldrich, C. (2003). *Simulations and the Future of Learning*. San Francisco: Pfeiffer.

Andersen, P.Ø. and Kampmann, J. (1996). *Børns Legekultur*. København: Munksgaard.

Armstrong, L. and Hamm, S. (1997). 'CD-roms: the giant rules: and even the game world's predators are feeling the pinch', *Business Week*.

Asplund, J. (1997). *Det Sociala Livets Elementära Former*. Göteborg: Korpen.

Avendon, E.M. and Sutton-Smith, B. (1971). *The Study of Games*. New York: John Wiley and Sons, Inc.

Bates, J. (2001). 'Everything you wanted to know about the sequel but were afraid to ask', *PC IGN*.

Bateson, G. (1972). *Steps to an Ecology of Mind*. Chicago: University of Chicago Press.

Beavis, C. (1997). 'Computer Games, Culture and Curriculum'. In I. Snyder and M. Joyce (eds.), *Page to Screen: Taking Literacy into the Electronic Era*. New York: Routledge.

Beavis, C. (1999a). Literacy, English and Computer Games. Paper presented at the the Power of Language, International Federation for the Teaching of English Seventh Conference, University of Warwick, UK.

Beavis, C. (1999b). Magic or Mayhem? New Texts and New Literacies in Technological Times. Paper presented at the annual conference, Australian Association for Research in Education and New Zealand Association for Research in Education, Melbourne.

Becker, K. (2001). 'Teaching with games – the Minesweeper and Asteroids experience', *The Journal of Computing in Small Colleges*, 17 (2), 22–32.

Becker, K. and Jacobsen, M. (2005). Games for Learning: Are Schools Ready for What's to Come? Paper presented at DiGRA 2005, Second International Conference.

Becta. (2001). 'Computer Games in Education Project'. www.becta.org. uk/research/research.cfm?section=1andid=519

Bergman, P. (2003). Digital Games and Learning: A Research Overview. Unpublished manuscript.

Betz, J.A. (1995). 'Computer games: increased learning in an interactive multidisciplinary environment' *Journal of Educational Technology Systems*, 24 (2), 195–205.

BioWare. (2004). 'Sponsor_Nvidia'. www.bioware.com/2million/sponsors/ sponsor_nvidia.html

Bloom, B.S., Engelhart, M.D., Furst, E.J., Hill, W.H. and Krathwohl, D.R. (1956). *Taxonomy of Educational Objectives: The Classification of Educational Goals: Handbook I: Cognitive Domain.* New York: David McKay Company.

Blossom, J. and Michaud, C. (1999). 'Postmortem: Lucas Learning's *Star Wars* DroidWorks', *Gamasutra*.

Boocock, S.S. and Schild, E.O. (1968). *Simulation Games in Learning.* London: Sage Publications.

Booth, J. and VanDeventer, S. (1997). An Informal Survey of Adult Attitudes About Learning From Cartoons and Videogames. Unpublished. Tampa, Florida.

Bowman, R.F. (1982). 'A Pac-Man theory of motivation. Tactical implications for classroom instruction', *Educational Technology*, 22 (9), 14–17.

Brake, D. (2002). 'Interview – Sid Meier'. www.mindjack.com/interviews/ sidmeier.html

Bransford, J.D., Brown, A.L. and Cocking, R.R. (1999). *How People Learn: Brain, Mind, Experience, and School.* Washington, DC: National Academy Press.

Bredemeier, M.E., and Greenblat, C.S. (1981). 'The educational effectiveness of simulation games: a synthesis of findings', *Simulation and Games*, 12 (3), 307–31.

Broderbund. (2003). www.broderbund.com/Product.asp?OID=4145761

Brody, H. (1993). 'Video games that teach?', *Technology Review*, 96 (8), 51–7.

Browder, S., Armstrong, L. and Judge, P.C. (1996). 'The disappearing CD-ROM players: small makers of kids' software sell out or get squeezed out', *Business Week*.

Brown, J. (24 October 2002). 'Payoff = points: a false equation', *New York Times*.

Brown, S.J., Lieberman, D.A., Gemeny, B.A., Fan, Y.C., Wilson, D.M. and Pasta, D.J. (1997). 'Educational video game for juvenile diabetes: results of a controlled trial', *Medical Informatics*, 22 (1), 77–89.

Bruner, J. (1991). *Acts of Meaning.* Cambridge: Harvard University Press.

Bruner, J. (1996). *Culture of Education*. Cambridge: Harvard University Press.

Bruner, J., Jolly, A. and Sylva, K. (1976). *Play: Its Role in Development and Education*. New York: Penguin Books.

Buckingham, D. (2003). *Media Education: Literacy, Learning, and Contemporary Culture*. Cambridge: Polity Press.

Buckingham, D., Carr, D., Burn, A. and Schott, G. (Forthcoming). *Videogames: Text, Narrative, Play*. Cambridge: Polity.

Buckingham, D. and Scanlon, M. (2002). *Education, Edutainment, and Learning in the Home*. Cambridge: Open University Press.

Butler, R.J., Markulis, P.M. and Strang, D.R. (1988). 'Where are we? an analysis of the methods and focus of the research on simulation gaming', *Simulation and Games*, 19(1), 3–26.

Butler, T. (1988). 'Games and simulations: creative education alternatives', *Tech Trends*.

Calvert, S.L. (1999). *Children's Journeys through the Information Age*. Boston: McGraw-Hill.

Campbell, D.T. and Stanley, J.C. (1969). *Experimental and Quasi-experimental Designs for Research*. Chicago: Houghton Mifflin Company.

Cassel, J., and Jenkins, H. (1998). *From Barbie to Mortal Kombat – Gender and Computer Games*. Cambridge: The MIT Press.

Cavallari, J., Hedberg, J. and Harper, B. (1992). 'Adventure games in education: a review', *Australian Journal of Educational Technology*, 8 (2), 172–184.

Cesarone, B. (1994). *Video Games and Children*, ERIC Clearinghouse on Elementary and Early Childhood Education.' Washington, DC: Office of Educational Research and Improvement.

Children's Software. (1998). 'Stanford Children's Software Stanford Conversation Transcripts'. www.childrenssoftware.com/stanfordtranscripts

Clegg, A.A. (1991). 'Games and Simulations in Social Studies Education'. In J.P. Shaver (ed.), *Handbook of Research on Social Studies Teaching and Learning*. New York: Macmillan.

Coleman, J. (1970). *The Role of Modern Technology in Relation to Simulations and Games for Learning*. Unpublished manuscript.

Coleman, J.S. (1967). 'Learning Through Games'. In J. Bruner, A. Jolly and K. Sylva (eds.), *Play: Its Role in Development and Evolution*. New York: Penguin Books.

Coleman, J.S., Livingstone, S.A., Fennessey, G.M., Edwards, K.J. and Kidder, S.J. (1973). 'The Hopkins' games program: conclusions from seven years of research', *Educational Researcher* (2), 3–7.

Coolican, H. (1994). *Research Methods and Statistics in Psychology*. London: Hodder and Stoughton.

Corbeil, P. (1999). 'Learning from the children: practical and theoretical reflections on playing and learning' *Simulation and Gaming*, 30 (2), 163–80.

Cotton, K. (1991). *Computer-Assisted Instruction.* Northwest Regional Educational Laboratory.

Crawford, C. (1982). *The Art of Computer Game Design.* Berkeley, CA: McGraw-Hill.

Crawford, C. (2003). *Chris Crawford on Game Design.* Boston: New Riders.

Csikszentmihalyi, M. (1992). *Flow: The Classic Work on how to Achieve Happiness.* New York: Harper Perennial.

Cuban, L. (2001). *Oversold and Overused: Computers in the Classroom.* Cambridge, MA: Harvard University Press.

Curtis, P. (1992). Mudding: Social Phenomena in Text-Based Virtual Realities. Paper presented at Directions and Implications of Advanced Computing, Berkeley, California.

Danielsen, O., Olesen, B.R., and Sørensen, B.H. (2002). 'From Computer-Based Educational Games to Actions in Everyday Life'. In O. Danielsen, J. Nielsen and B.H. Sørensen (eds.), *Learning and Narrativity in Digital Media* (pp. 67–81). Aarhus: Samfundslitteratur.

de Freitas, S. (2005). *Learning through Play. Using Educational Games and Simulations to Support Post-16 Learners.* London: London Learning and Skills Research Centre.

DeMaria, R. and Wilson, J.L. (2002). *High Score!: The Illustrated History of Electronic Games.* New York: McGraw-Hill/Osborne.

Dempsey, J.V., Rasmussen, K. and Lucassen, B. (1996). *The Instructional Gaming Literature: Implications and 99 Sources.* Thousand Oaks, CA: University of South Alabama.

Dewey, J. (1910). *How We Think.* New York: Prometheus Books.

Dewey, J. (1938). *Experience and Education.* New York: Simon and Schuster.

Din, F.S., and Caleo, J. (2000). Playing Computer Games versus Better Learning. Unpublished manuscript.

Döpping, J. (1995) 'A social theory of distribution of knowledge as translation' *Nordiske Udkast,* 23 (2), 17–33.

Dorn, D.S. (1989). 'Simulation games: one more tool on the pedagogical shelf', *Teaching Sociology,* 17 (1), 1–18.

Dorval, M. and Pepin, M. (1986). 'Effect of playing a video game on a measure of spatial visualization', *Perceptual Motor Skills,* 62 (1), 159–62.

Dowey, J.A. (1987). 'Computer games for dental health education in primary schools', *Health Education Journal,* 46 (3).

Drotner, K. (2001). *Medier for fremtiden – børn, unge og det nye medie-landskab.* Copenhagen: Høst og Søn.

Druckman, D. (1995). 'The Educational Effectiveness'. In D. Crookall and K. Arai (eds.), *Simulation and Gaming Across Disciplines and Cultures.* London: Sage Publications.

Duke, R.E. (1995). 'Opening Speech: Welcome and Challenge'. In D. Crookall and K. Arai (eds.), *Simulation and Gaming Across Disciplines and Cultures.* London: Sage Publications.

Duke, R.E., and Seidner, C.J. (1975). *Learning with Simulations and Games.* London: Sage Publications.

Educational Software Classics. (1999) 'The Oregon Trail'. ldt.stanford.edu/ ldt1999/Students/kemery/esc/otCompanyFrame.htm

Egenfeldt-Nielsen, S. (2001). *Digitale udfordringer. Informationsteknologi i en skole under forandring.* København: Gyldendal Uddannelse.

Egenfeldt-Nielsen, S. (2003a). *Bagom Computerspil – et undervisningsmateriale.* Copenhagen: Game-Research.

Egenfeldt-Nielsen, S. (2003b, 24 September). 'Computerspil på skoleskemaet'. *Berlingske Tidende.*

Egenfeldt-Nielsen, S. (2003c). Exploration in Computer Games – A New Starting Point. Paper presented at the DIGRA – Level up conference, Utrecht University.

Egenfeldt-Nielsen, S. (2003d). Keep the Monkey Rolling: Eye-Hand Coordination in Super Monkey Ball. Paper presented at the DIGRA – Level up conference, Utrecht University.

Egenfeldt-Nielsen, S. (2003e). 'Thoughts on learning in games and designing educational computer games', *Game-research.*

Egenfeldt-Nielsen, S. (2004). Designing Educational Computer Game Experiences. Unpublished manuscript.

Egenfeldt-Nielsen, S. (2005). Beyond Edutainment: Exploring the Educational Potential of Computer Games. Unpublished PhD dissertation, IT University, Copenhagen.

Egenfeldt-Nielsen, S. and Buch, T. (2006). The Learning Effects of Global Conflicts: Palestine Fornos. Media@terra.

Egenfeldt-Nielsen, S. and Smith, J.H. (2000). *Den digitale leg – om børn og computerspil.* Copenhagen: Hans Reitzels Forlag.

Egenfeldt-Nielsen, S. and Smith, J.H. (2002). 'Online gaming habits', *Game-research.*

Egenfeldt-Nielsen, S. and Smith, J.H. (2004). *Playing with Fire: How do Computer Games Influence Players?* Göteborg: Nordicom.

Elder, C. (1973). 'Problems in the structure and use of educational simulation', *Sociology of Education,* 46 (3), 335–54.

Ellis, H., Heppel, S., Kirriemuir, J., Krotoski, A. and McFarlane, A. (2006). *Unlimited Learning: Computer and Video Games in the Learning Landscape.* ELSPA.

EMU. (2004). 'Drabssag Melved'. http://drabssag.emu.dk/

ESA (2002). *Essential Facts about the Computer and Video Game Industry.* The Interactive Digital Software Association.

ESA. (2003). 'Industry Sales and Economic Data: Consumer Spending Poll'. www.theesa.com/industrysales.html

Fabricatore, C. (2000). Learning and Videogames: An Unexploited Synergy. Unpublished manuscript.

Facer, K. (2003). *Computer Games and Learning*. A NESTA Futurelab Discussion Document.

Facer, K., Furlong, J., Furlong, R. and Sutherland, R. (2003). '"Edutainment" Software: A Site for Cultures in Conflict'. In R. Sutherland, G. Claxton and A. Pollard (eds.), *Learning and Teaching Where Worldviews Meet*. London: Trentham Books.

Fagen, R. (1995). 'Animal Play, Games of Angels, Biology, and Brian'. In A.D. Pellegrini (ed.), *The Future of Play Theory: A Multidisciplinary Inquiry into the Contributions of Brian Sutton-Smith*. Albany: State University of New York Press.

Faria, A.I. (1990). 'Business Simulation Games After Thirty Years: Current Usage Levels'. In J.W. Gentry (ed.), *Guide to Business Gaming and Experiential Learning* (pp. 36–47). East Brunswick: Nichols/GP.

Federal Communications Commission. (2003). 'Television Technology – A Short History'. www.fcc.gov/omd/history/tv/

Ferguson, N. (1997). *Virtual History*. London: Picador.

Finnemann, N.O. (1999). 'Modernity Modernised – The Cultural Impact of Computerisation'. In P.A. Mayer (ed.), *Computer Media and Communication: A reader*. Oxford: Oxford University Press.

Flanagan, R. (2003). *Gould's Book of Fish*. London: Atlantic Books.

Fridberg, T. (1999). *7–15-åriges fritidsaktiviteter – Kultur- og fritidsundersøgelsen 1998*. Copenhagen: Socialforskningsinstituttet.

Funk, J.B. (1993). 'Video games: adolescent mediums', *State of the Art Reviews*, 4 (3), 589–98.

Funk, J. and Buchman, D. (1995). 'Video game controversies', *Paediatric Annals*, 24 (2), 91–4.

Gagnon, D. (1985). 'Videogames and spatial skills: an exploratory study', *Educational Communications and Technology Journal*, 33 (4), 263–75.

Gander, S. (2002). 'Does learning occur through gaming?', *Electronic Journal of Instructional Science and Technology*, 3 (2), 28–43.

Gardner, H. (1983). *Frames of Mind: The Theory of Multiple Intelligences*. New York: Basic Books.

Garson, D. (Unknown). 'PA 765: Quantitative Research in Public Administration'. www2.chass.ncsu.edu/garson/pa765/standard.htm

Gee, J.P. (2003). *What Video Games Have to Teach Us About Learning and Literacy*. New York: Palgrave-McMillan.

Gee, J.P. (2004a). Learning about Learning from a Video Game: Rise of Nations. Unpublished manuscript.

Gee, J.P. (2004b, 24 March). 'Learning by design: games as learning machines', *Gamasutra*.

Gee, J.P., Lieberman, D., Raybourn, E. and Rajeski, D. (2004). 'How Can Games Shape Future Behaviors'. www.watercoolergames.org/archives/000263.shtml#howcan

Gentry, J.W. (1990). *What is Experiential Learning?* New Jersey: Nichols.

Gleitman, H. (1995). *Psychology – Fourth Edition*. New York: Norton.

Goldstein, R. and Pratt, D. (2001). Michael's Computer Game: A Case of Open Modelling. Paper presented at the the Twenty-Fifth Annual Conference of the International Group for the Psychology of Mathematics, Utrecht, The Netherlands.

Good, T.L. and Brophy, J.E. (1990). *Educational Psychology: A Realistic Approach*. Fourth Edition. New York: Longman.

Grabe, M. and Dosmann, M. (1998). 'The potential of adventure games for the development of reading and study skills', *Journal of Computer-Based Instruction*, 15 (2), 72–7.

Gredler, M. (1992). *Designing and Evaluating Games and Simulations: A Process Approach*. London: Kogan Page Ltd.

Green, C.S. and Bavelier, D. (2003). 'Action video game modifies visual selective attention', *Nature* (423), 534–7.

Greenblat, C. (1981). 'Teaching with Simulation Games: A Review of Claims and Evidence'. In R.E. Duke and C. Greenblat (eds.), *Principles of Practice of Gaming-Simulation*. London: Sage Publications.

Greenblat, C. and Duke, R.E. (1981). *Gaming-Simulation: Rationale Applications*. London: Sage Publications.

Greenfield, P. (1984). *Mind and Media*. Cambridge: Harvard University Press.

Greenfield, P.M., Brannon, C. and Lohr, D. (1996). 'Two-Dimensional Representations of Movement Through Three-Dimensional Space: The Role of Video Game experience'. In P.M. Greenfield and R.R. Cocking (eds.), *Interacting With Video* (pp. 169–85). New Jersey: Ablex Publishing.

Griffith, J.L., Voloschin, P., Gibb, G.D., and Bailey, J.R. (1983). 'Differences in eye-hand motor coordination of video-game users and non-users', *Perceptual Motor Skills*, 57, 155–8.

Gros, B. (2003). 'The impact of digital games in education', *First Monday*, 8 (7).

Grundy, S. (1991). 'A computer adventure as a worthwhile educational experience', *Interchange*, 22 (4), 41–55.

Guba, E.G. and Lincoln, Y.S. (1989). *Fourth Generation Evaluation*. Newbury Park, California: Sage Publications.

Gugliemo, C. (1994). 'Class leader', *Wired*.

Hancock, C. and Osterweil, S. (1996). '*Zoombinis* and the art of mathematical play', *Hands On!*, 19 (1).

Healy, J.M. (1999). *FAILURE TO CONNECT: How Computers Affect Our Children's Minds*. New York: Touchstone.

Heaney, L.F. (1989). 'Computer adventure games: value and interest to teachers and pupils', *The International Journal of Educational Management*, 3 (4).

Helm, B. 'Educational games crank up the fun'. (2005). *Business Week*, 23 August.

Herring, R. (1984). 'Educational computer games', *Analog Computing*.

Højholt, C. and Witt, G. (1996). *Skolelivets socialpsykologi*. Copenhagen: Unge Pædagoger.

Hostetter, O. (2003). 'Video Games – The Necessity of Incorporating Video Games as part of Constructivist Learning'. www.game-research.com/ art_games_contructivist.asp

Hoyle, R.H., Harris, M.J. and Judd, C.M. (1991). *Research Methods in Social Relations*. Fort Worth, Philadelphia: Hartcourt Brace.

Hoyles, C., Noss, R. and Adamson, R. (2002). 'Rethinking the microworld idea', *Journal of Educational Computing Research*, 27 (1–2), 29–53.

Huizinga, J. (1986). *Homo Ludens: A Study of the Play-element in Culture*. Boston: Beacon Press.

Hunter, W. (2000). 'The Dot Eaters – Video Game History 101'. www. emuunlim.com/doteaters/

Jensen, J.F. (1999). '"Interactivity" – Tracking a New Concept in Media and Communication Studies'. In P.A. Mayer (ed.), *Computer Media and Communication: A Reader*. Oxford: Oxford University Press.

Jessen, C. (1995). 'Computeren i børnehaven – Rapport fra et forsøg-sprojekt'. *Tidsskrift for Børne-og Ungdomskultur* (35).

Jessen, C. (1998). 'Interpretive Communities: The Reception of Computer Games by Children and the Young'. www.carsten-jessen.dk/intercom.html

Jessen, C. (2001). *Børn, leg og computerspil*. Odense: Odense Universitetsforlag.

Jewitt, C. (2003). 'Re-thinking assessment: multimodality, literacy and computer-mediated learning', *Assessment in Education*, 10 (83–102).

Jillian, J.D., Upitis, R., Koch, C. and Young, J. (1999). 'The story of *Phoenix Quest*: how girls respond to a prototype language and mathematics computer game', *Gender and Education*, 11 (2), 207–23.

Johansson, M. and Küller, R. (2002). 'Traffic jam: psychological assessment of a gaming simulation', *Simulation and Gaming*, 33 (1), 67–88.

Jolicoeur, K. and Berger, D.E. (1998a). 'Implementing educational software and evaluating its academic effectiveness: part I', *Educational Technology*, 28 (10).

Jolicoeur, K. and Berger, D.E. (1998b). 'Implementing educational software and evaluating its academic effectiveness: part II', *Educational Technology*, 25 (10).

Jonassen, D. (2001). 'Learning From, In, and With Multimedia: An Ecological Psychology Perspective'. In S. Dijkstra, D. Jonassen and D. Sembill (eds.), *Multimedia Learning: Results and Perspectives*. Frankfurt am Main: Peter Lang.

Jones, M.G. (1998). Creating Engagement in Computer-based Learning Environments. Paper presented at the IT Forum.

Judd, C.M., Smith, E.R. and Kidder, L.H. (1991). *Research Methods in Social Relations*. Fort Worth, Philadelphia: Hartcourt Brace.

Juul, J. (2002) 'The Open and the Closed: Games of emergence and games of progression'. In *Computer Game and Digital Cultures Conference Proceedings*, ed. F. Müyrä, 323–329. Tampere: Tampere University Press.

Juul, J. (2003). Half-Real – Video Games Between Real Rules and Fictional Worlds. Unpublished PhD dissertation, IT University of Copenhagen, Copenhagen.

Kafai, Y. (1995). *Minds in Play: Computer Game Design as a Context for Children's Learning*. Hillsdale, NJ: Lawrence Erlbaum Associates.

Kafai, Y. (1996). 'Software by kids for kids', *Communications of the ACM*, 39 (4).

Kafai, Y.B. (2001). The Educational Potential of Electronic Games: From Games-To-Teach to Games-To-Learn. Paper presented at Playing by the Rules, Cultural Policy Center, University of Chicago.

Kafai, Y.B. and Resnick, M. (1996). *Constructionism in Practice: Designing, Thinking, and Learning in a Digital World*. Mawhaw, New Jersey: Lawrence Erlbaum Associates.

Kambouri, M., Schott, G., Mellar, H., Pavlou, V. and Thomas, S. (2003). Draft 3: Interim Report. London: Institute of Education.

Kaplan, R.M., and Saccuzzo, D.P. (1997). *Psychological Testing: Principles, Applications, and Issues*. Pacific Grove, CA: Brooks/Cole Publication.

Kashibuchi, M., Sakamoto, A. (2001). 'The educational effectiveness of a simulation/game in sex education', *Simulation and Gaming*, 32 (3), 331–43.

Kay, A. (1999). 'Computer Software'. In P.A. Mayer (ed.), *Computer Media and Communication: A Reader*. Oxford: Oxford University Press.

Kelly, G. (1963). *A Theory of Personality – The Psychology of Personal Constructs*. New York: Norton.

Kirkpatrick, G. (2003). 'The arrival of computer game studies'. *Ivory Tower Column*.

Kirriemuir, J., and McFarlane, A. (2002). *The Use of Computer Games in the Classroom*. Coventry: Becta.

Kirriemuir, J. and McFarlane, A. (2003). *Literature Review in Games and Learning*. Bristol: Nesta Future Lab.

Klawe, M.M. (1998). When Does the Use of Computer Games and Other Interactive Multimedia Software Help Students Learn Mathematics? Unpublished manuscript.

Klawe, M.M. and Phillips, E. (1995). A Classroom Study: Electronic Games Engage Children as Researchers. Paper presented at the CSCL 1995, Bloomington, Indiana.

Kliman, M. (1999). 'Choosing Mathematical Game Software for Girls and Boys'. www.terc.edu/mathequity/gw/html/ChoosingSoftwarepaper.html

Kline, S., Dyer-Witheford, N. and Greig, d. P. (2003). *Digital Play. The Interaction of Technology, Culture and Marketing*. Montreal: McGill-Queen's University Press.

Ko, S. (1999). *Primary School Children's Inferential Problem Solving in a Computer Game Context*. London: University of London.

Ko, S. (2002). 'An empirical analysis of children's thinking and learning in a computer game context', *Educational-Psychology*, 22 (2), 219–33.

Kolb, A.Y. and Kolb, D.A. (2003). 'Learning styles and learning spaces: enhancing experiential learning in higher education', *Academy of Management Learning and Education*, 4 (2), 193–212.

Kolb, D.A. (1984). *Experiential Learning: Experience as the Source of Learning and Development*. Englewood Cliffs, N.J: Prentice-Hall.

Konzack, L. (2003). *Edutainment: leg og lær med computermediet*. Aalborg: Aalborg Universitetsforlag.

Krathwohl, D.R., Bloom, B.S. and Masia, B.B. (1964). *Taxonomy of Educational Objectives: The Classification of Educational Goals: Handbook II: Affective Domain*. New York: David McKay Company.

Lauppert, T. (2004). 'Lemonade Stand'. http://members.chello.at/theador.lauppert/games/lemonade.htm

Lave, J. and Wenger, E. (1991). *Situated Learning: Legitimate Peripheral Participation*. Cambridge: Cambridge University Press.

Leddo, J. (1996). 'An intelligent tutoring game to teach scientific reasoning', *Journal of Instruction Delivery Systems*, 10 (4), 22–5.

Lee, J.L. (1994). *Effectiveness of the Use of Simulations in a Social Studies Classroom*. University of Virginia: ERIC.

Leeson, B. (Unknown). 'Origins of the Kriegsspiel. Kriegsspiel News'. http://myweb.tiscali.co.uk/kriegsspiel/kriegsspiel/origins.htm#

Leutner, D. (1993). 'Guided discovery learning with computer-based simulation games: effects of adaptive and non-adaptive instructional support', *Learning and Instruction*, 3 (2), 113–32.

Levin, J. (1981). 'Estimation techniques for arithmetic: everyday math and mathematics instruction', *Educational Studies in Mathematics*, 12, 421–34.

Leyland, B. (1996). How Can Computer Games Offer Deep Learning and Still be Fun? Paper presented at the Ascilite, Adelaide, Australia.

Lieberman, D.A. (2001). 'Management of chronic pediatric diseases with interactive health games: theory and research findings', *Journal of Ambulatory Care Management*, 24 (1), 26–38.

Linderoth, J. (19–22 August 2002). Making Sense of Computer Games: Learning With New Artefacts. Paper presented at Toys, Games and Media, London.

Littleton, K. and Light, P. (1999). *Learning with Computers: Analysing Productive Interaction*. London: Routledge.

Ljungstrøm, C. (1984). 'Differentiering og kvalificering: to væsensdimensioner i skole og uddannelsesforholdene', *Udkast*, 12 (2).

Lockyer, L., Wright, R., Curtis, S., Curtis, O. and Hodgson, A. (2003). Energy Balance: Design and Formative Evaluation of a Health Education Multimedia Game. Paper presented at EDMEDIA.

Loftus, G. and Loftus, E. (1983). *Mind at Play: The Psychology of Video Games*. New York: Basic Books.

Lopez, C.S. (2002). 'Le@rning in a Digitised Society'. In O. Danielsen, B.R. Olesen and B. H. Sørensen (eds.), *Learning and Narrativity in Digital Media*. Aarhus: Samfundslitteratur.

Lowery, B. and Knirk, F. (1983). 'Micro-computer video games and spatial visual acquisition', *Journal of Educational Technology Systems*, 11 (2), 155–66.

McCarty, C.T. (2001). Playing with Computer Games: An Exploration of Computer Game Simulations and Learning. Unpublished dissertation submitted in part fulfilment of the requirements of the MA (ICT in Education) Degree, University of London, London.

McFarlane, A., Sparrowhawk, A. and Heald, Y. (2002). *Report on the Educational Use of Games*. Cambridge: Teachers Evaluating Educational Multimedia.

McGrenere, J.L. (1996). *Design of Educational Electronic Multi-player Games: A Literature Review*. Vancouver: Department of Computer Science.

McMullen, D. (1987). *Drills vs. Games – Any Differences? A Pilot Study*. ERIC.

Macedonia, M. (2003). 'Games Soldiers Play'. www.spectrum.ieee.org/WEBONLY/publicfeature/mar02/mili.html

Magnussen, R. and Misfeldt, M. (2004, 6–8 December). Player Transformation of Educational Multiplayer Games. Paper presented at Other Players Conference, Copenhagen.

Makedon, A. (1984). 'Playful gaming', *Journal of Simulation and Games*, 15 (1), 25–64.

Malmberg, F. (2002). Personal correspondence with Paradox Entertainment regarding *Europa Universalis* game development.

Malone, T.W. (1980). What Makes Things Fun to Learn? Heuristics for Designing Instructional Computer Games. Paper presented at the Symposium on Small Systems Archive, Palo Alto, California, United States.

Malone, T.W., and Lepper, M. (1987a). 'Intrinsic Motivation and Instructional Effectiveness in Computer-based Education'. In Snow and Farr (eds.), *Aptitude Learning, and Instruction*. London: Lawrence Erlbaum Associates Publishers.

Malone, T.W. and Lepper, M. (1987b). Making Learning Fun: A Taxonomy of Intrinsic Motivation for Learning. In Snow and Farr (eds.), *Aptitude Learning, and Instruction*. London: Lawrence Erlbaum Associates Publishers.

Mamer, K. (2002). 'Ozark Softscape: Creators of MULE'. www.geocities.com/conspiracyprime/e2_ozark.htm

Markgren, P. (2004). 'Europa Universalis/IT-Gymnasiet Västerås'. In S. Egenfeldt-Nielsen (Ed.) (Email correspondence with teacher). Västerås.

Mayer, R. (2001). *Multimedia Learning*. New York: Cambridge University Press.

Mayer, R.E. and Moreno, R. (1999). 'A Cognitive Theory of Multimedia Learning: Implications for Design Principles'. In F.T. Durso, R.S. Nickerson, R.W. Schvaneveldt, S.T.D. Dumais, S. Lindsay and M.T.H. Chi (eds.), *Handbook of Applied Cognition*. New York: John Wiley and Sons.

Mellemfolkeligt Samvirke. (2003). www.globalisland.nu

Miller, C. (2000). 'Designing for kids: infusions of life, kisses of death', *Gamasutra*, 12 January.

Miller, C. (2002). Can *Sesame Street* bridge the Pacific Ocean? Linguistics senior thesis, Swarthmore College.

Miller, C., Lehman, J.F. and Koedinger, K. (1999). 'Goals and learning in microworlds', *Cognitive Science*, 23 (3), 305–36.

Mitchell, A. and Savill-Smith, C. (2004). *The Use of Computer and Video Games for Learning: A Review of the Literature*. Ultralab, London: Learning and Skills Development Agency.

Mortensen, P.O. and Svenstrup, C. (1998). *Giv dem da bare en computer med hjem – Bro@ager – et udviklingsprojekt*. København: Danmarks Lærerhøjskole.

Mouritsen, F. (2003). *Childhood and Children's Culture*. Portland, OR: International Specialized Book Service Inc.

MORI (2006). 'Close to 60% of UK Teachers want computer games in the classroom'. Futurelab. www.futurelab.org.uk/about_us/press_releases/pull.htm

Multimedieforeningen. (2004). 'Spilundervisning'. www.spilundervisning.dk

Murray, M., Mokros, J. and Rubin, A. (1998). 'Where's the math in computer games?', *Hands On!*, 21 (2).

Newman, J. (2004). *Videogames. Routledge Introductions to Media and Communications*. London: Routledge.

Noble, A., Best, D., Sidwell, C. and Strang, J. (2000). 'Is an arcade-style computer game an effective medium for providing drug education to school children?', *Education for Health*, 13 (3), 404–6.

Okagaki, L. and French, P. (1996). 'Effects of Video Game playing on Measures of Spatial Performance: Gender Effects in Late Adolescence'. In P. Greenfield and R. Cocking (eds.), *Interacting With Video*. New Jersey: Ablex Publishing.

Okan, Z. (2003). 'Edutainment: is learning at risk?', *British Journal of Educational Technology*, 34 (3), 255–64.

Olive, J. and Lobato, J. (2001). 'The Learning of Rational Number Concepts Using Technology'. In K. Heid, M. and G.W. Blume (eds.), *Research on Technology in the Learning and Teaching of Mathematics*. Greenwich, CT: Information Age Publishing, Inc.

Oliver, M. and Pelletier, C. (2004). Activity Theory and Learning from Digital Games: Implications for Game Design. Unpublished manuscript.

Packaged Facts. (1997). 'The Children's Educational Software Market', *Packaged Facts*.

Pahl, R.H. (1991). 'Finally, a good way to teach city government! a review of the computer simulation game *SimCity*', *Social-Studies*, 82 (4), 165–6.

Papert, S. (1980). *Mindstorms: Children, Computers, and Powerful Ideas*. New York: Basic Books.

Papert, S. (1996). *The Connected Family: Bridging the Digital Generation Gap*. Atlanta, GA: Longstreet Press.

Pearce, C. (2003). 'Into the labyrinth: defining games research', *Ivory Tower Column*.

Pillay, H., Brownlee, J. and Wilss, L. (1999). 'Cognition and recreational computer games: implications for educational technology', *Journal of Research on Computer in Education*, 32 (1), 203–16.

Plotz, D. (2003). 'Iraq: The Computer Game: What "Virtual World" Games can Teach the Real World about Reconstructing Iraq'. http://slate.msn.com/id/2084604

Prensky, M. (2001a). *Digital Game-Based Learning*. New York: McGraw-Hill.

Prensky, M. (2001b). What Kids Learn from Video Games: Five Learning Levels and their Implications for Public Policy. Paper presented at Playing by the Rules, Cultural Policy Centre, University of Chicago.

Prensky, M. (2004). 'The motivation of gameplay', *On the Horizon*, 10 (1).

Provenzo, E.F. (1992). 'What do video games teach?', *The Education Digest*, 56–8.

Quinn, C.N. (1997). Engaging Learning. Paper presented at the Instructional Technology Forum.

Randel, J.M., Morris, B.A., Wetzel, C.D. and Whitehill, B.V. (1992). 'the effectiveness of games for educational purposes: a review of recent research', *Simulation and Gaming*, 23 (3), 261–76.

Remus, W.E. (1981). 'Experimental design for analyzing data on games – or, even the best statistical methods do not replace good experimental Control'. *Simulation and Games*, 12 (1), 3–14.

Rieber, L.P. (1996). 'Seriously considering play: Designing interactive learning environments based on the blending of microworlds, simulations, and games', *Educational Technology Research and Development*, 44 (2), 43–58.

Roberts, N. (1976). *Simulation Gaming: A Critical Review*. Washington: US Department of Health and Welfare, National Institute of Education.

Robinett, W. (2004). 'Rocky boots'. www.warrenrobinett.com/rockysboots

Rollings, A. and Morris, D. (2000). *Game Architecture and Design*. Scottsdale: Coriolis.

Rosas, R.E.A. (2003). 'Beyond Nintendo: A design and assessment of educational video games for first and second grade students', *Computers and Education*, 40, 71–94.

Rousseau, J.J. (1993). *Emile*. London: J.M. Dent and Sons.

Ruben, B.D. (1999). 'Simulations, games, and experience-based learning: the quest for a new paradigm for teaching and learning', *Simulation-and-Gaming*, 30 (4), 498–505.

Rubin, A., O'Neil, K., Murray, M. and Ashley, J. (1997). What Kind of Educational Computer Games Would Girls Like? Paper presented at the AERA.

Saegesser, F. (1981). 'Simulation-gaming in the classroom. some obstacles and advantages', *Simulation and Games*, 12 (3), 281–94.

Saegesser, F. (1984). 'The introduction of play in schools: a philosophical analysis of the problems', *Simulation and Games*, 15(1), 75–96.

Saettler, P. (1968). *A History of Instructional Technology*. New York: McGraw-Hill.

Salen, K. and Zimmerman, E. (2003). *Rules of Play – Game Design Fundamentals*. Cambridge: The MIT Press.

Sandford, R., Ulicsak, M., Facer, Keri, K. and Rudd, T. (2006). *Teaching with Games*. Futurelab and EA.

Schank, R.C. (1999). *Dynamic Memory Revisited*. Cambridge: Cambridge University Press.

Scott, D. (1999). The Effect of Video Games on the Mental Rotation Abilities of Men and Women. Unpublished manuscript.

Sedighian, K. and Sedighian, A.S. (1996). Can Educational Computer Games Help Educators Learn About the Psychology of Learning Mathematics in Children? Paper presented at the Eighteenth Annual Meeting of the International Group for the Psychology of Mathematics Education, Florida.

Sedighian, K. and Sedighian, A.S. (1997). Aesthetic Response: Children's Reactions to Color and Graphics in Educational Software. Paper presented at ED-MEDIA 97: World Conference on Educational Multimedia and Hypermedia, Calgary, Canada.

Seidner, C.J. (1975). Teaching with Simulations and Games. In R.E. Duke and C.J. Seidner (eds.), *Learning with Simulations and Games*. London: Sage Publications.

Sluganski, R. (2001–2004). 'State of Adventure Gaming'. www.justadventure.com/Articles.shtm#SOAG

SocialImpactGames. (2004). www.socialimpactgames.com/modules.php?op=modloadandname=Newsandfile=indexandcatid=9andtopic=andallstories=1

Softbase. (2004). 'SoftBase Top 100 Educational Games'. http://softbase.150m.com/top73.html

Soloway, E. and Bielaczyc, K. (1995). Interactive Learning Environments: Where They've Come from and Where They're Going. Paper presented at Chi '95.

Sørensen, B.H. (2000). 'Multimedieaktører – Børns multimedieproduktion i skolen'. In B.H. Sørensen and S. Olesen (eds.), *Børn i en digital kultur – forskningsperspektiver*. Copenhagen: Gads Forlag.

Sørensen, E. (1997). Kan man lære noget af fiktion? Unpublished Dissertation submitted in part fulfilment of the requirements of the MA (Psychology) degree, Copenhagen University, Copenhagen.

Sørensen, E. (2001). 'Performing Spaces with 3D virtual Environments in an After-School Activity'. www.psy.ku.dk/estrid/INDHOLD/sorensen.pdf

Squire, K. (2003a). 'The Birth of Civilizations'. www.thinktv.org/education/ntti/ntti/lesson03/squire.html

Squire, K. (2003b). 'The Global Age: World History from 1450–1770'. www.thinktv.org/education/ntti/ntti/lesson03/squire.html

Squire, K. (2003c). 'Video games in education', *International Journal of Intelligent Simulations and Gaming*, 2 (1).

Squire, K. (2004). Replaying history. Unpublished dissertation submitted in part fulfilment of the requirements of the Doctor of Philosophy (Instructional Technology) Indiana University, Indiana.

Squire, K. (2005). 'Changing the game: what happens when video games enter the classroom?', *Innovate Journal of Online Education*, v1, 6.

Stearns, P.N. (2000). 'Student identities and world history teaching' *The History Teacher*, 33 (2), 185–91.

Stern, G. (24 April 1998). 'Life after twitch: an interview with Margo Nanny', *Gamasutra*.

Strein, W., and Kachman, W. (1984). 'Effects of computer games on young children's cooperative behavior: an exploratory study', *Journal of Research and Development in Education*, 19 (1), 40–3.

Subrahmanyam, K., and Greenfield, P. (1996). 'Effect of Video Game Practice'. In P. Greenfield and R. Cocking (eds.), *Interacting With Video*. New Jersey: Ablex Publishing.

Sutton-Smith, B. (1997). *The Ambiguity of Play*. Cambridge: Harvard University Press.

Sutton-Smith, B. and Kelly-Byrne, D. (1984). 'The Idealization of Play'. In P.K. Smith (ed.), *Play in Animals and Humans*. Oxford: Basil Blackwell Inc.

Tapscott, D. (1998). *Growing Up Digital*. New York: McGraw-Hill.

Taylor, J. (2003). Home Interactive Entertainment Market Update 2002–2003. Arcadia Investment Corp.

Thiagarajan, S. (1998). 'The myths and realities of simulations in performance technology', *Educational Technology*, 38 (5), 35–41.

Thomas, R., Cahill, J. and Santilli, L. (1997). 'Using an interactive computer game to increase skill and self-efficacy regarding safer sex negotiation: field test results'. *Health Education and Behavior: the Official Publication of the Society for Public Health Education*, 24 (1), 71–86.

Turnin, M.C., Couvaras, O., Jouret, B., Tauber, M.T., Bolzonella, C., Fabre, D. et al. (2000). 'Learning good eating habits playing computer games at school: a 2000 children evaluation', *Diabetes Research and Clinical Practice*, 50 (1001), 239.

Uddannelsesstyrelsen. (1999). *Undervisningsvejledning for gymnasiet: Historie med samfundskundskab*. Copenhagen: Undervisningsministeriet.

Van Sickle, R. (1986). 'A quantitative review of research on instructional simulation gaming: a twenty-year perspective', *Theory Research in Social Education*, 14 (3), 245–64.

VanDeventer, S. (1997). Expert Behaviour Among Outstanding Videogame-playing Children. Unpublished dissertation submitted in part fulfilment of the requirements of the Doctor of Philosophy (Curriculum and Instruction), University of South Florida, Florida.

Veen, W. (1995). 'Factors Affecting the Use of Computers in the Classroom: Four Case Studies'. In D. Watson and D. Tinsley (eds.), *Integrating Information Technology into Education*. London: Chapman and Hall.

Verbinski, G. (2003). 'Pirates of the Caribbean: Behind the scenes'. In J. Bruckheimer (Producer), *Pirates of the Caribbean*. USA: Buena Vista Pictures.

Veta. (2004). www.veta.com/

Vogel, H. (2001). 'Playing the Game: The Economics of the Computer Game Industry'. www.fathom.com/course/21701761

Vygotsky, L. (1986). *Thought and Language*. Cambridge, Massachusetts: MIT Press.

Walker de Felix, J. and Johnson, R.T. (1993). 'Learning from video games', *Computers in the Schools*, 9 (2–3), 199–33.

Walther, B.K. (2004, 23 March). 'Computerspil er dannelse' *Politiken*.

Wellington, W.J., and Faria, A.J. (1996). 'Team cohesion, player attitude, and performance expectations in simulations', *Simulation and Gaming*, 27 (1), 23–40.

Wenger, E. (1999). *Communities of Practice: Learning, Meaning, and Identity*. Cambridge: Cambridge University Press.

Wentworth, D.R. and Lewis, D.R. (1973). 'A review of research on instructional games and simulations in social studies education', *Social Education*, 37, 432–40.

Wertsch, J.V. (1991). *Voices of the Mind: A Sociocultural Approach to Mediated action*. Cambridge, MA: Harvard University Press.

Wertsch, J.V. (1998). *Mind as Action*. New York: Oxford University Press.

White, B.Y. (1984). 'Designing computer games to help physics students understand Newton's laws of motion', *Cognition and Instruction*, 1 (1), 69–108.

Whitebread, D. (1997). 'Developing Children's Problem-Solving: The Educational Uses of Adventure Games'. In A. McFarlane (ed.), *Information Technology and Authentic Learning*. London: Routledge.

Wiebe, J.H. and Martin, N.J. (1994). 'The impact of a computer-based adventure game on achievement and attitudes in geography', *Journal of Computing in Childhood Education*, 5 (1), 61–71.

Willis, J., Hovey, L. and Hovey, K.G. (1987). *Computer Simulations: A Source Book to Learning in an Electronic Environment.* New York: Garland Publishing, Inc.

Wolf, M.J.P. (2002). *The Medium of the Video Game.* Austin, Texas: University of Texas Press.

Wolfe, J. and Crookall, D. (1998). 'Developing a scientific knowledge of simulation/gaming', *Simulation and Gaming,* 29 (1), 7–19.

Woods, S. (2002). Fair Game? Possibilities for the Design and Implementation of Face-to-Face Social System Simulation Games in a Computer-Mediated Environment. Unpublished dissertation submitted in part fulfilment of the requirements of the Bachelor (Design) degree, Curtin University of Technology.

Woods, S. (2004). 'Loading the dice: the challenge of serious videogames' *Game Studies,* 4 (1).

Index

An 'f.' after a page number indicates inclusion of a figure; an 'n.' indicates a note; a 't.' indicates a table.